In: Green Research, Developments, and Programs

# RECYCLING AND GREEN PROGRAMS AT THE CAPITAL AND IN CONGRESS

# GREEN RESEARCH, DEVELOPMENTS, AND PROGRAMS SERIES

**Recycling and Green Programs at the Capital and in Congress**
*H.Y. Kim (Editor)*
2009. ISBN 978-1-60692-980-3

**In: Green Research, Developments, and Programs**

# RECYCLING AND GREEN PROGRAMS AT THE CAPITAL AND IN CONGRESS

**H. Y. KIM**
**EDITOR**

**Nova Science Publishers, Inc.**
*New York*

For permission to use material from this book please contact us:
Telephone 631-231-7269; Fax 631-231-8175
Web Site: http://www.novapublishers.com



**LIBRARY OF CONGRESS CATALOGING-IN-PUBLICATION DATA**
*Available upon request*
ISBN: 978-1-60692-980-3

*Published by Nova Science Publishers, Inc. ✦ New York*

# CONTENTS


| | | |
|---|---|---|
| **Preface** | | **vii** |
| **Chapter 1** | Green the Capitol Initiative. Submitted to Speaker Nancy Pelosi, Majority Leader Steny H. Hoyer<br>*Daniel P. Beard* | **1** |
| **Chapter 2** | Administering Green Programs in Congress: Issues and Options<br>*Jacob R. Straus* | **63** |
| **Chapter 3** | Recycling Programs in Congress: Legislative Development<br>and Architect of the Capitol Administration<br>*Jacob R. Straus* | **105** |
| **Chapter 4** | Architect of the Capitol: Progress in Improving Energy Efficiency and Options for Decreasing Greenhouse Gas Emissions<br>*United States Government Accountability Office* | **151** |
| **Chapter 5** | Economic and Other Implications of Switching from Coal to Natural Gas at the Capitol Power Plant and at Electricity-Generating Units Nationwide<br>*United States Government Accountability Office* | **163** |
| **Chapter 6** | Statement of Brendan Owens of the U.S. Green Building Council Before 191the Senate Committee on Rules and Administration 191on Improving Energy Efficiency, Increasing the Use of Renewable Sources of | |

| | | |
|---|---|---|
| | Energy, and Reducing the Carbon Footprint of the Capitol Complex,June 18, 2008 | **191** |
| **Chapter 7** | Executive Summary. Testimony of Jean Carroon, FAIA, 203Improving Energy Efficiency, Increasing the Use of Renewable Sources of Energy, and Reducing the Carbon Footprint of the Capitol Complex | **203** |
| **Chapter 8** | Testimony of Stephen T. Ayers, AIA, Acting Architect of the Capitol | **213** |
| **Chapter 9** | Testimony of Daniel P. Beard, Chief Administrative Officer US House of Representatives Before Select Committee on Energy Indepence and Global Warming, February 26, 2008. Food for Thought: Sustainability from Counter to Compost | **229** |
| **Index** | | **233** |

# Preface

In recent Congresses, the House of Representatives and the Senate have created separate greening programs. In addition, the Architect of the Capitol has developed green programs for the Capitol Complex.

The Architect of the Capitol also administers greening programs for the Capitol Complex. These programs include energy usage reduction programs for the House and Senate office buildings, the Capitol building, and other Capitol complex facilities; conservation measures for the Senate office buildings, the Capitol building, and other Capitol complex facilities; and green programs for the Capitol Grounds.

*Chapter 1* - On March 1, 2007, the Speaker and the Majority Leader directed the Chief Administrative Officer of the House to develop a "Green the Capitol Initiative" that would demonstrate leadership to the nation by providing an environmentally responsible and healthy working environment for employees.

Global warming and climate change are serious issues. Scientists agree that the introduction of carbon into the atmosphere is causing climate change. Efforts to reduce carbon emissions need to begin immediately. Such changes will have a positive impact on the environment and the economy.

This report on the "Green the Capitol Initiative" meets the directives set out in your letter. "We cannot ask the American people to address global warming and climate change issues," you noted, "without first carefully examining ways to reduce our own energy consumption and develop sustainable workplace practices." This report, and its recommendations, will enable the House to be a leader in sustainable operations.

Environmental responsibility is our duty to future generations. Now is the time to act to reduce our energy consumption as well as our energy dependence. To accomplish this, we will change the way we do business. A sustainable House Capitol complex will recognize the full environmental impact of our decisions on energy and water consumption, materials use and the quality of our workplace. By taking these steps, we not only reduce the impact of House operations on the environment, but also provide leadership by example.

*Chapter 2* - Programs to create an environmentally conscious workplace have long existed on Capitol Hill. Congress has been working to reduce consumption and conserve energy since the 1970s. Traditionally, these programs have been administered by the Architect of the Capitol. In recent Congresses, the House of Representatives and the Senate have created separate greening programs. In addition, the Architect of the Capitol has developed green programs for the Capitol Complex.

In the House of Representatives, the Chief Administrative Officer (CAO) manages green programs for individual Member offices, committee offices, and support offices. The administration of building-wide energy conservation programs is traditionally managed by the Architect of the Capitol. For the House, the CAO and Architect's program oversight is conducted by the Committee on House Administration. In the 110th Congress, the House of Representatives labeled all conservation and greening programs as part of the "Green the Capitol" initiative.

In the Senate, green programs in individual Senate offices, committee offices, and staff support offices are administered by the Architect of the Capitol, in coordination with the Secretary of the Senate and the Sergeant at Arms of the Senate, and with oversight provided by the Rules and Administration Committee. In the 110th Congress, the Architect of the Capitol's role in administering facilities-related programs on behalf of the Senate has remained unchanged.

The Architect of the Capitol also administers greening programs for the Capitol Complex. These programs include energy usage reduction programs for the House and Senate office buildings, the Capitol building, and other Capitol complex facilities; conservation measures for the Senate office buildings, the Capitol building, and other Capitol complex facilities; and green programs for the Capitol Grounds.

A number of policy options are potentially available to create an inter-chamber greening program on Capitol Hill. The options include creating a formal House greening program, creating a "Green the Senate" initiative, establishing an independent greening commission, creating a Capitol Complex-wide greening program, and continuing to use ad-hoc programming for greening issues.

For further analysis of general greening programs in Congress, see CRS Report RL34617, Recycling Programs in Congress: Legislative Development and Architect of the Capitol Administration, by Jacob R. Straus.

*Chapter 3* - The House of Representatives and the Senate created separate voluntary recycling programs in 1989, during the 101st Congress (1989-1991). Administered by the Architect of the Capitol, the recycling programs aimed to reduce the amount of material sent to landfills and establish the House and the Senate as leaders of the recycling movement.

The initial recycling programs in the House and Senate focused on the recycling of paper and the use of recycled paper, including white office paper, newspaper, and cardboard. While the program had modest beginnings, since 1992, when the General Services Administration (GSA) began managing the House and Senate recycling contracts, the House (9,939 tons) and the Senate (5,117 tons) have recycled a combined total of approximately 15,056 tons of paper.

At approximately the same time the House and Senate began recycling paper, they also began recycling bottles and cans. Since 1992, when GSA began managing the recycling of non-paper materials, the House (572 tons) and the Senate (198 tons) have recycled a combined total of approximately 770 tons of bottles and cans. This number has fluctuated as the increased use of plastic instead of glass bottles has decreased the total weight of recycled bottles and cans.

In 2001, the House and the Senate began recycling e-waste (e.g., computers, printers, and toner cartridges), construction, and demolition waste products (e.g., carpet, concrete, ceiling tiles, and scrap metal). The additional categories of recycling have allowed the House (23,000 tons) and the Senate (15,700 tons) to recycle almost 39,000 tons of materials that were not part of the initial recycling efforts. Overall, the expansion of the recycling program in both the House and Senate has resulted in an increase of total tons recycled and a decrease in total tons of waste transferred to landfills.

Recently, the recycling program has expanded to include the recycling of cell phones and the composting of food waste in the House of Representatives. In the FY2009 budget justification, the Architect of the Capitol has proposed legislative language to amend Title 2, United States Code concerning the collection and sale of recycled materials and the use of proceeds. The new language, if enacted, would allow the Architect to offset the initial cost of new House recycling programs by using current proceeds. The Senate, by law, currently designates recycling proceeds to the Senate fitness center.

For further analysis of recycling programs beyond those in the House and Senate, see CRS Report RS22807, Compact Fluorescent Light Bulbs (CFLs): Issues with Use and Disposal, by Linda Luther; CRS Report RL34 147, Managing Electronic Waste: An Analysis of State E-Waste Legislation, by Linda Luther; and CRS Report RL3 1505, Recycling Computers and Electronic Equipment: Legislative and Regulatory Approaches for 'E-Waste,' by James E. McCarthy.

Recycling can have multiple meanings. "To some, it is the stacking of newspapers and separating of cans and bottles from the trash. To others, it is the program that collects those materials. And, to still others, it is just another waste disposal program." [1] Recycling programs in the House of Representatives and the Senate have taken two approaches: recycling of material as part of the overall congressional waste disposal program and purchasing products made from recycled materials. In each case, the House and the Senate encourage participation through educational outreach [2].

*Chapter 4* - The Architect of the Capitol has made some progress toward implementing the recommendations in our April 2007 report but more opportunities remain. For example, AOC has prioritized a list of Capitol Hill buildings that need energy audits but has not developed a schedule for conducting the audits that explains the prioritization scheme or provides information on the anticipated costs. With respect to energy audits, AOC is conducting an energy audit of the U.S. Capitol Police Buildings and Grounds and plans to use $400,000 of fiscal year 2008 funds for energy audits of the Capitol Building and the Ford House Office Building. AOC has also requested $1.4 million for additional energy audits in its fiscal year 2009 budget request. In addition, AOC has contracted with a private firm to conduct preliminary audits of the Senate Office Buildings that could lead to more targeted audits and eventually identify cost-effective projects that would decrease energy use and related greenhouse gas emissions.

*Chapter 5* - Elevated concentrations of greenhouse gases—carbon dioxide, methane, nitrous oxide, and several synthetic chemicals—in the atmosphere resulting from the combustion of fossil fuels and other sources have the potential to cause significant changes in the earth's climate. These potential impacts include shifts in sea level and weather patterns and could pose threats to coastal and other infrastructure. Concerns about the potential impacts of climate change have led the Congress to consider legislation that would place binding, nationwide limits on greenhouse gas emissions, and the House of Representatives' leadership has initiated efforts to decrease emissions attributable to its operations. Nearly all of the greenhouse gas emissions from House operations consist of carbon dioxide and are associated with electricity purchased from utilities and the combustion of fossil fuels in the Capitol Power Plant (CPP), which provides steam and chilled water for heating and cooling the Capitol building and 23 surrounding facilities. The Architect of the Capitol (AOC) operates CPP.

*Chapter 6* - Buildings are responsible for 39% of U.S. CO2 emissions per year. In addition, buildings annually account for 39% of U.S. primary energy use; use 12.2% of all potable water or 15 trillion gallons per year; and consume 40% of raw materials globally. Green buildings create opportunities to mitigate these environmental impacts and also to generate financial savings. As an integral part of the physical and cultural fabric of communities, historic buildings play a critical role in this green revolution, inspiring civic engagement, enabling dense development near public transportation, and attracting integrated public services, among other amenities.

*Chapter 7* - In the United States, more than 40% of our carbon emissions are attributed to the construction and operation of buildings. While buildings represent a threat to the health of our planet, the reuse and greening of these structures also presents an enormous opportunity to reduce our nation's carbon emissions. Through improved energy efficiency and an increase in the use of renewable sources of energy at the Capitol Complex, the United States Senate has the opportunity to demonstrate to the American public the important role our older and historic buildings play in reducing carbon emissions.

*Chapter 8* - For the past four decades, the Office of the Architect of the Capitol (AOC) has undertaken initiatives and we continue to implement programs to improve energy efficiency and reduce the environmental impact of the Capitol complex. Our Agency's commitment to reducing energy consumption is integrated into our Strategic Plan, and is carried out through our mission to serve Congress as we serve as stewards of some 16.5 million square feet of buildings and nearly 450 acres of land.

*Chapter 9* - Our goal with the House food services operations is to make it a premier showcase of sustainable, green, and healthy food operations. The House food service touches virtually all of the visitors to the Capitol from constituents, citizen advocates to lobbyists, federal employees and the press corps. And of course there is the House staff and Members of Congress who eat here almost every working day.

In: Recycling and Green Programs at the Capital... ISBN 978-1-60692-980-3
Editor: H. Y. Kim, pp. 1-62 

*Chapter 1*

# GREEN THE CAPITOL INITIATIVE*

# SUBMITTED TO SPEAKER NANCY PELOSI, MAJORITY LEADER STENY H. HOYER

***Daniel P. Beard***

## EXECUTIVE SUMMARY REPORT TO THE SPEAKER AND MAJORITY LEADER

### Introduction

On March 1, 2007, the Speaker and the Majority Leader directed the Chief Administrative Officer of the House to develop a "Green the Capitol Initiative" that would demonstrate leadership to the nation by providing an environmentally responsible and healthy working environment for employees.

Global warming and climate change are serious issues. Scientists agree that the introduction of carbon into the atmosphere is causing climate change. Efforts to reduce carbon emissions need to begin immediately. Such changes will have a positive impact on the environment and the economy.

* Final Report dated June 21, 2007.

This report on the "Green the Capitol Initiative" meets the directives set out in your letter. "We cannot ask the American people to address global warming and climate change issues," you noted, "without first carefully examining ways to reduce our own energy consumption and develop sustainable workplace practices." This report, and its recommendations, will enable the House to be a leader in sustainable operations.

Environmental responsibility is our duty to future generations. Now is the time to act to reduce our energy consumption as well as our energy dependence. To accomplish this, we will change the way we do business. A sustainable House Capitol complex will recognize the full environmental impact of our decisions on energy and water consumption, materials use and the quality of our workplace. By taking these steps, we not only reduce the impact of House operations on the environment, but also provide leadership by example.

## Goals and Strategies

This report recommends that the House adopt three goals for future operations:

1. Operate the House a carbon -neutral manner by the end of the 110$^{th}$ in Congress
2. Reduce the carbon footprint of the House by cutting energy consumption by 50% in 10 years
3. Make House operations a model of sustainability

To achieve the goals outlined above, a wide variety of strategies will need to be implemented. For each goal below, a summary of implementing strategies is provided. These strategies provide the roadmap to reducing the carbon footprint of the House while operating in an environmentally sustainable manner.

### *Goal #1: Operate the House in a Carbon-Neutral Manner by the End of the 110$^{th}$ Congress (December, 2008)*

Climate change and global warming are serious issues. Scientists agree that the introduction of carbon dioxide (CO2) and other greenhouse gases into the atmosphere has serious effects. There are immediate steps the House can take to provide leadership to address global warming. The House can make the operations of the House carbon-neutral, so that its net carbon dioxide equivalent (CO2-e) emissions become zero.

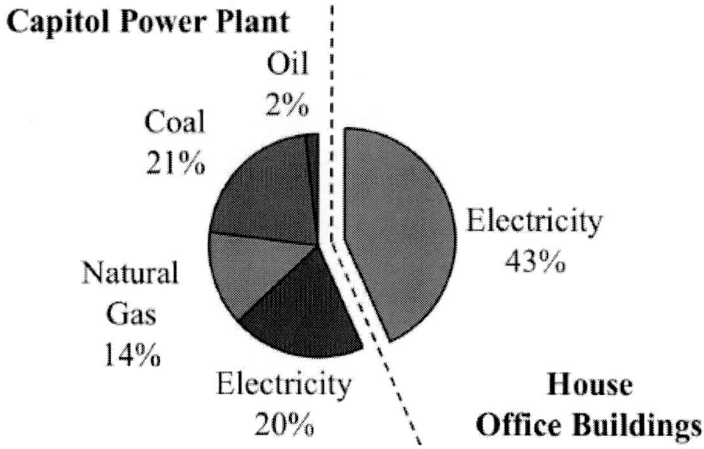


Figure ES - 1. Total 2006 Carbon Dioxide-Equivalent Emissions for House Buildings.

Using data developed by the Government Accountability Office, and reviewed by Lawrence Berkeley National Laboratory, it is estimated that the operation of the House complex was responsible for 91,000 tons [1] of CO2-e emissions in fiscal year 2006.

This value is equivalent to the annual CO2-e emissions of 17,200 cars [2]. Figure ES-1 shows the sources for the CO2-e emissions for the House buildings by fuel type. Electricity is purchased from the local utility and provided directly to the buildings. Heating and cooling for the buildings is provided by the Capitol Power Plant (CPP), located on site. The CPP no longer produces electricity.

Three strategies are recommended to achieve carbon neutrality for the House buildings:

1. Purchase electricity generated from renewable sources
2. Switch from using coal, oil, and natural gas at the CPP to natural gas only

Purchase offsets for the remaining carbon emissions

**Strategy #1: Purchase Renewable Power for Electricity Use**

Electricity use is the largest source of CO2-e emissions from House operations. To achieve the goal of making operations carbon-neutral the Chief Administrative Officer (CAO) and the Architect of the Capitol (AOC) have negotiated with our energy service provider to purchase 100% of the electricity needs, approximately 103,000 megawatt-hours per year, from renewable sources beginning October 1, 2007. The cost of electric power generated from renewable sources is an additional $520,000 and that amount has been included in the Fiscal Year 2008 Legislative Branch Appropriations bill. By implementing this recommendation the House will eliminate 57,000 tons of the total CO2-e emissions annually or the equivalent of removing 11,000 cars from the road.

**Strategy #2: Operate the CPP with Natural Gas**

The second strategy is to reduce the CO2-e emissions from the coal burned at the CPP to meet the needs of the House of Representatives. It is recommended that the CPP use natural gas instead of coal to meet the needs of the House. By taking this action, CO2-e emissions from the CPP can be lowered by 30% from the 2006 level, which is the equivalent of taking 1,900 cars off the road each year. Because the boilers already have dual-fuel capabilities, they can be switched to natural gas and can use alternate fuel, either coal or oil, as emergency back-up. The total cost to implement this recommendation in Fiscal Year 2008 is $2.75 million. Money to purchase the natural gas is included in the Legislative Branch Appropriations bill.

**Strategy #3: Purchase Carbon Offsets on the Chicago Climate Exchange**

Even by using electricity from renewable sources and switching the generation of steam to natural gas, the House will still need to offset 24,000 tons of carbon emissions to achieve the goal of carbon-neutral operations. Therefore, it is recommended that all our remaining carbon emissions be offset by purchasing from the Chicago Climate Exchange carbon financial instrument contracts or carbon credits specifically for projects in the United States. These carbon financial instruments will be permanently retired so that the carbon credits cannot be used again. The Chicago Climate Exchange has been notified of the House's intent to initiate this action. The cost of offsetting 24,000 tons of greenhouse gases is estimated to be approximately $95,000. Money is available in CAO's Fiscal Year 2008 budget to make these purchases. The CAO will purchase CO2-e offsets equal to House-attributable emissions on an annual basis.

***Goal #2: Reduce the Carbon Footprint of the House by Cutting Energy Consumption by 50% in 10 Years***

While the House can achieve carbon neutrality by the end of the 110th Congress, the long-term goal should be to lower our carbon emissions, or the "carbon footprint," by reducing energy consumption. Cost-effective investments in energy efficiency will pay for themselves and reduce the House's annual operating costs. The goal of reducing the House's energy use by 50% over the next 10 years should be adopted. The specific strategies identified in the following pages outline the steps needed to achieve this goal. After careful examination of the current carbon emission and energy use of the House and analyzing the recommendations contained in this report, it is feasible for the House to achieve the 50% energy reduction goal. In carrying out this goal, every opportunity will be taken to purchase American-made, energy-efficient technologies.

Before detailing each of those recommendations and outlining its effects, it is important to provide the following background on the energy use and carbon footprint of House operations. Figure ES-2 estimates where energy was used during 2006 in the House office buildings, based on data from AOC and additional analyses. To reduce total House energy use by 50% over the next ten years, energy use will have to be reduced five percentage points per year. This is more than twice the Energy Policy Act (EPAct) of 2005 requirement of 2% reductions in energy use per year for federal buildings.

The largest use of energy in the House buildings is for cooling (3 8%) followed by heating (28%), lighting (17%), office equipment (7% ), and miscellaneous other uses (10%), such as ventilation fans, elevators, and other equipment and appliances. Figure ES-3 shows how the proposed goal for cutting energy use by 50% by 2017 will be achieved. The reductions mandated under the 2005 Energy Policy Act are indicated by the blue dotted line. The proposed strategy more than doubles those savings.

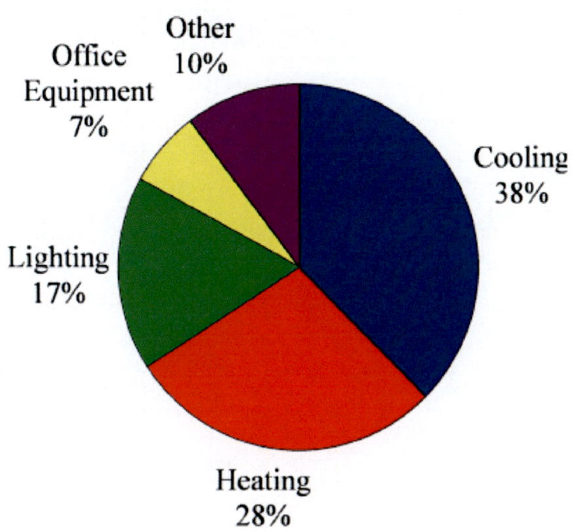


Figure ES-2. Total Energy Use for House Buildings by End Use.

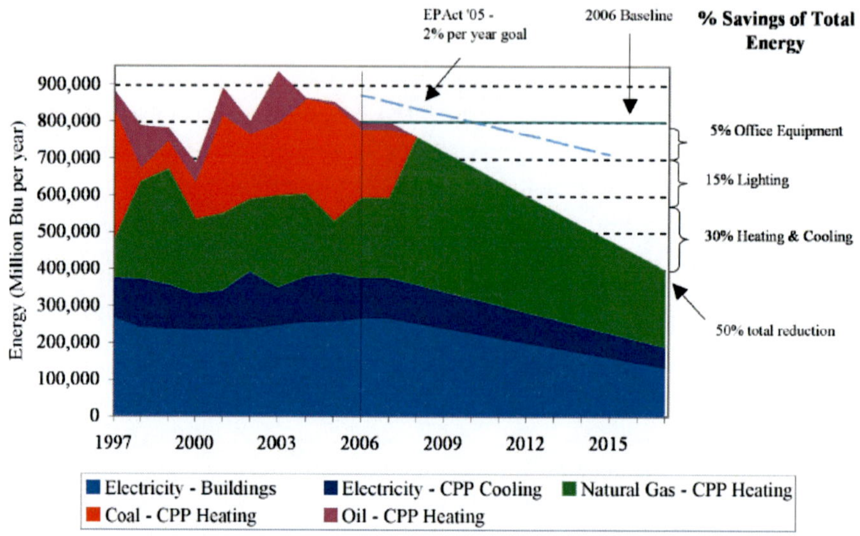


Figure ES-3. Energy reduction scenario for the House attributable consumption due to improved efficiency measures.

To achieve the 50% goal, the House will have to employ an optimal mix of life-cycle cost- effective investments in energy efficiency. Figure ES-4 shows how the increased costs necessary to achieve the carbon-neutral strategy will be repaid through energy savings actions.

Figure ES-4 shows that over a 10-year period, the reduced demand for energy from the cost- effective energy retrofits pays for the increased premium for electricity produced by renewable sources, the costs of switching to natural gas, and the purchase of carbon offsets. These estimates do not include the savings from eliminating fly ash disposal from burning coal, as well as from other direct and indirect environmental benefits. Investments in energy efficiency should not be delayed if appropriated funds are not available.

Congress in Energy Policy Act of 2005 recognized the value of alternative financing mechanisms as a means to leverage private -sector funds to make improvements in public-sector operations. Through alternative financing mechanisms private parties provide funding for energy efficiency projects and they are repaid by the savings. The use of such alternative financing mechanisms where appropriate to move projects forward is a sound approach to help reach the energy efficiency goals.

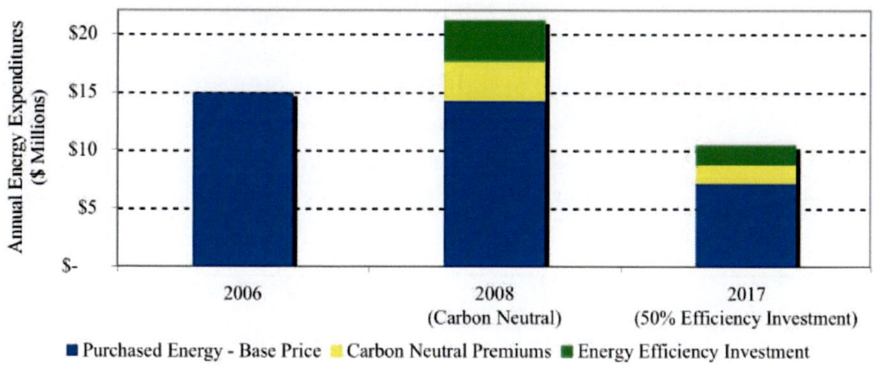


Figure ES-4. Total carbon-neutral scenario costs.

Two sets of specific actions should be taken: (1) reducing energy consumption in House office buildings and (2) reducing energy consumption at the CPP. This initiative will maximize the use of American products and services.

(1) Recommendations for House office building operations:

- Use metering, commissioning, and tracking to improve operating efficiency and management
- Install/upgrade steam meters for all House buildings
  - Install/upgrade chilled water meters for all House buildings
  - Optimize major steam and chilled water systems for energy efficiency during different seasons
  - Use utility tracking to monitor energy use during various times of day to identify energy savings opportunities
- Install energy efficient lighting
  - Retrofit ceiling lamps, fixtures, and controls to increase energy efficiency
  - Evaluate motion-activated lighting in offices, service corridors, tunnels, and parking areas to reduce energy use
  - Replace desk lamps with energy-efficient bulbs
  - Conduct high-efficiency ceiling lighting pilot program
  - Evaluate exterior building lighting to reduce energy use
- Adopt new technologies and optimal operating practices for electronics and office equipment
  - Change computer operations to allow staff to centrally power-down equipment when unused for significant periods such as nights and weekends

  - Maximize power management efforts present in existing electronic equipment through periodic audits and employee education
  - Develop a preferred list of Energy Star-qualified office electronics
  - Devise strategies to consolidate equipment
- Update heating, ventilation, and air conditioning equipment and practices
  - Retrofit motors, fan drives, pumps, and valves with energy-efficient models.
  - Modify CAV equipment and controls so that air-handling systems operate as VAV systems
  - Seal air distribution ducts to minimize air leakage
  - Optimize fan schedules to avoid unnecessary equipment operation
- Make computer rooms and servers more energy efficient
  - Improve operational control of data center auxiliary cooling and power systems
  - Consolidate servers distributed throughout House buildings into dedicated server rooms
  - Consolidate many lightly-used servers into fully-utilized server systems
  - Adjust air distribution in computer rooms for thermal optimization
- Evaluate food service practices, elevator and vending machine energy efficiency, hot water use, laundry and dry cleaning services, fitness center operations, and other House services for energy savings opportunities
  - Inventory current equipment and schedules to identify energy savings opportunities
  - Install new energy-efficient equipment and operating strategies emphasizing products made in America

(2) The CPP is the largest single source of carbon emissions on the Capitol Hill. As noted earlier, switching to natural gas will reduce the CO2-e emissions of the CPP by 30%. The plant's operation has also been controversial because of visual and health concerns among Capitol Hill residents. It is important for Congress to take a leadership role in modernizing and updating this facility. It is recommended that the committees of jurisdiction be instructed to review the plant's operation, and develop appropriation guidance, including legislation if necessary, to make the plant a model of efficient operations and sustainability. This legislation should be passed by the end of the 110th Congress.

Making changes to the CPP will take many years to plan, finance, and implement. During this interim period, the following actions should be taken to optimize operations of the CPP to maximize energy efficiency and reduce energy consumption:

- Improve steam production efficiency
  - Evaluate reducing boiler steam pressure output from 200 PSI to 150 PSI
  - Implement best practices for operations and maintenance Monitor energy efficiency performance
- Improve chilled water production efficiency
  - Implement best practices for operations and maintenance Retrofit motors with premium efficient motors
  - Evaluate retrofit potential of variable-speed drives on pump motors Monitor energy efficiency performance
  - Evaluate new efficient chillers for West Refrigeration Plant
- Improve steam and chilled water distribution systems
  - Improve maintenance of steam traps, increasing steam system distribution efficiency
  - Determine need for new insulation of all distribution lines to reduce heating and cooling losses
  - Adjust steam delivery pressures where practicable to follow heat load requirements in Capitol buildings

***Goal #3: Make House Operations a Model of Sustainability***

In addition to improving the way the House consumes energy, the House should provide an environmentally sustainable and healthy working environment for employees. The House has the opportunity to lead by example by making its business operations a model of sustainability. In order to achieve this goal, every attempt will be made to purchase American-made environmentally sustainable products.

**Strategy #1: Direct the CAO to Oversee Implementation of "Green the Capitol Initiative"**

The Office of the CAO should be charged with responsibility to oversee implementation of the "Green the Capitol Initiative" for the House of Representatives. This includes working with the AOC and other offices to improve the sustainability of the day -to-day operations of the House office buildings including maintenance, finance, transportation, childcare, and food service.

**Strategy #2: Develop a House Sustainability Plan**

In June 2007, the CAO convened a meeting with three sustainability leaders from major universities that are championing sustainability. Representatives from Harvard, Yale, and the University of California provided briefings on their goals, operations, and successes. A key component of their success has been a sustainability plan that provides focus and direction to reform efforts. It is recommended the CAO develop and implement a House Sustainability Plan as a dynamic document intended to provide a roadmap for major steps toward sustainability over the next 20 years and to identify timetables for specific actions.

The CAO and the AOC should be directed to take the following specific actions under the Sustainability Plan:

- Improve indoor water use efficiency
  - Install additional water meters Analyze water consumption and quality patterns
  - Install low flow water fixtures
- Adopt sustainable practices for site and landscape
  - Implement conservation measures for irrigation
  - Improve storm water control to reduce runoff
  - Decrease pesticide use to improve runoff water quality
  - Expand tree canopy
- Improve employee access to transit options and reduce transportation energy use
  - Demonstrate a commitment to alternate fuels through installation of an E-85 ethanol fueling station
  - Replace the current House motor vehicle fleet with efficient, hybrid, or alternative fuel vehicles
  - Establish an employee transit coordinator position
  - Centralize the House transit benefit progra m and increase the benefit level Implement a Bike to Work program
  - Implement a car sharing program
- Implement sustainable practices in the House's food service system
  - Purchase serviceware products recommended through the U.S. EPA Environmentally Preferable Purchasing Program
  - Establish goals for supply of locally and organically produced food
- Reduce environmental impact of materials through purchase of locally or regionally produced products, and standardize where possible to reduce inventory and procurement costs

- Specify low-VOC paints, furniture, carpet, and other furnishings emphasizing products made in America
- Specify office furnishing containing recycled content, bio-based products, or
- certified wood, emphasizing products made in America Purchase office electronics certified through the Electronic Product Environmental Assessment Tool (EPEAT)
- Procure 100% recycled and 30% post-consumer content paper and recommend measures to reduce paper consumption
- Divert 50% of the building occupant waste stream through improved recycling program
- Purchase cleaning supplies that meet the requirements of Green Seal Standard for Industrial and Institutional Cleaners, Standard GS-37; and for floor products, Standard GS-40

**Strategy #3: Leadership, Education, and Outreach**

The CAO should pursue networking and outreach with the Senate, universities, businesses, local and state governments, and others to remain current on sustainability practices and CO2-e emission reduction opportunities. The networking can showcase the House's leadership role and facilitate the exchange of ideas and information on environmentally sustainable issues. This activity could include hosting green summits on sustainability. The CAO should also work with the AOC to make sustainability a mission-critical element of the AOC's business practices.

Recommendations for specific actions include:

- Prepare a checklist for sustainable office operations for use by Members of Congress and other Capitol Hill offices
- The House should take a leadership role in networking with the Senate, universities, businesses, and local and state governments including hosting green summits
- Hold a green expo for House offices to demonstrate the latest in green products or services available from commercial vendors
- Work with the AOC to make sustainability a mission-critical element
- Provide energy efficiency and sustainability materials for Capitol Hill visitors

**Strategy #4: Develop Mechanisms for Evaluating Success and Reporting Progress**

The CAO should track benchmarks for energy consumption and CO2-e emissions monthly and prepare annual reports documenting progress on the complementary goals of carbon neutrality and sustainable operations. Energy and CO2-e emissions data will be made available on a website, both as an educational tool and to provide feedback to House staff.

# CONCLUSION

This report provides a roadmap for carbon neutrality, energy efficiency, and operating in an environmentally sustainable fashion. It demonstrates that the House can operate in a carbon neutral manner now and begin to implement energy efficiency measures today. The report provides the way forward to cutting the House's energy use by 50% in 10 years. It shows how the House can do business in an environmentally sustainable manner. Implementing these goals is a good investment for the American taxpayer, the environment, and our children's future.

# KEY TERMS

*Carbon dioxide:* Carbon dioxide is a chemical compound composed of one carbon atom and two oxygen atoms. It is often referred to by its chemical formula CO2. It is present in the Earth's atmosphere at a concentration of approximately 0.04% and is an important greenhouse gas. The unit that is used in this report is short tons of carbon dioxide-equivalents or CO2-e.

*Carbon footprint:* The net amount of CO2-e generated by an institution, business, household, individual, or other entity from all of its activities, usually estimated during a certain period such as a year.

*Carbon-neutral:* An adjective describing buildings or operations that produce no net contribution to carbon dioxide-equivalent emissions.

*Carbon offset:* An action that reduces the net carbon dioxide-equivalent emissions of an individual or organization, through investment in emissions reduction action by another individual or organization.

*Cogeneration:* Cogeneration, also called combined heat and power (CHP), is the use of a heat engine or a power station to simultaneously generate both electricity and useful heat.

*Global warming:* Global warming is the observed increase in the average temperature of the Earth's near-surface air and oceans , and its projected continuation. The cause is an increase in carbon dioxide emissions, primarily from the combustion of carbon (fossil) fuels and other greenhouse gases.

*Renewable energy:* Renewable energies derived from resources that are regenerative, or for all practical purposes, cannot be depleted. Because of their renewable nature, these energy sources are fundamentally different from finite fossil fuels. They produce fewer greenhouse gases and other pollutants as fossil fuel combustion.

*Sustainability:* Capable of being continued with minimal long-term effect on the environment. Sustainability relates to the continuity of economic, social, institutional and environmental aspects of society.

*Ton of CO2-e*: English short tons (1 ton = 2000 pounds), used in this report for CO2-e. Ton of cooling: 1 ton of cooling = 12,000 Btu/hour.

## ACRONYMS, UNITS, AND CONVERSIONS

| | |
|---|---|
| AOC | Architect of the Capitol |
| BOMA | Building Owners and Managers Association International |
| CAO | Chief Administrative Officer |
| CAV | Constant air volume |
| CFL | Compact fluorescent lamp |
| CPP | Capitol Power Plant |
| CRAC | Computer-room air conditioner |
| CRT | Cathode ray tube |
| DDOT | District Department of Transportation |
| EPAct | Energy Policy Act (of 1992 or 2005) |
| EPEAT | Electronic Product Environmental Assessment Tool |
| FEMP | Federal Energy Management Program |
| GAO | Government Accountability Office |
| GPO | Government Printing Office |
| HOB | House office building |
| HVAC | Heating, ventilating and air-conditioning |
| IT | Information technology |
| LBNL | Lawrence Berkeley National Laboratory |
| LCD | Liquid crystal display |
| LED | Light-emitting diode |
| MACS | Members Allowance Checklist for Sustainability |

| | |
|---|---|
| UPS | Uninterruptible power supplies |
| VAV | Variable air volume |
| VOCs | Volatile organic compounds |
| WMATA | Washington Metropolitan Area Transit Authority |
| ZEB | Zero energy building |
| MBtu | Million British thermal unit |
| MWh | Mega-watt hour (106 Watt-hours) (1 MWh = 3.4 12 MBtu) |
| PSI | Pound per square inch |

# INTRODUCTION

On March 1, 2007, Speaker Nancy Pelosi and Majority Leader Steny H. Hoyer directed the CAO to develop a series of preliminary recommendations to reduce the environmental effects associated with the operation of the House office building complex. As they noted, "the House of Representatives should demonstrate leadership to the nation by providing an environmentally- responsible and healthy working environment for our employees. In addition, the House complex should be a showcase for sustainability. The House cannot ask the American people to address global warming and climate change issues without first carefully examining ways to reduce our energy consumption and practice sustainable workplace practices."

As a result of this directive, the CAO has undertaken a review of the House operating procedures with respect to energy conservation, sustainability and related matters, and offers the following recommendations to "Green the Capitol."

Several studies have recently been completed, or are currently under way, that characterize the energy use and carbon dioxide equivalent emissions (CO2-e) of the Capitol area complex. The AOC is preparing an overall Sustainability Plan. The AOC is completing an assessment of the energy retrofits that can be undertaken as part of its overall facilities planning process. The Government Accountability Office (GAO) has issued a report documenting detailed analysis of the energy use and CO2-e emissions for the Capitol complex and outlined its "carbon footprint." The House Science Committee is proposing demonstration offices to showcase energy-efficient and sustainable practices. Recommendations have been made by Carnegie Mellon University and others on specific measures that can be taken, both as short-term actions and through improved specifications for future retrofits. The Vermont Energy Investment Corporation, a non-profit entity, has offered recommendations to Congressman Peter Welch on the best way to insure carbon-neutral operations for his office in the Longworth Building. Various other energy audits and surveys have been conducted in the past.

Energy management has been on the Capitol's agenda for some years. While the potential for further gains is substantial, notable precedents exist in the House's use of energy-efficient technologies, and operational practices that enhance energy efficiency. Examples of these practices are listed in Appendix B.

This report expands on current practice, drawing on the prior studies, reports, and recommendations, as well as other sources. It presents a framework in which all of these recommendations, and others, can be reviewed and implemented.

# PART ONE: GOALS AND STRATEGIES

This report contains three goals:

1. Operate the House in a carbon-neutral manner by the end of the 110$^{th}$ Congress
2. Reduce the carbon footprint of the House by cutting energy consumption by 50% in 10 years
3. Make House operations a model of sustainability

To achieve the goals outlined above, a wide variety of strategies will need to be implemented. For each goal below, a summary of implementation strategies is provided. These strategies provide the roadmap to reducing the carbon footprint of the House while operating in an environmentally sustainable manner.

## Goal #1: Operate the House in a Carbon-Neutral Manner by the End of the 110$^{th}$ Congress

Climate change and global warming are serious issues caused primarily by the introduction of carbon dioxide (CO2) and other greenhouse gases into the atmosphere [3].

There are immediate steps the House can take to provide leadership to address glob al warming. The House can make the operations of the House carbon-neutral, so that its net carbon dioxide equivalent (CO2-e) emissions become zero.

Using data developed by the Government Accountability Office, and reviewed by Lawrence Berkeley National Laboratory, it is estimated that in 2006 the operation of the House complex was responsible for approximately 91,000 tons [4] of CO2-e emissions in fiscal year 2006. This value is equivalent to the annual CO2-e emissions of 17,200 cars [5]. Figure 1 shows the sources for the CO2-e emissions for the House buildings by fuel type.

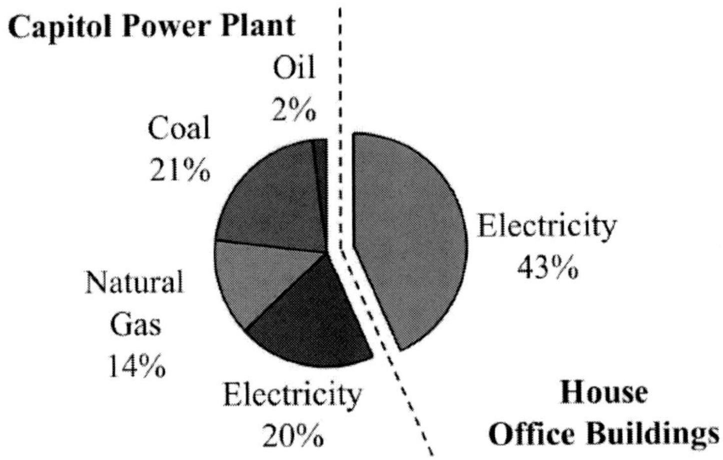


Figure 1. Total 2006 Carbon Dioxide-Equivalent Emissions for House Buildings [Source GAO 2007].

The largest source of CO2-e emissions for the House buildings is from the electricity purchased by the House and other Legislative Branch agencies. Electricity comprises 63% of CO2-e emissions and is generated offsite from several sources: coal (53%), nuclear (37%), natural gas (7%), renewables (2%), and fuel oil (1%). Combustion of fossil fuels in the CPP boilers generates steam to heat the buildings and accounts for the remaining 37% of the House CO2-e emissions. The power plant's boilers are fired using coal (43% of the 2006 boiler output), natural gas (52%), and oil (5%); the relative amounts of fuel used vary widely from year to year.

Figure 2 illustrates that there has been no clear trend in CO2-e emissions for the past 10 years, with the drop in 1998-2001 for central steam due to fuel switching for the boilers in the CPP. The data [6] in Figure 2 use CO2-e emissions factors from GAO 2007.

Figure 3 shows the CO2-e emissions by type of energy from the House buildings and the House- attributable portion of the CPP output. This graph illustrates the need for reduction of emissions from electricity use and fuel use addressed by the strategies below. Historically, the use of different percentages of coal, natural gas and oil has varied widely from year to year; for example, in

1998, coal was considerably reduced, and the difference was made up in natural gas and oil.

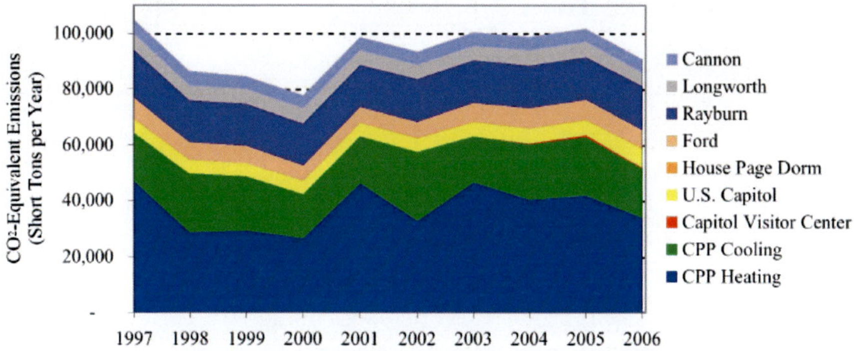


Figure 2. Total Carbon Dioxide-Equivalent Emissions for the House Buildings 1997-2006.

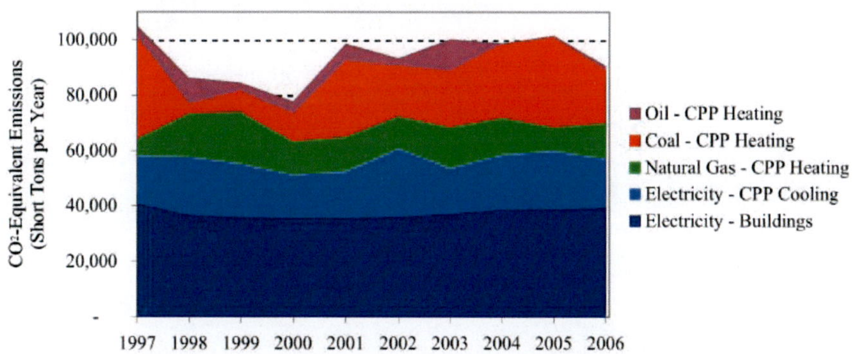


Figure 3. Carbon Dioxide-Equivalent Emissions by Type of Energy.

Figure 4 shows proposed strategies for achieving carbon neutrality for the House buildings. As shown by the vertical line, the baseline year is 2006. The first strategy is to offset CO2-e emissions from electricity use by purchasing electricity generated from renewable sources. The second strategy is to reduce the carbon emissions from the fossil fuel use at the CPP. By switching from coal, oil, and natural gas use to natural gas only, the CO2-e emissions of the CPP required to meet the House's needs can be lowered 30%. The third strategy is to offset the remaining fossil fuel use by purchasing carbon offsets.

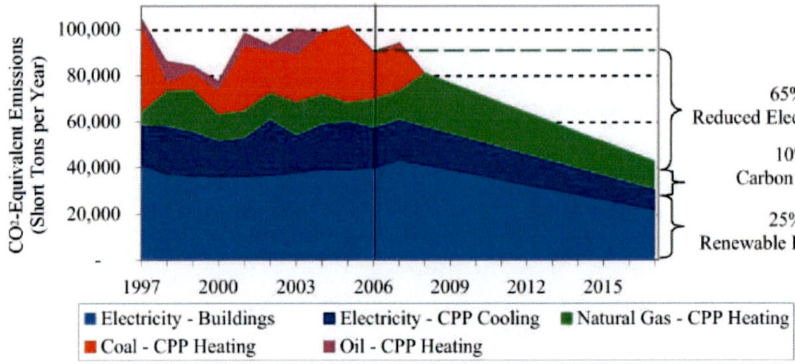


Figure 4. Carbon Dioxide-Equivalent Emissions Reduction Scenario.

**Strategy #1: Purchase renewable power for electricity use**

The purchase of electricity is the largest source of CO2-e emissions from the operations of the House. To achieve the goal of making House operations carbon-neutral, the CAO and the AOC have negotiated to purchase 100% of the electricity needs, approximately 103,000 megawatt- hours per year, using renewable power starting October 1, 2007. The electricity cost premium to purchase power generated from renewable sources is an additional $520,000 and that amount has been included in the Fiscal Year 2008 Legislative Branch Appropriations bill. This increased cost will be offset over the long run by energy conservation actions. By implementing this recommendation, the House buildings will eliminate 57,000 tons of CO2-e emissions, or the equivalent of removing 11,000 cars from the road.

**Strategy #2: Operate the CPP with Natural Gas**

The second strategy is to reduce the CO2-e emissions from the coal burned at the CPP to meet the needs of the House of Representatives. The CPP should use natural gas instead of coal to meet the needs of the House. By taking this action, CO2-e emissions from the CPP can be lowered by 30% from their 2006 level. Because the boilers already have dual-fuel capabilities, they can be switched to natural gas and can use their alternate fuel either coal or oil as emergency back-up. The total cost to implement this recommendation in Fiscal Year 2008 is $2.75 million. Money to purchase the natural gas is included in the Legislative Branch Appropriations bill. Implementing this recommendation will eliminate over 10,000 tons of CO2-e emissions, the equivalent of removing 1,900 cars from the road.

The switch to natural gas will also dramatically reduce other pollutant emissions from the CPP. More than 95% of sulfur oxides (SOx) and at least 50% of nitrogen oxides (NOx) and carbon monoxide could be eliminated. Onsite testing and further analysis is needed to determine the actual reductions possible. The CPP already monitors stack emissions, so relevant data may be available or obtained. The cost of removing fly ash from the coal-fired boilers, expected to double or triple in coming years, would be eliminated. The dual-fueled boilers can be switched to natural gas immediately if directed.

**Strategy #3: Purchase Carbon Offsets on the Chicago Climate Exchange**

Even by using electricity from renewable sources and switching the generation of steam to natural gas, the House will still have to offset 24,000 tons of carbon emissions to achieve the goal of carbon-neutral operations. Therefore, it is recommended that all remaining carbon emissions be offset by purchasing Carbon Financial Instrument (CFI) contracts, or carbon credits, specifically for projects in the United States from the Chicago Climate Exchange. The Carbon Financial Instrument is the financial instrument developed by the Chicago Climate Exchange (CCX) to facilitate price-transparent, cash-transaction emissions trading based upon emissions reductions and emissions offsets by CCX Members and Participant Members. Each CFI sold represents the emission reduction of 100 metric tons of carbon dioxide. CFIs are assigned unique serial numbers that are tracked in the CCX database called a registry. CFIs are traded in similar fashion to traditional commodities such as corn and wheat. These carbon financial instruments will be retired permanently so that the carbon credits cannot be used again. The Chicago Climate Exchange has been notified of the House's intent to initiate this action. The cost of offsetting 24,000 tons of greenhouse gases is estimated to be approximately $95,000. Money is available in CAO's Fiscal Year 2008 budget to make these purchases. The CAO will purchase CO2-e offsets equal to House-attributable emissions on an annual basis.

## Goal #2: Reduce the Carbon Footprint of the House by Cutting Energy Consumption by 50% in 10 Years

While the House can achieve carbon neutrality immediately, the long-term goal is to lower carbon emissions, or the carbon footprint, by improving energy efficiency. Cost-effective investments in energy efficiency will pay for themselves and reduce the House's annual operating costs. The goal of reducing the House's energy use by 50% over the next 10 years should be adopted. The specific strategies identified below outline the steps needed to achieve this goal. After careful examination of the current carbon emission and energy use of the House and analyzing the recommendations contained in this report, it is feasible for the House to achieve the 50% energy reduction goal. In carrying out this goal, every opportunity will be taken to purchase American-made energy efficiency technologies.

Before detailing each of those recommendations and outlining the effects, it is important to provide the following background on the energy use and carbon footprint of House operations.

### *Characteristics of the House Building Complex*

The House buildings represent a diverse mix of office and support spaces, and include historical buildings as well as the new Capitol Visitor Center, currently under construction. The House complex can be viewed as a small campus within the larger Capitol complex.

The House building complex described in this report consists of seven buildings in the Capitol complex, accounting for 6.1 million square feet, roughly 40% of the 15.4 million square feet of the total Capitol complex area (see Table 1, which does not include the CPP).

**Table 1. Characteristics of the House Buildings**

| Building Name | Year Built | 2006 Floor Area [square feet] |
|---|---|---|
| Cannon House Office Building | 1908 | 888,536 |
| Longworth House Office Building | 1933 | 682,791 |
| Rayburn House Office Building (inc. E & W Underground Garages) | 1965 | 2,971,469 |
| Ford House Office Building | 1939 | 594,730 |
| House Page Dorm | 1940 | 44,986 |
| U.S. Capitol[A] | 1793 | 421,800 |
| Capitol Visitors Center | (under construction) | 580,000 |
| TOTAL | | 6,122,312 |

[A]Only one-half of the Capitol floor area is under House jurisdiction.

***Energy Consumption for the House Buildings***

Energy is supplied to the House buildings from several sources. Electricity is purchased from the local utility and provided directly to the buildings. The buildings are on a district steam and chilled water loop supplied by the CPP, located on site. The CPP does not produce electricity, but purchases electricity to operate the chillers. The boilers of the plant primarily use coal or natural gas to produce steam that is distributed to many of the buildings. Some of the buildings, for example, the Ford House Office Building, have other suppliers of heating and cooling energy.

Table 2 shows total energy consumption in House buildings. The table includes energy consumption, primarily electricity, metered at each House building, electricity used by the CPP to provide chilled water to House buildings, and fuel used by the CPP boilers to provide steam heat to House buildings.

**Table 2. 2006 House Buildings Energy Consumption**

| Building Name | Metered Electricity (MWh) | Electricity (Million Btu) | Total Fuel (Million Btu) | Total Energy (Million Btu) |
|---|---|---|---|---|
| Cannon HOB | 9,126 | 31,138 | | 31,138 |
| LongworthHOB | 8,761 | 29,893 | | 29,893 |
| Rayburn HOB plus East & West Underground Garages | 28,046 | 95,694 | | 95,694 |
| Ford HOB | 11,745 | 40,074 | 22,992 | 63,066 |
| House Page Dorm | 393 | 1,342 | | 1,342 |
| U.S. Capitol | 12,709 | 43,363 | | 43,363 |
| Capitol Visitors Center | 431 | 1,472 | | 1,472 |
| CapitolPowerPlant@31% | 32,199 | 109,862 | 433,259 | 543,121 |
| TOTAL | 103,411 | 352,838 | 456,251 | 809,089 |

Source: Architect of the Capitol 2007 HOB = House Office Building.

The CPP provides chilled water and steam throughout the Capitol complex, not just to House buildings. Because metered consumption of chilled water and steam is not available for each House building, LBNL had to estimate of the percentage of total CPP output that was attributable to the House buildings. Based on square footage data for buildings served by the CPP, they estimated that 31% of the CPP output is attributable to House buildings. LBNL calculated chilled water and steam energy consumption to the House buildings by applying that 31% factor to total CPP electricity and fuel consumption.

In 2006, the total annual energy use for the House buildings was an estimated 809,100 million Btu (MBtu) expressed as site energy (not source energy).

Figure 5 shows that for the past ten years there is no clear trend in total energy consumption for the House buildings. Central steam predominates, followed by central chilled water from the CPP. There are numerous opportunities for investing in cost-effective energy efficiency measures in the House office buildings and at the CPP. Figure 6 shows where energy was used in 2006 in the House office buildings. To reduce total House energy use by 50% over the next ten years, energy use will have to be reduced five percentage points per year. This is more than twice the Energy Policy Act (EPAct) of 2005 requirement of 2% reductions in energy use per year for federal buildings. The largest use of energy in the House buildings is for cooling (38%), followed by heating (28%), lighting (17%), office equipment (7%), and other uses (10%), such as ventilation fans, elevators, hot water and other equipment and appliances.

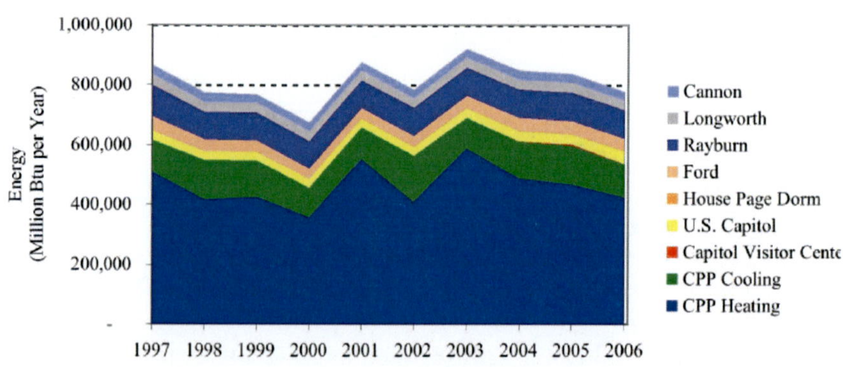


Figure 5. Total Energy Consumption for House Buildings 1997-2006.

The total 2006 annual electricity consumption for the House buildings, including the 31% factor at the CPP for the chilled water, is 103,000 MWh (Table 3). This is roughly the same electricity consumption as that of 8,600 U.S. homes.

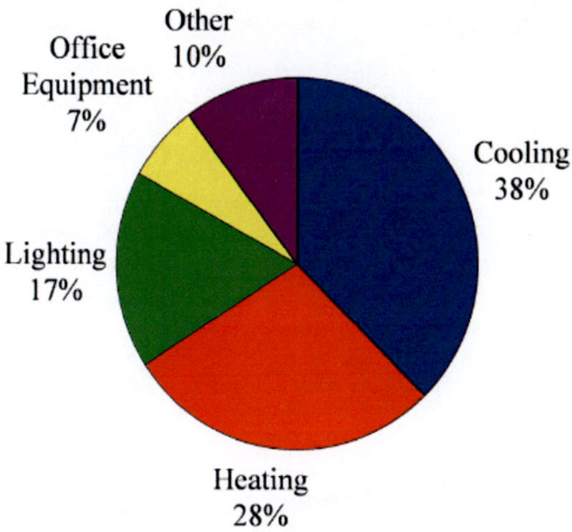


Figure 6. Total Energy Use (site) for House Buildings.

**Table 3. Trend in Electricity Consumption for House Buildings and CPP, 2003-2006**

| House Buildings Electricity (MWh) | | | | | 2006 Change from 2003 Baseline | |
|---|---|---|---|---|---|---|
| | FY 03 | FY 04 | FY 05 | FY 06 | MWh | % |
| Cannon HOB | 9,057 | 9,205 | 8,890 | 9,126 | 69 | 1% |
| Longworth HOB | 9,173 | 9,867 | 9,560 | 8,761 | -412 | -4.5% |
| Rayburn HOB | 27,485 | 27,399 | 27,774 | 28,046 | 561 | 2% |
| FordHOB | 11,836 | 12,749 | 12,748 | 11,745 | -91 | -1% |
| House Page Dorm | 410 | 439 | 409 | 393 | -16, | -4% |
| U.S. Capitol (House only) | 9,403 | 9,663 | 9,682 | 12,709 | 3,306 | 35% |
| House Total (kWh) | 67,471 | 70,894 | 71,665 | 71,212 | 3,741 | 5.5% |
| Capitol Power Plant @ 31% | 34,214 | | | 32,199 | 14,917 | -6% |
| TOTAL HOUSE & CAPITOL POWER PLANT | 101,685 | | | 103,411 | 29,850 | 1.7% |

Source: Architect of the Capitol 2007.

Table 3 also shows a 2% increase in electricity consumption by 2006 from the FY03 baseline established by the Energy Policy Act of 2005, with an even greater increase in electricity use in the House buildings. The power consumption at the CPP has been decreasing over the same period.

Figure 7 shows the proposed goal for reducing energy use by 50% in ten years. The reductions mandated for federal buildings under the Energy Policy Act of 2005 (EPAct 2005) are indicated by the blue line. Per the EPAct 2005, beginning in 2006, a building must use 2% less per year than its 2003 energy use. The proposed strategy for the House complex nearly doubles those savings.

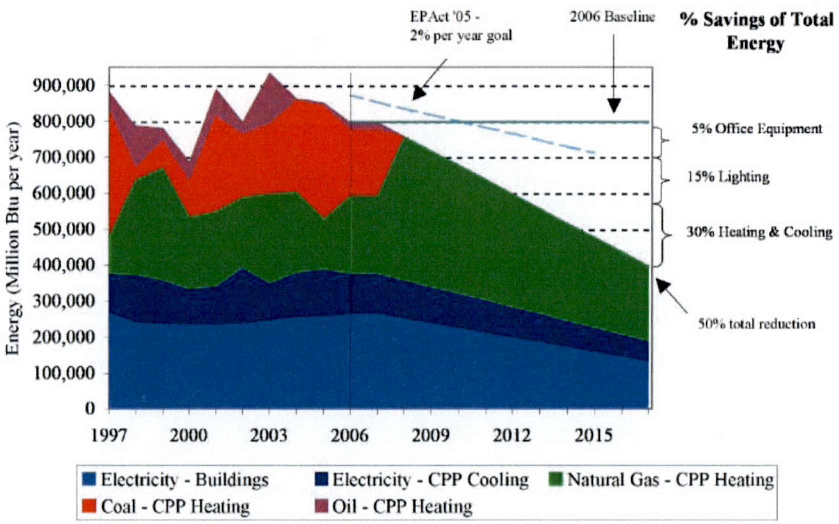


Figure 7. Energy reduction scenario due to improved efficiency measures.

Figure 8 shows that the House buildings' energy costs have risen dramatically in recent years, more than doubling in the past 10 years.

Figure 9 shows the costs, energy consumption and CO2-e emissions indexed to their 1996 values.

The overall strategy proposed is to pursue an optimal mix of life-cycle cost-effective investments in energy reduction and the most cost-effective ways to reduce CO2-e emissions.

Figure 10 shows one scenario for reduced costs from pursuing carbon-neutral strategies. In this scenario, the reduced demand for energy from the cost - effective, energy-efficiency retrofits pays for the increased premium for electricity generated by renewables, the costs of switching from coal to natural gas, and the purchased carbon offsets. These estimates do not include the additional savings from avoiding disposal of fly ash from burning coal, as well as other direct and indirect environmental benefits.

Investments in energy efficiency should not be delayed if appropriated funds are not available. Congress, in the Energy Policy Act of 2005, recognized the value of alternative financing mechanisms as a means to leverage private-sector funds to make improvements in public-sector operations. The use of such alternative financing mechanisms where appropriate to move projects forward is a sound approach to help reach the energy efficiency goals.

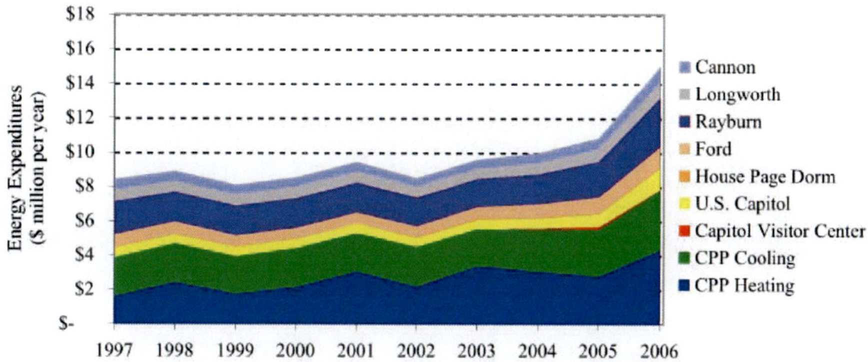


Figure 8. Annual Energy Expenditure for Key End Uses and Buildings.

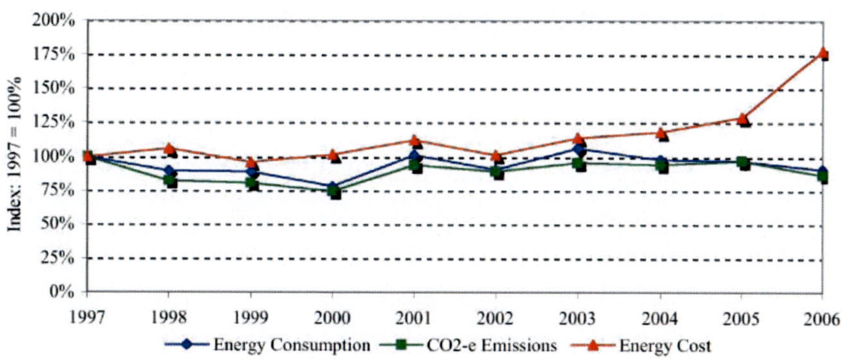


Figure 9. Trends in Costs, Energy, and Emissions.

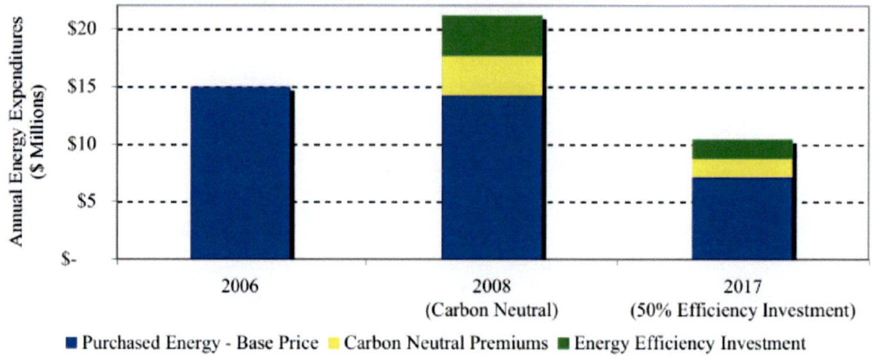


Figure 10. Total carbon-neutral scenario costs.

## Goal #3: Make House Operations a Model of Sustainability

In addition to improving the way the House consumes energy, the House should provide an environmentally sustainable and healthy working environment for employees. The House has the opportunity to lead by example by making its business operations a model of sustainability.

### *Strategy #1: Direct the CAO to Oversee Implementation of "Green the Capitol Initiative"*

It is recommended that the office of the CAO be charged with the responsibility to oversee implementation of the "Green the Capitol Initiative" for the House of Representatives. This includes working with the AOC and other offices to improve the sustainability of the day-to-day operations of the House office buildings, including maintenance, finance, travel, childcare, and food service.

### *Strategy #2: Develop a House Sustainability Plan*

In June 2007, the CAO convened a meeting with three sustainability leaders from major universities that are championing sustainability. Representatives from Harvard, Yale, and the University of California provided briefings on their goals, operations, and successes. A key component of their success has been a sustainability plan to give focus and direction to reform efforts. It is recommended that the CAO be charged with responsibility to develop and implement a House Sustainability Plan as a dynamic document intended to provide a roadmap for major steps toward sustainability over the next 20 years and which will identify timetables for specific actions.

***Strategy #3: Pursue Networking, Outreach, and Coordination***

The CAO should work to pursue networking, outreach, and coordination with several groups, including the Senate, to undertake activities on sustainability and CO2-e emissions reduction. The CAO should work with the AOC to make sustainability a mission-critical element of their business model. The CAO should undertake outreach efforts, including hosting a series of greening summits, to better understand where the House can improve its effort and inform the public of the House's accomplishments.

***Strategy #4: Mechanisms for Evaluating Success and Reporting Progress***

The CAO should track benchmarks monthly on energy use and CO2-e emissions and prepare an annual report documenting progress on the twin goals of carbon neutrality and sustainable operations. Energy and CO2-e emissions data will be made available on a website, both as an educational tool and as a way to provide feedback to House staff and other interested parties.

# PART TWO: DETAILED RECOMMENDATIONS

Part Two of the report presents the detailed recommendations for each of the goals identified in Part One.

## Recommendations for Goal #1

The recommended approaches for achieving Goal #1, *Operate the House in a carbon-neutral manner by the end of the 110$^{th}$ Congress*, have been addressed in Part One as specific strategies.

## Recommendations for Goal #2

The recommended strategies for Goal #2, Reduce the carbon footprint of the House by cutting energy consumption by 50% in 10 years, are described in two sections:

- Actions to reduce energy consumption in House office buildings
- Actions to reduce energy consumption at the CPP

### *Actions to Reduce Energy Consumption in House Office Buildings*

Three of the strategies towards achieving carbon neutrality – purchasing renewable electricity, fuel switching at CPP, and purchasing carbon offsets – can be implemented quickly. The next step is to make improvements in House energy use. By implementing these improvements through investment in energy-efficient technologies and changes in operating practices, the House can reduce its ongoing cost of operations while maintaining carbon neutrality.

The starting point to improving the energy efficiency of House buildings is to understand where energy is being consumed. This applies throughout the Capitol complex. There are two major areas where investment in energy efficiency technologies ca n be made: in House buildings themselves, and at the CPP. The following three sections illustrate these actions.

### *Metering, Commissioning, and Tracking*

Understanding how much energy is being used and where it is being consumed is critical to effective energy management. Meters for all energy flows (electricity, natural gas, steam, chilled water, condensate return) should be installed throughout the Capitol complex. This data must then be regularly collected, widely circulated, and effectively used.

### *House Buildings and Meters*

Reliable and up-to-date energy consumption information is vital to efficiently operate the Capitol buildings. It is also important to track progress in achieving the emissions goals.

It is therefore recommended that the calibration of present meters and loads served by them is verified. Additional steam and chilled water meters should be installed and maintained in House buildings where necessary to understand the system's performance. It is recommended that real- time tracking be developed to determine whether or not benchmarks for load shapes, schedules, and other energy efficiency measures are being achieved. Finally, House staff, building managers, and CPP staff should be provided with real-time information with easy-to-understand graphics on building energy use and $CO_2$-e emissions.

This proposed emissions-information display system can also serve as a model for other government and commercial buildings.

### *Benchmarking and Commissioning*

The place to begin saving energy and improving the work environment is with a comprehensive review of energy use patterns and the condition of existing energy-using equipment and control systems. Lawrence Berkeley National Lab's preliminary review of energy consumption data and trends has identified buildings in the House complex that are twice as energy-intensive as others, with significant cooling energy use in winter, and uncharacteristically high energy use during low-occupancy days and hours. These findings indicate large opportunities for reducing energy use and CO2-e emissions by commissioning the House's buildings.

Tuning up the House's buildings is a process known as "commissioning." Commissioning has been shown to yield, on average, 15% energy savings often in less than a year. Retrocommissioning means commissioning an existing building rather than a new building. Periodic retro-commissioning is recommended to ensure that benchmarks for energy and CO2-e emissions savings continue to be met. Commissioning requires no capital investment, and by helping reduce baseline energy use, it minimizes the cost and maximizes the energy savings from subsequent equipment retrofits. Commissioning is also the primary way to identify and resolve non-energy problems, such as poor comfort conditions, and provide additional benefits to staff. Preliminary walk-throughs conducted during the preparation of this report identified many commissioning opportunities in the House complex that would yield significant energy savings at low cost.

*Specific recommendations for metering, commissioning, and tracking:*

- Verify calibration of present meters and loads
- Install steam meters and chilled water meters
- Develop utility tracking screens of benchmarked load shapes, schedules, etc.
- Provide Congressional staff, building managers, and CPP staff with real-time information Commission (retro-commission) major systems

### *Lighting*

It is recommended that all the overhead lighting in the House buildings be updated with modern, energy-efficient lighting components. These fixtures should be refitted with high-performance electronic ballasts and lamps. This measure will reduce the lighting loads in the House suites and meeting rooms from 2.5 watts per square foot to under 1 watt per square foot while improving lighting quality. This action will reduce the energy and carbon footprint from the House buildings' lighting by more than 50% – the equivalent of eliminating over 7,130 tons of CO2-e emissions or taking 1,340 cars off the road. Motion sensors and daylight controls will be installed where practical and periodically reviewed for wider application as technologies mature and prices drop.

There are many tunnels and service corridors connecting the Capitol buildings that are lit continuously even though they are very sparsely used at night. Newly-available, two-level or bilevel fluorescent lighting provides a low light level during unoccupied hours and brings the light level to full intensity when anyone enters the tunnel or corridor. By using occupancy sensors to dim lighting of service areas to a low-energy state when unoccupied, the lighting energy consumption will be greatly reduced without reducing security. It is also recommended that the AOC investigate the feasibility of two-step lighting for the parking garages in the House complex.

Table lamps and floor-standing lamps are common in the House buildings and most use inefficient light bulbs. Incandescent bulbs in 2000 desk lamps in the House office buildings were replaced with modern compact fluorescent lamps (CFLs) on Earth Day (April 22, 2007). By the date of this report, June 21, 2007, these CFLs have already paidfor themselves in lower electricity charges. By completing the conversion of the remaining 10,000 table and floor lamps in the House office complex to CFLs by 2008, the House will save $245,000 in electric power costs every year. Every new Energy Star CFL will use only a fourth of the electricity and last 8 to 10 times longer than the incandescent lamp it replaced. Replacing 12,000 CFLs in the House complex is the equivalent to removing 255 cars from the road.

The goal should be to refit all the incandescent sockets in the House complex including the many specialty applications (such as 3-way bulbs, small chandelier lamps, and dimmable lamps) that have inhibited previous high-efficiency lamp replacement programs. Because there are now inexpensive high-efficiency lamps available for these applications, it is recommend that AOC maintain a robust inventory of these efficient lamps.

It is recommended that energy efficiency be promoted among the 7,000 staff of the House by making high-efficiency lamps available at cost in the House Office Supply Store. If all staff members installed just one high-efficiency lamp in their home to replace a standard incandescent bulb used 3 hours/day, it would have the cumulative effect of removing 150 cars from the road.

Given the anticipated increase in high-efficiency lamp usage, the AOC should be directed to expand their lamp disposal program to include the proper collection of used high-efficiency lamps.

Exterior building lighting needs to be evaluated to identify energy-efficiency opportunities. This evaluation needs to balance energy savings, security, and the public visibility of building lighting with the potential energy savings.

*Specific recommendations for lighting:*

- Replace the inefficient overhead lighting with high-performance fluorescent lighting and improved controls
- Install motion-activated "two-level" lighting in service corridors, tunnels and parking areas
- Upgrade all desk lamps and floor -standing lamps with high-efficiency lamps
- Make high-efficiency lamps available at cost in the House office supply store.
- Direct AOC to collect high-efficiency lamps as part of its lamp disposal program
- Evaluate exterior building lighting

### *Office Equipment and Other Electronics*

Office equipment and other electronics are responsible for roughly 20% of total electricity use in the Capitol buildings. Desktop computers, displays, printers, and copiers consume the majority of this electricity, so the focus should be on these devices. A combination of improved operating practices and new, efficient equipment could reduce electricity use of office equipment and electronics by 50%.

Recommendations for reducing energy use, ranked roughly in order of potential energy savings, are described next. Making changes in computer operations, back-ups, upgrades, and maintenance, will allow staff to safely power-down computers and related equipment during nights and weekends. All energy-saving features on equipment, such as sleep modes, should be enabled. Staff should be advised on ways to effectively consolidate printer and copier operations within offices. Replacing all CRT televisions with LCD models, possibly through bulk purchase, will save energy with the added benefit of increasing ergonomic comfort. Finally, only equipment complying with Energy Star specifications should be purchased.

In addition to providing electricity and CO2-e emissions savings, these measures have the important side benefits of space efficiencies, improved thermal characteristics and acoustic comfort in offices. Other efficiency measures for more specific opportunities will be described elsewhere.

*Specific recommendations for office equipment and other electronics:*

- Change computer operations to allow staff to centrally power-down equipment when unused for significant periods such as nights and weekends
- Maximize power management efforts present in existing electronic equipment through periodic audits and employee education
- Develop a preferred list of Energy Star-qualified office electronics
- Devise strategies to consolidate equipment

### *Heating, Ventilating and Air Conditioning (HVAC)*

Together, the CPP and Capitol complex buildings form a typical district heating and cooling system. This system consists of three main components: a "power" plant, [7] a distribution system and multiple buildings with various end uses. Figure 10 illustrates the connections between a generic plant and a generic space heating and cooling system in a building, along with some of the important energy and water flows.

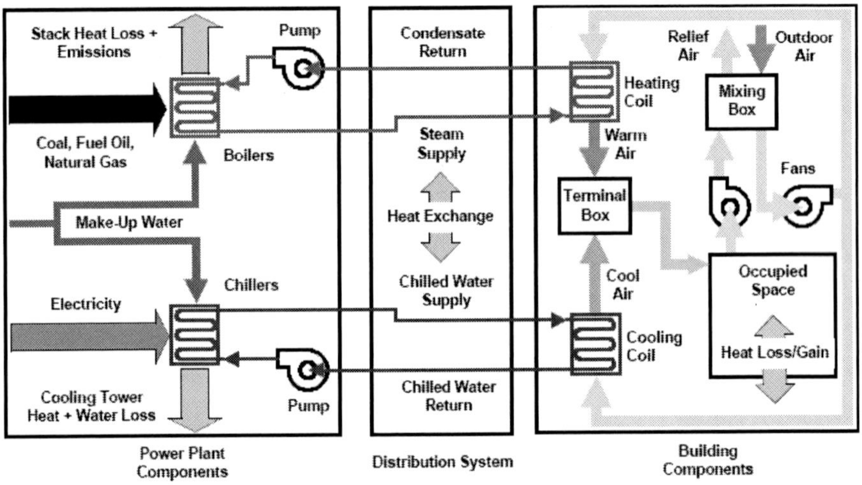


Figure 10. District Heating and Cooling System Schematic.

It is essential to recognize that the effects of the power plant, distribution system, and building inefficiencies are multiplicative. For example, to heat a conditioned space, if 40% of the steam and chilled water energy supplied to the buildings is wasted before it reaches the conditioned spaces, 15% of the energy supplied to the distribution system pipes is wasted before it reaches the buildings, and 25% of the energy supplied to the plant is wasted before it reaches the distribution system, then the net efficiency, fuel to end use, is reduced to only about 38%. This means that about 62% of the energy supplied to the plant is ultimately wasted, or conversely, the plant must supply about 2.6 times more energy than the building end uses require. It also means that actions to reduce CPP energy use should include improvements to the HVAC and distribution systems.

Consultants who have carried out energy audits of the Rayburn House Office Building and the Capitol Building have recommended several improvements to increase HVAC energy efficiency, such as replacing faulty equipment and using motors and pumps that are more efficient. However, the recommendations have not included two major opportunities that are available at relatively low cost: reducing duct leakage, and improving the operation of constant-speed fans that circulate hot and cool air.

Electricity used by fans to circulate hot and cool air in large commercial buildings is typically 30 to 50% of the total HVAC site energy use. Recent field data indicate that duct leakage can result in fan energy increases of 25 to 35%. It is possible to almost eliminate this energy waste by sealing the ducts using aerosol-based sealants or a similar technology. New wireless-based sensor and control technology has recently become available to enable constant air volume (CAV) air-handling systems to operate as variable air volume (VAV) systems. This will help reduce fan speeds and energy use, as well as reduce unnecessary heating and cooling. To use this wireless technology, fan drives need to be upgraded, but there is no need to replace other air distribution components. Potential energy savings from duct leakage sealing and improving fan operation could be as much as 30 to 50% of supply fan energy consumption, plus about 30 to 40% of the other heating, cooling, and HVAC auxiliary equipment energy consumption.

It is recommended that duct leakage tests and an analysis of available fan speed control technologies be conducted to better assess the potential energy savings. It is also recommended that fan schedules be optimized to avoid unnecessary equipment operation, further reducing energy use.

Ventilation air is supplied to each House building by its HVAC system, by building leakage, and in some cases, by open windows. Large reductions, (greater than 50%), in ventilation -related energy use may be possible if ventilation rates can be reduced without harming health and reducing work performance. It is recommended that detailed analyses be conducted and supplemented by onsite testing to select appropriate ventilation rates and technologies. It is also recommended that long-term monitoring be conducted to verify acceptable or superior indoor air quality. Specific efforts should include improving existing equipment and installing new equipment as needed to: a) measure and control ventilation rates such as measurement systems for HVAC outdoor airflows, demand-controlled ventilation systems for spaces with highly variable occupancy; b) calibrate and maintain ventilation economizer controls; c) re-circulate return air for 100% outdoor air systems where possible; d) recover ventilation heat that would be otherwise discharged outdoors; and e) implement improved particle filtration and add gas-phase air cleaning. Related efforts should include providing guidance to building operators and occupants about indoor pollutant source control to reduce the amount of ventilation needed.

*Specific recommendations for heating, ventilation, and air conditioning (HVAC) :*

- Retrofit motors, fan drives, pumps, and valves with energy-efficient models
- Modify CAV equipment and controls so that air-handling systems operate as VAV systems
- Seal air distribution ducts to minimize air leakage
- Optimize fan schedules to avoid unnecessary equipment operation

### *Information Technology Equipment and Data Centers*

Computer servers, network equipment and storage devices are collectively known as information technology (IT) equipment. IT equipment consumes a significant amount of electricity itself, but its energy consumption impact is magnified by the cooling that must be provided for the equipment. Opportunities for energy efficiency are similarly divided between improvements to the energy performance of the equipment itself and enhancements to the ways in which the operating environment of the equipment is maintained.

House IT systems are operated two ways: distributed operation, in which IT equipment is dispersed throughout Member and Committee offices in the House office buildings; and centralized operation, in which IT equipment is located in dedicated data center facilities.

### *Distributed IT Equipment Energy Savings Opportunities*

Energy savings opportunities in distributed IT equipment operation are available through careful attention to power management and process scheduling. These include: enabling sleep modes to allow equipment to reduce power when not actively providing computational services, powering off equipment when its services are not needed, and scheduling services carefully.

Server consolidation can also provide energy savings. Moving various IT functions to one server instead of spreading those functions across multiple machines can reduce the energy consumption associated with those IT functions while providing equal services. If IT functions are consolidated into centralized operations, the services available from the hardware can often be enhanced.

Beyond operational management, substantial energy savings are available from transitioning distributed IT equipment into a centralized operations model because of the cooling loads associated with the distributed IT equipment. Systems that are sprinkled throughout Member and committee offices require levels of power reliability and space conditioning that are much higher than the requirements for other office operations. For example, House office building ventilation systems do not have the degree of control that can allow air conditioning to be supplied solely to one small space housing a file server. As a result, one cluster of IT equipment in a particular office can often drive the space conditioning supply requirements for a large portion of the building, leading to enormous energy loses in unneeded cooling supplied to that large area. In some cases, offices in the same HVAC zone require heating in their space to override the cooling that is being delivered for the IT equipment.

Centralized data center facilities, by contrast, are designed to deliver focused space conditioning (and other infrastructure services like high -quality, reliable power) to meet the unique needs of IT equipment. Making the transition to a centralized IT equipment model would increase space available in the House office buildings currently used by IT equipment, as well as reduce the noise and the cooling loads on the HVAC systems that are overwhelmed in many areas. This will have the added benefit of improving thermal and acoustical comfort in the office. Consolidation would significantly reduce the number of servers that need to be purchased, housed, powered, cooled, and maintained, with corresponding energy, emissions, and other operating cost savings. Consolidation opportunities could be facilitated by the office moves at each new Congress.

*Specific recommendations for distributed IT equipment:*

- Specify energy management capability, energy efficiency, and environmentally - benign materials as desired product criteria in new purchases. Where applicable, use the Electronic Performance Environmental Assessment Tool (EPEAT) to guide purchasing decisions
- Enable power management to minimize unnecessary energy consumption

- Consolidate multiple servers into a smaller number of servers with higher utilization
- Consider energy consumption implications of service scheduling and maximize opportunities for IT equipment to be powered down or off
- Wherever possible, shift from distributed IT equipment to a centralized model that can be design-optimized for IT equipment operation

***Data Center Energy Savings Opportunities***

The opportunities for energy savings for servers and data centers are similarly divided into the energy savings potential of the IT equipment itself and the potential for improvement in energy efficiency of the dedicated services supporting the IT equipment, such as space conditioning and reliable power.

Operational improvements include efficiency improvements that require essentially no capital investment. Operating the existing stock of IT equipment with greater detail to power management could result in savings of 20% of existing energy consumption.

Energy efficiency levels achieved by the most efficient existing facilities today go well beyond those operational savings. These facilities build on the enhancements from improved operational maintenance. Specific improvements req uire more capital investment, planning and engineering. The technologies in this scenario are available today but are not widely used in the Capitol. Potential savings could be 45% of existing energy consumption. It should be noted that in state- of-the-art new data centers, reductions of energy use by approximately 66% are possible.

Improved operational control of computer-room air conditioners (CRACs) and Uninterruptible Power Supplies (UPSs) is recommended. There should be coordinated controls of CRACs in any data center room to eliminate simultaneous humidification and de-humidification. Also, temperature and humidity setpoints that are consistent with the IT equipment manufacturers' recommended range should be used. Finally, CRACs should operate double-conversion UPSs in bypass mode, when this feature is available and the switchover time to battery/inverter operation is consistent with the IT equipment requirements.

An evaluation of current computer rooms and servers needs to be done to develop ways to consolidate distributed servers. Opportunities are likely to include both consolidating the servers to fewer locations as well as consolidating to fewer physical servers, including virtualization.

An evaluation and adjustment of air distribution in computer rooms for thermal optimization should be conducted. In the current data centers, modeling tools are already being used to improve air-flow management. This is critical to effective and efficient data center operation. These tools need to be used to help configure and optimize the centers as modifications are made. Improved air-flow management, including hot aisle/cold aisle isolation, and the elimination of bypasses and leaks in the room and within racks should be pursued.

Finally, power management functions in servers and storage equipment need to be enabled to reduce energy use during light demand.

*Specific recommendations for data centers:*

- Specify energy management capability, energy efficiency, and environmentally- benign materials as desired product criteria in new purchases. Where applicable, use the Electronic Performance Environmental Assessment Tool (EPEAT) to guide purchasing decisions
- Enable power management functions in servers and storage equipment
- Turn off test and lab equipment when not in use.
- Install sensor -based lighting in server rooms and ensure lights (other than emergency lighting) are turned off during prolonged inactivity periods
- Evaluate current computer rooms and servers and find ways to consolidate distributed servers
- Improve operational control of CRACs and UPSs
- Evaluate and adjust air distribution in computer rooms for thermal optimization. Develop and enforce controls for the introduction of new equipment to maintain optimal equipment thermal performance within the space
- Perform a comprehensive energy efficiency assessment in the existing data centers to identify specific energy reduction opportunities and savings targets
- Institute an ongoing energy management process to continually monitor and improve the energy performance of data centers

### *Other End Uses*

Other end uses where energy efficiency opportunities exist are food service, vending machines, hot water, laundry, dry cleaning, gyms, elevators, escalators, and others. Each of these areas should be evaluated for energy efficiency investments.

## Actions to Reduce Energy Consumption at the CPP

The CPP is the largest single source of carbon emissions on Capitol Hill. It is important for Congress to take a leadership role in modernizing and updating this facility. It is recommended that the committees of jurisdiction review the plant's operation, and develop legislation to make the plant a model of efficient operations and sustainability. This legislation should be passed by the end of the 110$^{th}$ Congress.

Making changes to the CPP will take many years to plan, finance, and implement. During this interim period, it is recommended that the following actions be taken to optimize operations of the CPP to maximize energy efficiency and reduce energy consumption.

### *Boiler Plant*

The CPP produces high-pressure steam using seven dual -fuel boilers: two that are fired using coal or natural gas and five that are fired using oil or natural gas. Well-tuned, generic boilers have "fuel-to-steam" efficiencies in the range of 70 to 85% at full load, but the efficiency drops rapidly as less steam is needed. There can be further efficiency losses of 10 to 15% due to soot and scale contamination of the boiler heat transfer surfaces and poor water quality control practices. In combination at full load, as much as 45% of the energy in the fuel could be wasted.

The AOC is already planning to address one of the larger opportunities for energy savings: adding controls so that one or more boilers are operated at or near full load as much as possible. A variety of other e nergy -saving opportunities exist. These include: using natural gas only to fire the boilers instead of a combination of coal, oil, and natural gas; reducing boiler steam pressure from 200 PSI to 150 PSI reducing fuel usage by about 5%; and assessing opportunities to improve existing operation and maintenance programs such as regular cleaning to minimize boiler contamination, returning more condensate to the CPP, recovering more heat from the stacks to reduce the energy needed to preheat water for the boilers and resetting the steam supply pressure in mild weather to optimize the tradeoff between lowest acceptable steam pressure and piping pressure losses. Boiler performance needs to be monitored to measure the effects of these changes and to fine -tune equipment operation. This information should be available real-time, in an easy-to-use graphical format, for each component and for the overall boiler plant so that the operations staff can monitor and control it as well as flag components in need of maintenance or repair.

*Specific recommendations for the boiler plant*:

- Switch to using natural gas only
- Evaluate reduction of steam pressure generated by the CPP boilers from 200 PSI to 150 PSI
- Implement best practices for operations and maintenance
- Monitor performance

***Chiller Plant***

There are a number of strategies that can be implemented at the CPP chiller plant to save energy, money, and CO2-e emissions. While further study will be needed to more precisely determine the possible savings, there appear to be opportunities for 10 to 20% savings in the electricity used for the overall chiller plant, which is comprised of the chillers, chilled water and condensing water pumps, cooling towers, water-side economizer heat exchangers, interconnecting piping and valves, and controls.

***Implement Best Practices for Operations and Maintenance***

The CPP chiller plant is undergoing modification, relocation, and modernization of the major equipment and controls, offering new opportunities for energy efficient operation. The plant already appears to have an excellent maintenance program. Specific opportunities for energy efficient plant operation, some of which are already being implemented, include:

- Operate the most efficient available chillers for any given load
- Operate the cooling towers at the best operating point given the tradeoff between tower fan and chiller compressor power
- Continue to explore chilled water temperature reset strategies to deliver the highest acceptable chilled water temperature
- In winter and shoulder months, operate the water-side economizer system in the best combination of series or parallel configuration to obtain "free" cooling, again with fan vs. chiller power in mind
- Investigate the opportunity to reset the chilled water supply pressure to follow the load
- Operate the new chillers' synchronous motors to control the plant power factor

For cooling tower, water-side economizer, and chilled water supply pressure reset optimization, further study and analysis will be needed, and ideally software written, to inform the operators on the most efficient configuration for the combination of load, chilled water temperature, and wet-bulb temperature.

### *Retrofit Motors with Premium Efficiency Motors*

It is recommended that a study be performed to assess the opportunity for replacing existing motors with premium efficiency motors. In particular, the older west-plant cooling tower fan motors seem to be optimum candidates.

### *Evaluate Retrofit Potential of Variable-Speed Drives on Pump Motors*

The new chilled-water secondary pumps are equipped with variable-speed drives, and there is a planned conversion of the older pumps to two-speed operation; the option to make the latter pumps completely variable should be investigated, as variable speed pumping would fully support parallel operation and pressure reset in the most energy-efficient manner. Also, the condensing water pumps should be studied for variable-speed operation, which would allow further optimization of the condensing side of the plant and the current strategy of throttling flows could be minimized.

### *Monitor Performance*

The key delivery variables of chilled water supply temperature and pressure are paramount in the monitoring of the plant. The metric for efficient supply of temperature and pressure should be overall plant kW per ton of cooling supplied, including all power consumed by chillers, chilled and condensing water pumps, and cooling tower fans. This information should be available real- time, in an easy-to-use graphical format, for each component and for the overall chiller plant so that the operations staff can monitor and control it, as well as flag components in need of maintenance or repair.

*Specific recommendations for the chiller plant:*

- Implement best practices for operations and maintenance
- Retrofit motors with premium efficiency motors
- Evaluate retrofit potential of variable -speed drives on pump motors
- Monitor performance
- Evaluate new efficient chillers for West Refrigeration Plant

### *Distribution System*

Two capital-intensive improvements should be considered to improve distribution system performance:

Steam traps are used to remove water from steam lines as well as at the thousands of heat exchangers in the buildings, and are often a critical source of energy inefficiency. Although the AOC has an excellent trap maintenance program in place, many traps cannot be maintained easily, such as in the Longworth building. The problem of maintaining steam traps can be reduced by changing steam distribution to hot water, where feasible. The AOC is already considering such a change in the Longworth building.

The steam and chilled water pipes that connect the CPP to the buildings that it serves are located in an extremely hot environment throughout the year due to heat losses from the steam pipes. Energy losses associated with steam line leakage and inadequate insulation can be in the range of 5 to 20% of the energy entering the steam line. An audit is needed to quantify the savings opportunities from lowering steam temperatures and pressures and improving the pipe insulation.

*Specific recommendations for the distribution system:*

- Improve maintenance of steam traps, increasing steam system distribution efficiency
- Determine need for new insulation of all distribution lines to reduce heating and cooling losses

### *CPP Alternatives*

One major opportunity that the House should consider further is the conversion of the CPP to be a combined heat and power (CHP) system, also known as a cogeneration system. Such a system would generate electrical power on site, and energy that would normally be wasted in offsite electricity generation (as much as two thirds of the energy input) could be used to produce steam and chilled water for use onsite.

A CHP system can save at least 50% of the combined energy that otherwise would be required to separately genera te electricity off site plus steam and chilled water onsite. The conversion is capital-intensive and requires further study. A report requested by the AOC for such a system will be available this summer.

## RECOMMENDATIONS FOR GOAL #3

The recommended strategies for Goal #3, Make House operations *a model of sustainability*, are described in the following sections:

- Water Management
- Landscape Management
- Transportation and Alternative Fuels
- Food Service
- Procurement, Materials, Recycling, and Cleaning
- Leadership, Education, and Outreach

In order to achieve this goal, every attempt will be made to purchase American-made environmentally sustainable products.

## Water Management

Water use needs to be managed in three areas: indoor water consumption, outdoor irrigation use, and stormwater runoff. Irrigation water and runoff are discussed further in the following section on Landscaping. Reducing water usage has a secondary impact on the carbon footprint as it saves energy for water pumping and for wastewater treatment.

According to the AOC, water is the only purchased utility not tracked by the AOC's online Utility Tracking and Management program (AOC 2007). Instead, AOC staff maintains water consumption and billing data separately. Data are available for 67 meters within the Capitol complex. Water consumption for offsite facilities is not included in this information. The 67 meters account for all campus water consumption, including landscape irrigation and CPP cooling tower use. Water is metered by supply volume only. There is no separate metering of sewer volume.

Since FY 2003, water consumption tracked by these meters rose 8.9 percent, from 438 million gallons to 478 million gallons. CPP water consumption was relatively stable during this time, but in FY 2003, much of the Capitol complex irrigation system was shut down while backflow preventers were installed. This condition may have produced an artificially low baseline volume. Increased consumption could also result from aging infrastructure.

A storm water management rain garden was installed in 2004. The rain garden gathers rain water, which the vegetation not only utilizes for growth, but also processes oil and other manmade products cleaning the storm water prior to draining into the sewage system.

In FY 2006, AOC developed a preliminary analysis of improved water metering for the Capitol campus. This includes consideration of separate metering of supply and sewer volume since water that is evaporated from cooling towers or used for landscape irrigation does not incur sew er volume charges. AOC also plans an initial edit of its Design Standards for irrigation systems. In FY 2007, AOC will meet with the District of Columbia Water and Sewer Authority to upgrade water metering to improve the Agency's ability to trace and address water consumption inefficiencies. AOC also plans to include water usage in the online Utility Tracking and Management program in FY 2007.

Annual water use for landscaping is shown in Table 4.

**Table 4. Annual water use for landscaping (gallons per year)**

| | 2003 | 2004 | 2005 | 2006 |
|---|---|---|---|---|
| Total landscaping water consumed, irrigation and fountains (based on meters that are irrigation-only) | 77,806,212 | 105,425,364 | 57,817,408 | 91,360,720 |

Source: AOC 2007.

Currently there is considerably less information available on water consumption and costs or wastewater volumes and costs than exists on energy consumption and costs. To reduce water consumption, use water more efficiently, and determine energy savings from reduced water demand, more information is needed about water use and costs related to Capitol facilities. It is recommended that additional meters to track building water use be installed. Tests should also be conducted regularly to determine water quality.

Water-consuming equipment in the House buildings includes faucets and toilets in bathrooms, dishwashers, food steamers, pre-rinse spray valves and icemakers in food service, and clothes washers, dishwashers, showers, tub-spout diverters, faucets, and toilets. Replacing such equipment with high-efficiency products, either low-flow or water-free, will reduce water consumption.

*Specific recommendations for water:*

- Analyze water consumption
- Analyze water quality
- Install additional water meters
- Evaluate potential for water-efficient fixtures and follow EPA recommended practices
- Install low-flow and water-free fixtures

## Landscape Management

Like buildings, outdoor spaces can conserve resources. They can also degrade or wastefully consume resources. Unlike buildings, green outdoor spaces have the capacity to enhance and regenerate natural resources. No environmental audit of a building complex is complete without consideration of the design and care of the grounds. In the best case, well-designed grounds enhance watershed health and biodiversity. In the worst case, grounds support little or no life and send polluted stormwater downstream. There is always room to further strengthen and celebrate natural heritage, and there is no place more appropriate to do so than on the historic landscape of the Capitol grounds. Greening the Capitol grounds can be accomplished incrementally by integrating a number of improvements in design features and maintenance practices:

### *Stormwater Management*

The Capitol complex has the opportunity to provide a relief for excessive stormwater runoff. The Capitol complex is served by District of Columbia's combined sewer system, which means that excessive stormwater runoff leads to sewage overflows, which is the primary source of pollution in the Anacostia and Potomac Rivers. Stormwater runoff from paved surfaces and lawns can carry pollutants, overwhelm urban infrastructure, erode stream channels, and degrade aquatic habitats.

In addition to green roof technology, porous pavements and rain gardens are strategies that can vastly improve the stormwater performance of the parking lots and other paved areas on the Capitol grounds. A rain garden area can be designed to be periodically saturated with stormwater, providing another layer of protection against excessive runoff. Parking lot runoff tends to be particularly polluted due to automobile fluids carried by stormwater. These strategies, in addition to collecting stormwater, can help filter out contaminants.

*Specific recommendations for storm water management*:

- Use porous pavements to replace impervious surfaces, increasing infiltration of stormwater into the soil
- Establish rain gardens, stormwater planters, and tree boxes to serve as collection points for stormwater runoff

### *Irrigation Water Efficiency*

The Capitol complex should also encourage sound water resource management. Emphasis should be placed on careful and efficient use of water to meet the needs of the Capitol complex. Water already on site should be used as much as possible. Irrigation needs could also be reduced by using indigenous plants.

*Specific recommendations for irrigation water efficiency:*

- Replace on-site water use with high efficiency irrigation, including captured rainwater or recycled site water
- Perform a soil/climate analysis to determine appropriate landscape type and design landscape with indigenous plants to reduce or eliminate irrigation requirements

### *Biodiversity*

To the extent compatible with historic landscape preservation, simple landscapes like lawns should be enhanced with other forms of vegetation that more fully achieve the health, richness, and complexity of the natural world. Biodiversity encompasses the potential richness and complexity of plant and animal life supported by microbe-rich soil. A single site's contribution to biodiversity provides pleasure to its users as well as an incremental increase in habitat for desirable species. As this country's population grows and land consumption rises, tended gardens in urban areas can provide increasingly significant supplemental habitat, particularly to plant, bird, and insect species.

*Specific recommendation for biodiversity:*

- Explore vegetation that could be added to the Capitol grounds that would enhance biodiversity

### *Expand Tree Canopy Coverage*

Trees offer many benefits to counter air pollution, water pollution, stormwater runoff, heat island effect, and other urban environmental ills. Trees sequester carbon and provide a reduction of carbon in the atmosphere. One ten-year-old tree can sequester 5 to 20 pounds of carbon per year; 100 ten-year-old trees will sequester up to a ton of carbon each year [8]. They act as giant filters as they convey water from their roots through their leaves and cool the air through evapotranspiration.

Research shows that the leaves of trees are like cups and can hold up to one-tenth of an inch of rainwater – an amount of rainfall that can trigger a discharge in some sewer-sheds.9 Trees should be planted in parking lots to shade vehicles and pavement on hot days. This also decreases the "heat island effect" associated with excessive temperatures in the city. Trees in parking lots can also mitigate the evaporative emissions from vehicles [10].

*Specific recommendation for expanding tree canopy coverage:*

- Strategically plant trees around the Capitol grounds for shade, helping with rainwater and carbon sequestration benefits
- Reconfigure the parking lots to permit intermittent tree planting

### *Improved Maintenance Practices*

Maintenance of green spaces can generate pollution. Chemical fertilizers and pesticides can pollute air and water and harm biodiversity both on- site and off-site. A wide variety of machinery is used to maintain the extensive lawns and the landscape of the Capitol complex. Opportunities should be examined to reduce or eliminate various machinery used in landscape maintenance. Regular application of compost impro ves soil and plant health and retains soil moisture. Composting also provides a means for recycling plant clippings and other organic wastes.

*Specific recommendation for improved maintenance practices:*

- Reduce or eliminate various machinery use in landscape maintenance
- Reduce chemical fertilizer and pesticide application
- Provide for regular compost application emphasizing using plant material generated on site

## Transportation and Alternative Fuels

There are 7,000 people employed in various capacities in the House. Each day they make at least two trips – one to get to work and one to get home – for a total of 14,000 trips each day or 70,000 trips each week. In addition, there are thousands of visitors daily to the House office buildings and the Capitol. The majority of these journeys to and from work are made by car. This pattern is similar to the regional norm, but significantly higher than the District of Columbia itself, where fewer than half of residents drive to work..

The impact of transportation on CO2-e emissions is enormous – estimates vary from one quarter to one third of all CO2-e emissions nationwide. The potential to reduce the carbon footprint of the House by addressing commuting issues is quite significant.

From a commuter perspective there are significant programs to help reduce the impact of House employee's current commuter trends – Transit Benefit Programs, Bike and Walk to Work Programs, and Telecommuting Programs.

***Alternative Fuel Infrastructure and Vehicles***

The House maintains its own fleet of vehicles, both cars and trucks. These are predominantly lower-efficiency vehicles, and should be replaced with efficient, hybrid, or alternate fuel vehicles.

An important element of decreasing our environmental foot print is moving towards alternative transportation fuels. The House will show leadership by providing such infrastructure.

*Specific recommendations for Alternative fuel infrastructure:*

- An E-85 ethanol fueling station should be installed to provide for alternative fuel vehicles

***Establish an Em ployee Transportation Coordinator Position***

Changing the travel behavior of House members and staff will require time. To assist in this change process, the creation of a CAO staff position to properly manage the implementation of all commuter related recommendations and other transportation management strategies is recommended. Such an individual would work with regional transportation management agencies such as the Commuter Connections program at the Metropolitan Washington Council of Governments, as well as with the District Department of Transportation to provide valuable services and information to Capitol Hill employees.

*Specific recommendations for the Employee Transportation Coordinator:*

- Implement programs that would encourage House employees to util ize an alternative commuting method
- Expand information and education programs to support and encourage alternate modes of commuting
- Implement, administer and promote a guaranteed or emergency ride home program

- Collect and analyze data on travel to, from and within the House office buildings and Capitol complex
- Coordinate with House offices, U.S. Capitol Police, the AOC, District Department of Transportation, Washington Metropolitan Area Transit Authority and other agencies
- Develop a comprehensive website an d materials on commuting alternatives to encourage Hill employers to choose alternatives to commuting by car

***Centralize the Cost of the House Transit Benefit Program and Increase the Benefit Level***

Offering transit benefits demonstrates to House employees and the community that the House is an environmental leader and is committed to a sustainable future.

*Specific recommendations to centralize the cost ofHouse transit benefits*:

- Increase the House Transit Benefit Program limit to $200, once legislation is passed
- Fund the cost of the House Transit Benefit program in a centralized place, in the same manner as other House employee benefits, and at no direct cost to House employing offices
- Implement the WMATA Smart Benefits program for House employees in the Capitol complex. SmartBenefits is a web -based program that lets employers conveniently load the dollar value of an employee's Metrochek transit, Van Pool and Metro station parking benefits directly to an employee's SmarTrip® card
- Implement a guaranteed or emergency ride home program tailored to the House's circumstances and work practices to provide a back -up to those who can and would like to take public transportation to work

***Implement a Bike to Work Program***

Bicycling is a healthy, quiet, clean, economical, and fun way to get to work. Thousands of Washington area employees bike to work every day. The House currently provides bike racks in a number of their parking lots however, the racks are old and located in non secure areas. The House should adopt the bicycle parking guidelines of the Association of Pedestrian and Bicycle Professionals. Short-term bicycle parking for staff and visitors should use the inverted U design; longer term and secure parking should be provided with lockable cages.

*Specific Recommendations to implement a Bike to Work Program*:

- Adopt the bicycle parking guidelines of the Association of Pedestrian and Bicycle Professionals
- Improve the parking infrastructure for cyclists
- To the maximum extent feasible, provide showers and changing facilities in each House building. House buildings should provide at least four showers, two rooms, two stalls each, with two of them being accessible to the disabled
- Provide one lockable gym locker for every long-term bicycle parking space provided
- Implement a Guaranteed or Emergency Ride Home Program tailored to the House's circumstances and work practices to provide a back-up to those who can and would like to bicycle to work
- Provide information on bike commuting including a map of bike parking locations, locations of showers and gym, bike maps of the Capitol area, and information on bike education classes
- Review options for a bike-sharing program that would be available for House members and staff

Coordinate with the AOC and the District Department of Transportation to provide safe bicycling conditions and facilities for bicyclists on the Capitol complex.

***Improve Telecommuting Capabilities***

The use of telecommuting, also known as telework, for House employees should be encouraged. In addition to the reduced CO2-e emissions, increased telecommuting capabilities ensure the continuity of business operations for the House in the event of an emergency. Additional benefits include enabling House offices to attract and retain a diverse and talented work force, encourage affordable traffic patterns, better address work and family demands, reduce the number of daily commuters, and further the goals of the Clean Air Act.

*Specific Recommendations to improve telecommuting capabilities*:

- Review current House telecommuting policies and individual House office practices regarding telecommuting

- Explore the viability and use of telecommuting centers in the Washington Metropolitan area considering costs, locations, availability of spaces, and computer security
- Develop telecommuting pil ot programs, in the House, to determine the most effective telework arrangements, tailored to the House's circumstances and work practices
- Expand information and education programs, for House offices, to support and encourage telework as an alternate to commuting

***Car Sharing***

The CAO should explore the feasibility of offering car -sharing services at the House. There is a segment of the House community that does not own vehicles. Some individuals in this group live within close proximity to the Hill and other s split their time between their home states and DC. Having access to a vehicle, on an as-needed basis, would aid them in running errands, reaching medical appointments, shopping, etc. Their primary mode of transportation would remain public transportation but they would have the option of using a car share vehicle when public transportation was not practical for a given errand. The House has an opportunity to address the need for providing a car service and at the same time offer an environmentally-friendly solution using the car sharing model. For some users, car sharing reduces the dependence on automobiles and increases usage of more environmentally-friendly forms of transportation. According to the Department of Transportation, "a single car-sharing vehicle can be used by 6 to 10 households, thus reducing parking and traffic congestion." Car sharing could be limited to personal use as initially described above. However, adopting models currently in use in several cities, the House could use cars for official business during the day and then those same cars could be used by staff after hours to optimize vehicle use.

*Specific recommendations for car sharing*:

- Explore the feasibility of offering car-sharing services at the House

## Food Service

As part of the "Green the Capitol Initiative," the CAO Service Management team will partnered with its food service contractors to integrate environmentally-conscious measures into Capitol campus dining facilities.

It is recommended that other sustainable food service programs, including introducing organic foods into menu rotations, composting of food wastes, using ecologically-safer cleaning supplies, and installing air-curtains on walk-in coolers be investigated. Furthermore, it is the recommendation that all future equipment purchases adhere to Energy Star and/or Federal Energy Management Program (FEMP) energy-efficient guidelines. The AOC has committed, in the upcoming Longworth Food Court kitchen renovation to use Energy Star and/or FEMP equipment.

Finally, it is recommended that the global foodservice industry be monitored for new and innovative ways to bring sustainable dining initiatives to the House. To this end, allying with an established "green" food organization should be explored.

*Specific recommendations for food service*:

- Purchase locally-grown food products when possible
- Purchase a reasonable predetermined amount of organic food products
- Utilize sustainable "green" cleaning supplies
- Comply and participate with all present and future campus recycling programs
- Place strong emphasis on waste reduction and prepare to document reductions on an annual basis
- Evaluate the feasibility of implementing composting to reduce waste streams
- Use earth-friendly or biodegradable carry-out and catering food containers
- Use paper carry-out food containers that contain high levels of recycled content
- Maximize opportunities to reduce overall packaging required for food, such as using paper wraps rather than traditional bulkier carry-out containers
- Strictly limit wherever possible, plastic or Styrofoam cups, plates, bowls and other carry-out food containers
- Explore the future use of biodegradable flatware
- Use paper napkins made with high levels of post-consumer recycled content
- Educate customers about the advantages of a sustainable food service
- Investigate sustainable food service programs
- Purchase only Energy Star or FEMP-designated products

Monitor for innovation opportunities and ally with "green" food organizations.

## Procurement, Materials, Recycling, and Cleaning

### *Procurement and Materials*

It is recommended the House establish best practices for procurement of paper, furniture, paints, carpets, office equipment, etc. The House is a major purchaser of products and services, and should demonstrate leadership by making purchases that pro mote sustainability.

Various guidelines should be used in the procurement process. Energy Star or FEMP products have been determined by the appropriate federal agencies to be life-cycle cost effective in normal operations and will contribute significantly to reduced consumption of energy. The Electronic Product Environmental Assessment Tool (EPEAT) system helps evaluate, compare and select electronic equipment based on its environmental attributes. EPEAT-certified electronic devices are low in heavy metals and high in recycled plastic content. Purchasing wood products certified by the Sustainable Forests Initiative or the Forest Stewardship Council will make a contribution toward insuring bio-diverse forests for future generations.

Volatile organic compounds (VOCs) are emitted by adhesive, sealants, paints, coating, and carpets. VOCs are major components affecting indoor air quality and they contribute to climate change. Emphasis should be put on purchasing products that emit low quantities of VOCs.

*Specific recommendations for procurement:*

- Purchase only Energy Star or FEMP-designated products when available
- Purchase only EPEAT-certified office equipment when available
- Purchase only adhesive, sealants, paints, coating, and carpets that emit very low quantities of volatile organic compounds emphasizing made in America products
- Purchase only furnishings that contain recycled products or wood certified as sustainable by the Sustainable Forests Initiative, the Forest Stewardship Council or similar programs

### *Recycling and Cleaning*

The House needs to review current practices and make recommendations for best practices for recycling, green cleaning and custodial practices. These might include training from associations such as BOMA, incentives, best practices for sustainable operations and maintenance.

The House needs to reduce the environmental impact of materials, through purchase of locally or regionally produced products, and standardize where possible to reduce inventory and procurement costs.

The House needs to significantly improve its current recycling program. A goal of recycling 50% of the waste stream is achievable. Other opportunities for recycling such as obsolete office equipment need to be explored. Also the House should increase the purchase of paper products containing high or 100% recycled content.

Many cleaning products contain toxic substances. Switching to green cleaning materials can improve the health ofjanitorial staff and office workers. Cleaning supplies used in the House should at a minimum meet the requirements of Green Seal Standard for Industrial and Institutional Cleaners, Standard GS -37; and for floor products, Standard GS-40.

*Specific recommendations for recycling and cleaning:*

- Divert 50% of the building occupant waste stream through an improved recycling program
- Examine other recycling opportunities such as obsolete office equipment
- Procure 100% recycled and 30% post-consumer content paper and recommend measures to reduce paper consumption
- Purchase cleaning supplies that at a minimum meet the requirements of Green Seal Standard for Industrial and Institutional Cleaners

## Leadership, Education, and Outreach

The CAO should pursue networking and outreach with the Senate, universities, businesses, local and state governments, and others to remain current on sustainability practices and CO2-e emission reduction opportunities. The networking can showcase the House's leadership role and facilitate the exchange of ideas and information on environmentally sustainable issues. This activity could include hosting green summits on sustainability. The CAO should also work with the AOC to make sustainability a mission-critical element of the AOC's business practices.

The CAO should initiate education programs for House staff and Member offices on sustainability practices. This activity should include holding green expositions to disseminate information and learn about new green products and services. A checklist could be created for Members and staff to use to reduce energy and implement sustainability practices; for example, using easy-to-access switches for shutting off office equipment or encouraging public transportation. In such a program, staff would be rewarded for additional innovative ideas and for overall performance.

Energy efficiency and sustainability information should also be provided to the visitors of the House. These educational materials should be available in the Capitol Visitors Center and in Member offices.

*Specific recommendations for leadership, education and outreach*:

- Prepare a checklist for sustainable office operations for use by Members of Congress and other Capitol Hill offices
- The House should take a leadership role in networking with the Senate, universities, businesses, and local and state governments including hosting green summits
- Hold a green expo for House offices to demonstrate the latest in green products or services available from commercial vendors
- Work with the AOC to make sustainability a mission-critical element
- Provide energy efficiency and sustainability materials for Capitol Hill visitors

## Develop Mechanisms for Evaluating Success and Reporting Progress

The CAO should track benchmarks for energy consumption and CO2-e emissions monthly and prepare annual reports documenting progress on the complementary goals of carbon neutrality and sustainable operations. Energy and CO2-e emissions reports and data will be made available through the Sustainability website, both as an educational tool and to provide feedback to House staff.

## CONCLUSION

This report provides a roadmap for carbon neutrality, energy efficiency, and operating in an environmentally sustainable fashion. It demonstrates that the House can operate in a carbon neutral manner now and begin to implement energy efficiency measures today. The report provides the way forward to cutting the House's energy use by 50% in 10 years. It shows how the House can do business in an environmentally sustainable manner. Implementing these goals is a good investment for the American taxpayer, the environment, and our children's future.

## REFERENCES

Architect of the Capitol, July 2000. Comprehensive Energy Conservation and Management Plan.

Architect of the Capitol, January 2006 (draft). Capitol Complex Master Plan: Sustainability Framework Plan.

Architect of the Capitol, September 4, 2006 [Initial Draft]. "Quick turnaround energy saving strategies for the Architect of the Capitol," submitted by Carnegie Mellon University, Center for Building Performance and Diagnostics.

Architect of the Capitol, March 16, 2002. "Boehlert Energy Efficiency Initiative for the House Science Committee Spaces: Rayburn House Office Building submitted by Andy Walker, NREL.

Architect of the Capitol and House Science Committee, August 1, 2006. "Baseline Environmental Quality Assessment & Preliminary Retrofit Options Analysis for Energy and Sustainability, Ford and Rayburn House Office Buildings," prepared by Carnegie Mellon University, Center for Building Performance and Diagnostics.

Architect of the Capitol, March 2007. "2006 Annual Report, Energy and Water Management and Conservation."

ASHRAE 2004. Thermal Guidelines for Data Processing Environments. TC 9.9 Mission Critical Facilities. Atlanta, Georgia: American Society of Heating, Refrigerating, and Air-Conditioning Engineers.

Brown, Rich, 2007, Lawrence Berkeley National Laboratory, personal communication. Chicago Climate Exchange. http://www.chicago climatex.com/

Chief Administrative Officer, April 19, 2007. Beard, Daniel P. Preliminary Report: Green the Capitol Initiative.

Government Accountability Office, April 2007. "Energy audits are key to strategy for greenhouse gas emissions. GAO Report GAO-07-5 16.

Lawrence Berkeley National Laboratory, 2007. Data Centers: Best-Practice Summaries. (http://hightech.lbl.gov/datacenters-bpg.html)

Carnegie Mellon University, Center for Building Performance and Diagnostics, September 2006 (draft). Guidelines for Strategic Environmental Investment.

U.S. Environmental Protection Agency, http://www.fueleconomy.gov/

## ACKNOWLEDGMENTS

This report was overseen by Daniel P. Beard, Chief Administrative Officer of the House, with Grant Scherling, Senior Advisor to the CAO, providing management and direction, and Perry Plumart for editorial and technical assistance.

Technical support was provided by staff from *Lawrence Berkeley National Laboratory*, including Barbara Atkinson, Peter Biermayer, Rich Brown, Rick Diamond, Camilla Dunham- Whitehead, Ryan Firestone, Steve Greenberg, Don Medley, Anthony Ma, Alan Meier, Evan Mills, Bruce Nordman, Christopher Payne, Mary Ann Piette, Francis Rubinstein, Steve Selkowitz, Craig Wray, and Peng Xu.

Staff of the *Architect of the Capitol*, including Mike Azarcon, Jim Calendar, Tom Costello, Eric Goodman, Greg Green, Charles Iliff, Brian Klein, Mike Laser, William Miller, Dan Murphy, Theon Parker, Dave Pilkins, Chris Potter, Louis Scalfari, Toby Virts, John Williams, Rick Wilmoth, and Beverly Wood.

We would like to acknowledge and thank the following individuals and organizations for their contribution to this report:

Staff of the *Office of the ChiefAdministrative Officer*

Stephanie Sand, Sara Vermillion, and Terry Dorn, *Government Accountability Office* Nina Baird, *Carnegie Mellon University*

Leith Sharp, *Harvard University*

Julie Newman, *Yale University*

Matt St. Clair, *University of California*

Ron Paich, *Postal Square*

Dennis Carey and Ray Creeley, *Government Printing Office*

Roxanne Blackwell and Nancy Somerville, *American Society of Landscape Architects*

# APPENDIX A. RECOMMENDATIONS FROM GREEN THE CAPITOL PRELIMINARY REPORT, APRIL 2007

## Recommendation 1: Operate the House in a Carbon Neutral Manner

Climate change and global warming are serious issues caused primarily by the introduction of carbon into the atmosphere. One way the House can begin to address this problem is to work toward undertaking our operations in a carbon neutral manner. This will mean taking steps to reduce the greenhouse gas emissions our complex creates through its operations. Global warming is an international problem, but there are steps we can take to provide leadership for solving these issues locally.

The most important step is to adopt a policy of making the operations of the House carbon neutral.

Accordingly, it is recommended the House operate in a carbon neutral manner at the earliest possible date, but no later than the end of the 1 10th Congress. By implementing this recommendation, we will be eliminating the impact of 91,000 tons of carbon dioxide emissions annually, which is the equivalent of taking 17,200 cars off the road each year.

## Recommendation 2: Shift to 100 Percent Renewable Electric Power

The purchase of electricity is the largest source of carbon dioxide emissions from the operations of the House. In order to achieve our goal of making our operations carbon neutral, my office, working with the Architect 103,000 megawatt-hours per year) from renewable sources at the earliest possible date. The cost of electric power generated from renewable sources can be up to 20% more than power generated from traditional sources.

This increase in cost will be offset over the long run by the energy conservation actions I am recommending. By implementing this recommendation, we will eliminate 57,000 tons of the total greenhouse gas emissions annually, or the equivalent of removing 11,000 cars from the roads.

## Recommendation 3: Aggressively Improve Energy Efficiency

There are a series of immediate steps House offices can take to reduce energy use. I recommend we take the following actions:

(a) Immediately convert 2,000 desk lamps in the House office buildings to compact fluorescent lamps (CFL). In addition, within six months take the steps necessary to convert the remaining 10,000 desk lamps to CFLs. Replacing 12,000 CFLs is the equivalent to removing 255 cars from the road, and it will yield a $245,000 savings in electric power costs to the House per year.

(b) Direct the CAO and Architect of the Capitol to no longer purchase standard incandescent replacement bulbs with funds made available by the House. Standard incandescent bulbs consume four times the energy of compact fluorescents and it is time for the House to eliminate their use.

(c) Instruct the Architect to convert the overhead House ceiling lights to high efficiency lighting and controls at the earliest possible date. Such action has the potential to reduce lighting energy from these sources by as much as 50 percent. This action will eliminate 7,130 tons of greenhouse gas emissions, which is equivalent to 1,340 cars.

(d) Promote energy efficiency among the 7,000 staff of the House by making CFLs available at cost in the House office supply store. If all staff members installed just one CFL bulb for their own use, it would have a cumulative effect of removing 150 cars from the road.

(e) Direct the Architect to expand their fluorescent lamp disposal program to include the proper collection of used CFLs.

## Recommendation 4: Adopt Sustainable Business Practices

Our office is a major purchaser of products and services, and we should demonstrate leadership by making purchases that promote sustainability. Therefore, I recommend the following actions:

(a) Purchase only Energy Star or Federal Energy Management Program-designated products where such designations are available. These products have been determined by the appropriate Federal agencies to be life-cycle cost effective in normal operations and will contribute significantly to reduced consumption of energy.

(b) Purchase office equipment that is certified using the Electronic Product Environmental Assessment Tool (EPEAT) system. This system helps evaluate, compare and select electronic equipment based on its environmental attributes. EPEAT certified electronic devices are low in heavy metals and high in recycled plastic content.
(c) Give priority to the purchase of climate neutral products that offset the life cycle contribution of greenhouse gas emissions. Specifically, purchase only adhesive, sealants, paints, coating, and carpets that emit very low quantities of volatile organic compounds. Volatile organic compounds are major components affecting indoor air quality and they contribute to climate change.
(d) Purchase only furnishings that contain recycled products or wood certified as sustainable by the Sustainable Forests Initiative, the Forest Stewardship Council or similar programs. Implementing this recommendation will make a small contribution toward insuring biodiverse forests for future generations.
(e) Direct the Architect to finalize the installation of an Ethanol-85 tank, pump, and related infrastructure for the use of official vehicles within the next six months.

## Recommendation 5: Continued Leadership on Sustainability Issues

It is important for Members and staff to continue to provide leadership on climate change and sustainability issues. To assist in maintaining this continuing commitment, I recommend the following actions:

(a) Hold a "Green Expo" for House offices to demonstrate the latest in green products or services available to offices from commercial vendors.
(b) Establish a sustainability education program for House employees providing guidance on how employees can make a contribution to impacting climate change and sustainability at home and in the work place.
(c) Establish a "Green Revolving Fund" where revenues received from various sources will be placed in a revolving fund to be used to undertake energy and water conservation initiatives that offset greenhouse gas emissions.

## Recommendation 6: Offset to Insure Carbon Neutral Operations

It is likely that even by implementing all the recommendations outlined above, the House will not be operating in a carbon neutral manner. As a result, we will have to develop a strategy for offsetting as much as 34,000 tons of greenhouse gas emissions by either: (1) Purchasing offset credits in the domestic market, or (2) Contributing a per ton payment, based on the current domestic market, of carbon dioxide equivalents emitted by the CPP boilers and placing these funds in the Green Revolving Fund to be used to directly mitigate the emissions. Since the domestic offset market is in its infancy and lacks uniform standards, it is important the House carefully screen any offset purchases. Between now and June 30, I will undertake a review of possible investments and determine their acceptability. If an acceptable offset cannot be secured, depositing the offset monies in the Green Revolving Fund would provide us with an acceptable alternative.

# Appendix B. Examples of Current Good Practices for House Buildings

## Energy Supply

- An existing policy purchases 3% of all electric power with from wind-generated sources
- The Central Power Plant is able to switch among fuels, allowing the option of lower CO2-e emission operation with no capital investment

## Energy-Efficient Technologies

- Select motors have been upgraded to energy-efficient models
- Failed motor starters are replaced with variable -frequency drives, giving them soft-start capability now and maximum flexibility for more sophisticated control modifications later
- The Ford Building has implemented efficient low-e, spectrally-selective windows
- Many light fixtures have been retrofitted to compact fluorescent lamps

- Fluorescent tube lighting with bi-level switching is inst alled in congressional suites throughout the Rayburn Building
- A water-side economizer in the Central Power Plant can operate in lieu of, or in combination with, the chillers
- Outside-air economizers with differential enthalpy controls are used at some buildings
- In one building, heat is being recovered from the condensed steam and preheats domestic hot water

## Efficient Management & Operations

- Energy expenses are tracked and analyzed using "Energy Guru" software
- A computerized energy management control system is used in parts of some buildings
- An existing design guideline calls for direct digital control energy management systems in new buildings and renovations
- Some air-handling equipment is shut down during unoccupied hours; other equipment is set back
- The chilled water temperature is reset upwards at the Central Power Plant in the winter
- A good maintenance program is in place (e.g., replacements of filters and belts, and attention to basic controls functionality)

## References

[1] Tons = English short tons (1 ton = 2000 pounds).

[2] Estimates were derived using coefficients for CO2-e emissions from the GAO April 2007 report and conversion factors for equivalent number of cars from the U.S. EPA (www.fueleconomy.gov).

[3] Greenhouse gas emissions are referred to as carbon dioxide-equivalent emissions (CO2-e), in short tons.

[4] Tons = English short tons (1 ton = 2000 pounds).

[5] Estimates were derived using coefficients for CO2-e emissions from the GAO April 2007 report and conversion factors for equivalent number of cars from the U.S. EPA (www.fueleconomy.gov).

[6] Fuel consumption from 2007 to 2017 has been weather-normalized to the long-term average degree-days from 1997 to 2006. Weather normalization means that one year's energy use data is adjusted to reflect what the energy consumption would have been if average weather conditions had occurred instead in the same location over the time period of interest.

[7] Although the CPP was originally equipped with steam turbines, it has not generated electricity since the early 1950s.

[8] U.S. Department of Energy, Energy Information Administration, "Method for Calculating Carbon Sequestration by Trees in Urban and Suburban Settings," 1998.

[9] Casey Trees and Limno-Tech, "The Green Build-Out Model: Quantifying the Stormwater Management Benefits of Trees and Green Roofs in Washington, DC," 2007.

[10] David J. Nowak, USDA Forest Service, "The Effects of Urban Trees on Air Quality."

In: Recycling and Green Programs at the Capital... ISBN 978-1-60692-980-3
Editor: H. Y. Kim, pp. 63-103 

*Chapter 2*

# ADMINISTERING GREEN PROGRAMS IN CONGRESS: ISSUES AND OPTIONS*

*Jacob R. Straus*

## ABSTRACT

Programs to create an environmentally conscious workplace have long existed on Capitol Hill. Congress has been working to reduce consumption and conserve energy since the 1970s. Traditionally, these programs have been administered by the Architect of the Capitol. In recent Congresses, the House of Representatives and the Senate have created separate greening programs. In addition, the Architect of the Capitol has developed green programs for the Capitol Complex.

In the House of Representatives, the Chief Administrative Officer (CAO) manages green programs for individual Member offices, committee offices, and support offices. The administration of building-wide energy conservation programs is traditionally managed by the Architect of the Capitol. For the House, the CAO and Architect's program oversight is conducted by the Committee on House Administration. In the 1 10th Congress, the House of Representatives labeled all conservation and greening programs as part of the "Green the Capitol" initiative.

In the Senate, green programs in individual Senate offices, committee offices, and staff support offices are administered by the Architect of the Capitol, in coordination with the Secretary of the Senate and the Sergeant at Arms of the Senate, and with oversight provided by the Rules and

* Excerpted from CRS Report RL34694, dated October 6, 2008.

Administration Committee. In the 110th Congress, the Architect of the Capitol's role in administering facilities-related programs on behalf of the Senate has remained unchanged.

The Architect of the Capitol also administers greening programs for the Capitol Complex. These programs include energy usage reduction programs for the House and Senate office buildings, the Capitol building, and other Capitol complex facilities; conservation measures for the Senate office buildings, the Capitol building, and other Capitol complex facilities; and green programs for the Capitol Grounds.

A number of policy options are potentially available to create an inter-chamber greening program on Capitol Hill. The options include creating a formal House greening program, creating a "Green the Senate" initiative, establishing an independent greening commission, creating a Capitol Complex-wide greening program, and continuing to use ad-hoc programming for greening issues.

Programs designed to create an environmentally friendly work environment and conserve energy have gained a higher profile in the 1 10th Congress (2007-2009). In March 2007, the House of Representatives created the "Green the Capitol" initiative with the goal of making the House "carbon neutral" by the end of the 1 10th Congress [1]. The "Green the Capitol" initiative expanded energy reduction and greening programs for the House and encouraged cooperation with efforts in the Senate and in the Capitol Complex.

In general, the House and the Senate have developed separate greening programs. In the House, these programs are administered by the Chief Administrative Officer (CAO) in cooperation with the Architect of the Capitol, and with the oversight of the Committee on House Administration. In the Senate, greening programs are administered by the Architect of the Capitol in coordination with the Secretary of the Senate and the Sergeant at Arms of the Senate, with the oversight of the Committee on Rules and Administration. In addition, the Architect of the Capitol administers greening initiatives for the Capitol Complex, including energy usage programs for the House and Senate office buildings and the Capitol building.

## HOUSE OF REPRESENTATIVES

Implementation of greening programs in the House is divided between the Architect of the Capitol and the CAO. In general, the Architect is responsible for building and facilities maintenance, while the CAO is responsible for the interior of Member, committee, and support staff offices. In some ways, the relationship between the Architect and CAO is similar to the relationship between condominium owners and their building. The owner (the CAO) is responsible for maintenance of inside spaces including paint, carpet, furniture, and appliances, while the building (Architect) is responsible for maintenance of walls and general facilities operation such as heating, cooling, and building repairs. The following sections discuss the role of the CAO in implementing the "Green the Capitol" initiative and the role of the Architect in other greening projects.

## "Green the Capitol" Initiative

In March 2007, Speaker Nancy Pelosi, Majority Leader Steny Hoyer, and the then chair of the Committee on House Administration, the late Juanita Millender-McDonald, asked CAO Daniel Beard and his Senate counterparts to "undertake a 'Green the Capitol' initiative to ensure that the House institutes the most up-to-date industry and government standards for green building and green operating procedures" [2]. The letter further asked the CAO to provide a preliminary report by April 30, 2007 and a final report, with recommendations, by June 30, 2007.

As a result of the March 2007 letter, the CAO conducted a study to understand "House operating procedures with respect to energy conservation, sustainability and related matters" [3]. The results of the study were presented to the House in two reports. The preliminary report was issued on April 19, 2007, and the final report was issued on June 21, 2007.

*Preliminary Report.* Using figures from the Government Accountability Office (GAO) and the Lawrence Berkeley National Laboratory, the CAO estimated that the House was responsible for 91,000 tons of greenhouse gas emissions, equivalent to the emissions of 17,200 cars, in FY2006 [4]. Based on these numbers, the preliminary report included six recommendations to reduce greenhouse gas emissions in the House. These six preliminary recommendations were

1. operate the House in a carbon neutral manner;
2. shift to 100 percent renewable electric power;
3. aggressively improve energy efficiency;
4. adopt sustainable business practices;
5. maintain leadership on sustainability issues; and
6. insure carbon neutral operations with offsets.

The preliminary report also included broad options for implementing the six recommendations [5].

*Final Report.* In the final report, the CAO created three goals for the "Green the Capitol" initiative based on the six initial recommendations. These three goals are

- operate the House in a carbon-neutral manner by the end of the 110th Congress;
- reduce the House's carbon footprint by cutting energy consumption by 50 percent in 10 years; and
- make House operations a model of sustainability [6].

To achieve these goals, the final report provided a "roadmap to reduc[e] the carbon footprint of the House while operating in an environmentally sustainable manner." [7] While the three goals are broad, the report suggests strategies for implementation. Table 1 lists the goals and recommended implementation strategies.

The CAO has since created a greening agenda for the House of Representatives to reduce energy consumption and make the House "carbon neutral"8 by the end of the 1 10th Congress. In announcing the release of the final report, Speaker of the House Pelosi summarized the initiative and its importance: "This plan is an essential first step, because it not only will make the House a better place to work and live near, but it will also make our institution a model — one that cares about what kind of planet our children will inherit." [9].

*Six-Month Progress Report.* In December 2007, six months after the "Green the Capitol" initiative began, the CAO issued a report on the progress made in meeting the initiative's goals. In his comments introducing the report, the CAO stated: "In just six months we have made significant inroads toward our goal of carbon neutrality and vastly improved energy efficiency. Based on our success thus far, and with the help of our committed and environmentally-conscious employees, I am confident that goal is well within our grasp" [10].

**Table 1. Implementation Strategies for Final Report Goals**

| Goal | Recommended Strategy |
|---|---|
| Operate the House in a carbon-neutral manner by the end of the 1 10th Congress (December 2008) | - Purchase renewable power for electricity use;<br>- Operate the Capitol Power Plant with natural gas; and<br>- Purchase carbon offsets on the Chicago Climate Exchange. |
| Reduce the carbon footprint of the House by cutting energy consumption by 50% in 10 years | - Reduce energy consumption in House office buildings; and<br>- Reduce energy consumption at the Capitol Power Plant. |
| Make House operations a model of sustainability | - Direct the CAO to oversee implementation of "Green the Capitol Initiative";<br>- Develop a House sustainability plan;<br>- Conduct leadership, education, and outreach; and<br>- Develop mechanisms for evaluating success and reporting progress. |

Source: U.S. Congress, House Chief Administrative Officer, Green the Capitol Initiative Final Report, 1 10th Cong., 1st sess. [http://speaker.gov/pdf/GTCI621full2.pdf], accessed July 10, 2008, pp. 2-14.

The six-month progress report also contained a list of completed and ongoing projects. These projects, described in more detail below, included initiating a study to relight the Capitol Dome, purchasing carbon credits on the Chicago Climate Exchange, holding a "Green the Capitol Expo" to highlight alternative forms of transportation, initiating a car sharing program, purchasing renewable electricity and additional natural gas for the Capitol Power Plant, serving "fair trade" coffee in House food service venues, composting food and material waste from the cafeteria, and installing compact florescent light bulbs throughout the House [11].

*"Green the Capitol" Programs.* "Green the Capitol" programs seek to reduce energy consumption to meet the House goal of carbon neutrality by the end of the $110^{th}$ Congress. The details of many of these projects are contained in the preliminary report, final report, and the six month progress report, which are noted earlier in this CRS report. Other information can be found in testimony

given by the CAO at committee hearings, in "Green the Capitol" newsletters, and press releases.

*Relighting of the Capitol Dome.* On October 19, 2007, the CAO issued a Request for Proposal (RFP)12 to design a lighting scheme for the Capitol Building Dome using "more energy efficient lighting" [13]. The RFP specified that the "work will include the lighting of the interior and exterior of the Capitol Dome. The design shall describe the role of the lighting in enhancing the exterior and the architecture of the building at night and shall emphasize methods for incorporating energy saving lighting design and sustainability as part of the overall effort" [14].

On March 4, 2008, a contract to design a new configuration for the Capitol Dome was awarded to The Lighting Practice of Philadelphia [15]. The Lighting Practice contract will cost $671,400 and was chosen from among five proposals ranging in cost from $521,306 to $1,348,268 and "offered the lowest cost and the most technically acceptable design" [16]. Funds for the lighting design project will be disbursed from the CAO's operating budget [17]. A future RFP is to be issued by the Architect for the implementation of the design.

*Compact Fluorescent Light Bulbs.* The House is currently in the process of changing approximately 30,000 light bulbs from standard incandescent bulbs to more energy efficient compact fluorescent light bulbs (CFL). CFLs use approximately one-fifth to one-quarter the energy of incandescent light bulbs and can last up to 10 times longer than incandescent light bulbs [18]. According to the fact sheet accompanying the "Green the Capitol" six-month progress report, approximately 7,000 of 30,000 light bulbs had been changed as of December 2007 [19].

*Low VOC (volatile organic compounds) Carpets.* In preparation for the transition to the 111th Congress (2009-20 1 1), the CAO issued an RFP for the installation of new carpet for Member offices [20]. As part of the installation of new carpet, the CAO sought a vendor who could offer carpets that contained low levels of volatile organic compounds, [21] which are often associated with "sick building syndrome." [22].

*Carbon Offsets.* A carbon offset is defined as "tradeable carbon-emissions permits" [23]. Carbon offsets can be purchased on market-based exchanges, such as the Chicago Climate Exchange [24]. Carbon offsets are purchased as a way to counterbalance emissions that are not easily remedied through other programs. For example, in November 2007, the House purchased $90,500 in carbon credits to offset the burning of natural gas in the Capitol Power Plant to heat and cool the House Office Buildings [25]. In a press release, Representative Rahm Emanuel summarized the goal of carbon offsets in the House.

> Under the leadership of House Speaker Nancy Pelosi (CA-8) and Majority Leader Steny Hoyer (MD-5), the House will become carbon neutral by purchasing wind power for electricity used by the House, by substituting the House's portion of the use of the Capitol Power Plant natural gas for coal, and to offset the carbon emitted from burning natural gas, the House will purchase carbon offsets. After taking into account the other changes made under the Green the Capitol Initiative, the House is offsetting 30,000 tons of carbon through the purchase of carbon financial instrument contracts or carbon credits through CCX [Chicago Climate Exchange], totaling approximately $90,000. Funding for the purchase of these carbon offsets is available in the Chief Administrative Officer's Fiscal Year 2008 budget [26].

For FY2009, the CAO has requested $125,000 for the purchase of carbon offsets. The CAO testified that he hopes the House will not need to purchase carbon credits to remain carbon neutral in FY2009. If, however, the purchase of credits is necessary "then the Chicago Climate Exchange, like the New York Stock Exchange, is a marketplace where prices fluctuate depending on supply and demand. Accordingly, in the event that we need to purchase the same amount of carbon credits in FY2009, as we did in FY2008, we would expect a potential increase in the purchase price" [27].

*Natural Gas in the Capitol Power Plant.* The House has decided to stop using coal to generate steam in the power plant. Instead, the House is working to use only natural gas to generate the steam necessary to operate the heating and cooling system in the House Office Buildings and in the House portion of the Capitol building [28]. Because the House office buildings do not receive steam separately from other buildings, the House has directed the Architect to purchase additional natural gas so that the proportion of steam supplied to the House will no longer be generated with coal and fuel oil [29].

In testimony before the House Committee on Transportation and Infrastructure, the CAO stated:

> I think it is important to add to this debate, though, that if we switch to 100 percent natural gas, we would certainly have a significantly reduced environmental footprint and carbon footprint. Right now, the Congress is the proud owner and operator of a facility that is the second largest point source pollution in the District of Columbia. And so, I think there is a significant environmental benefit associated with moving to 100 percent gas [30].

In a statement on the House floor, Representative Jay Inslee reiterated the CAO's statement on the importance of switching to natural gas at the Capitol Power Plant and suggested that the House could further reduce its emissions.

> Switching from coal, first, to natural gas in our power plant, which reduces carbon dioxide something like 20 to 30 percent. We're then taking a look at the possibility of going to a totally renewable fuel of wood pellets [from trees] grown in New Hampshire and some other places which would go to essentially zero CO2 on a net basis [31]

In May 2008, the GAO completed a report on the implications of switching from coal to natural gas at the Capitol Power Plant. The Capitol Power Plant uses a combination of coal, natural gas, and fuel oil to generate the steam necessary to heat and cool the Capitol Complex. From 2001 to 2007, "[t]he percentage of energy input from each fuel has varied from year to year, with an average fuel mix of 43 percent natural gas, 47 percent coal, and 10 percent fuel oil" [32]. Additionally, GAO reported that to complete the "Green the Capitol" goal of using only natural gas to supply steam to the House would require a 38% increase in the use of natural gas.

> Based on available data and key assumptions about the plant's operation and future fuel costs, we estimated that fulfilling the Green the Capitol initiative's fuel-switching directive would require the plant to increase its natural gas use by 38 percent relative to its baseline level of fuel consumption between 2001 and 2007. As a portion of the plant's total fuel mix, natural gas would increase from about 43 percent of overall energy input to about 60 percent of input. Using information from the AOC on its fuel expenditures and fuel price projections from EIA [Energy Information Administration], we estimate that implementing the fuel-switching directive could range in cost from $1.0 to $1.8 million in fiscal year 2008 [33].

*Car Sharing.* On November 1, 2007, the House began a car sharing pilot program with four cars located in Rayburn parking garage. The program is designed to encourage "Hill staffers to use public transportation to commute to work, and the car share program for meetings and appointments off the Hill." [34] Partnered with Zipcar, the House has a fleet of four hybrid cars, located in the Rayburn garage [35]. Zipcars parked in the Rayburn garage are available only for the use of House Members and staff, but otherwise operate with the same rules and regulations as other Zipcars [36]. House Members and staff can use the Zipcars outside of work hours.

In a speech on the House floor, Representative Earl Blumenhauer discussed the benefits for a car sharing program.

> Car sharing ...is a very successful business around the country. It's recently on the GSA schedule. I'm pleased to have a small part in encouraging that to happen here on Capitol Hill. We now have over 100 employees that have signed up for it. There are cars that are parked here that people can use before or after hours for business or after hours on their own time...[37]

The CAO testified before the House Appropriations Committee's Subcommittee on the Legislative Branch that 272 individuals had signed up for Zipcars through the House program, that 38% of registrants were actively making reservations, and that "[s]ince November 1, 2007, the on-campus vehicles have been driven a total of 290.5 hours or 8.7 percent of available hours. House participants have used off-campus vehicles for a total of 1736 hours since the inception of the program" [38].

*Bicycle Programs.* On March 21, 2008, the CAO issued an RFP to create a House bicycle sharing program. In the RFP, the CAO stated that:

> The House is interested in acquiring the services of a contractor to provide and maintain at least 30 bicycles. Additional bicycles may be ordered later depending on the success of the program and subject to availability of funding. The contractor will deliver the bicycles fully assembled and ready for use and provide ongoing preventative and remedial maintenance [39].

The "Wheels4Wellness" program is free of charge to House staff and employees who sign up at the House fitness center [40]. The bike-sharing program is designed to "allow employees to checkout bicycles from self-service racks in six locations on the House side of the Capitol" [41]. Bicycles can be checked out from First Call in room B227 of the Longworth House Office Building or from the CAO's HR office in room 102 of the Ford House Office Building between 8:00 a.m. and 5:00 p.m. [42]. Bicycles are located in lot one behind the Cannon House Office Building, lot four behind the Rayburn House Office Building, and lot nine across from the Ford House Office Building [43]. The bicycles cannot be kept overnight [44].

*Purchase of Renewable Electricity.* During FY2007, the House purchased renewable energy from Pepco, their energy supplier. On May 11, 2007, Stephen T. Ayers, acting Architect of the Capitol, testified before the House Committee on Transportation and Infrastructure on climate change and energy independence. As part of his testimony, Mr. Ayers stated that the Architect has "contracted with

GSA and Pepco for three percent renewable energy in FY2007 and is currently in discussions with Pepco as we assess the budget implications to increase this percentage to the maximum percentage that is reasonable" [45]

*Food Service.* In 2005, the Architect began a search for a food service vendor for the Capitol Visitor Center [46]. As part of the search process, the House and the Senate were provided the option of contracting with the Architect's vendor for House and Senate food services operations, respectively. In August 2007, the Architect chose Restaurant Associates of New York City as the official food vendor for the Capitol Visitor Center. Following the Architect's decision, the House independently contracted with Restaurant Associates to provide food service in the Longworth, Rayburn, and Cannon House Office Buildings, the House wing of the Capitol, and the Members' Dining Room [47]. The contract went into effect on December 17, 2007.

As part of the contract, Restaurant Associates (RA) has agreed to operate the House cafeteria and restaurants in an environmentally friendly manner. "At the US House of Representatives, RA is determined to impact both the health and wellness of our guests, and the quality of our community and the environment." [48] RA initiated the following programs:

- purchasing organic food, when possible;
- purchasing local food grown within 150 miles of the Capitol, when possible;
- purchasing sustainable seafood;
- serving food with zero trans-fat;
- serving fair trade coffee;
- serving cage free eggs;
- composting food and biodegradable container waste; and
- installing white boards to reduce printing of signs.

There has been considerable attention on two of the programs that RA has initiated. The fair trade coffee program and the composting program have been discussed in the CAO's Six-Month Progress Report, on the floor of the House, or during hearings.

*Fair Trade Coffee.* To ensure that coffee was purchased under "fair market conditions," the House has begun to serve "Pura Vida Coffee, which specializes in organic and bird-friendly, shade-grown beans" [49]. In a speech on the House floor, Representative Sam Farr explained the importance of fair trade coffee. "They [Restaurant Associates] are going to provide all fair trade coffee, which is the coffee that is paid the best price because you grow it for organic conditions, for taking care of the employees, paying good wages of doing it environmentally sensitive, and Starbucks and everyone else is participating in this" [50].

Composting. The House of Representatives began composting food waste and biodegradable food containers and utensils in partnership with the House restaurant food vendor in December 2007 [51]. Between December 2007 and April 2008, the House reduced the volume of materials sent to the landfill by 120 tons [52].

In testimony before the Select Committee on Energy Independence and Global Warming on February 26, 2008, CAO Daniel Beard described the process for composting of food service waste and its benefits for the reduction of transportation costs of waste materials.

> We send the compostable food service items along with all of the food waste from the front of the cafeteria and from the kitchens to a pulper. The pulper is like a giant garbage disposal that breaks down and dewaters the compost material. This reduces the volume of the compost material by a ratio of 10-1 and reduces the weight by as much as 4-1. The result is reduced hauling costs and reduced tipping fees by 60%-75%. [53]

The House is expanding the composting program to include individual Member offices. In testimony before the House Committee on Transportation and Infrastructure's Subcommittee on Economic Development, Public Buildings, and Emergency Management, the CAO talked about the program's expansion. "The House has completely revamped its paper recycling program to ensure compostable food waste is picked up from Member offices"[54]. Bins to collect compostable materials within individual offices are available through the House recycling program office [55].

## Other Green Initiatives

The House also has greening programs that operate outside of the "Green the Capitol" initiative. These programs are administered by the Architect of the Capitol and oversight is provided by the Committee on House Administration, the Transportation and Infrastructure Committee's Subcommittee on Economic Development, Public Buildings, and Emergency Management, and during the 1 10th Congress the Select Committee on Energy Independence and Global Warming [56].

*Architect of the Capitol.* The Architect of the Capitol is responsible for the facilities and buildings in the Capitol Complex. As part of this role, the Architect is responsible for the administration of the House recycling program and is generally responsible for the reduction of energy usage throughout the Capitol Complex.

*Recycling.* The House recycling program was established by the adoption of H.Res. 104 in the 101st Congress (1989-1991).57 Created as a voluntary program, focused on recycling paper, the recycling program has grown to include bottles, cans, e-waste (i.e., computers, printers, and toner cartridges), and construction materials (i.e., carpet, concrete, ceiling tiles and scrap metal). In calendar year 2007, the House recycled approximately 1,400 tons of paper, 21.5 tons of bottles and cans, and 294 tons of e-waste and construction material [58].

The recycling program operates separately from the "Green the Capitol" initiative. The "Green the Capitol" initiative, however, has begun recycling materials not previously recycled by the Architect. These items include the composting of food waste, corn-based biodegradable forks, spoons, and knives, and sugar cane-based biodegradable carry out containers from the House restaurants. The personal cell phones of House staff have also been collected and recycled [59].

*Committee Programs.* The Committee on House Administration and the Transportation and Infrastructure Committee's Subcommittee on Economic Development, Public Buildings, and Emergency Management have held hearings and discussions on greening issues in the House. These hearings have concentrated on the Architect's energy reduction programs as well as the CAO's "Greening the Capitol" initiative. Additionally, the Committee on House Administration has begun to organize programs, such as a tire inflation workshop, to assist individual staff members reduce their energy consumption during their commute to work.

*Proper Tire Inflation.* On July 28, 2008, Representative Vernon Ehlers, Ranking Member of the Committee on House Administration, sent a Dear Colleague letter announcing a program to check staff vehicles for proper tire inflation. In his letter, Representative Ehlers stated "[t]he Department of Energy estimates that 1.2 billion gallons of fuel were wasted in 2005 as a result of driving on underinflated tires. With gas prices at an all time high, the simple step of keeping tires inflated will help ease pain at the pump, as well as reduce carbon emissions, a major threat to the environment" [60]. The program took place on July 30, and offered free tire inspections to participants.

*Legislative Proposals.* While the Architect administers the majority of greening programs not officially part of "Greening the Capitol," other legislative proposals have also been introduced to create green programs. In the 110th Congress, two bills have been introduced that would create green programs. H.R. 6474, introduced by Representative Zoe Lofgren would allow the CAO of the House to create projects to promote energy efficiency and reduce energy consumption in the House. H.R. 6171, introduced by Representative Dan Lungren, would create a Congressional commission [61] on energy in the National Capitol Region.

*Demonstration Projects.* On July 10, 2008, Representative Lofgren and Representative Zack Wamp introduced H.R. 6474 "[t]o authorize the Chief Administrative Officer of the House of Representatives to carry out a series of demonstration projects to promote the use of innovative technologies in reducing energy consumption and promoting energy efficiency and cost savings in the House of Representatives" [62]. The bill would authorize $5 million for both FY2009 and 2010 for the CAO to carry out short term demonstration projects that promote innovative technology to reduce energy consumption and promote energy efficiency and cost savings in the House [63].

During the markup session on July 30, Representative Ehlers proposed three amendments to the bill. The amendments would have (1) provided the authority to carry out the demonstration projects to the Architect of the Capitol instead of the CAO, (2) required the CAO to consult with the Architect on demonstration projects, and (3) clarified the responsibility of the CAO and the Architect for building related projects [64]. All three amendments were defeated by voice vote. The bill was ordered reported by voice vote.

*National Capitol Energy Commission.* On June 3, 2008, Representative Dan Lungren introduced H.R. 6171, the "National Capital Region Leadership in Environmental and Energy Stewardship Commission Act." The bill would create a Congressional commission to analyze the environmental and energy footprint of the federal government in the National Capitol Region, hold a nationwide competition to find innovative solutions to reduce or eliminate federal government facility emissions, analyze existing and new technologies, recommend solutions to eliminate emissions and reduce energy consumption, and submit a report to Congress with recommendations and draft legislation [65]. The bill was referred to Committee on Oversight and Government Reform.

## SENATE

Unlike the House of Representatives, the Senate does not have a formal name for its greening activities. The Senate, however, is engaged in greening activities, such as the replacement of light bulbs, the installation of energy efficient building systems, and the development of green programs in the Senate cafeterias.

## Administration

While the Senate does not have a formal greening program, the Architect of the Capitol, under the guidance of the Senate Committee on Rules and Administration, has created a greening program for the Senate office buildings and the Senate wing of the Capitol. In creating greening programs, the Architect aims to improve client (i.e., individual Member, committee, and support staff offices) satisfaction and to improve energy efficiency [66]. The Sergeant at Arms also administers greening and energy savings initiatives related to computer technology and security for the Senate.

## Greening Programs

Senate greening programs are focused on the reduction of energy consumption and lessening overall Senate energy costs. The details of many of these projects were discussed during a Senate Committee on Rules and Administration hearing and in conversations with the Architect's office.

*Recycling*. The Senate recycling program was established by the adoption of S.Res. 99 in the 101st Congress (1989-1991) [67]. Created as a voluntary program focused on recycling paper, the recycling program has grown to include bottles, cans, e-waste (i.e., computers, printers, and toner cartridges), and construction materials (i.e., carpet, concrete, ceiling tiles and scrap metal). In calendar year 2007, the Senate recycled approximately 700 tons of paper, 10 tons of bottles and cans, and 292 tons of e-waste and construction material [68].

*Lighting Programs*. The Architect has developed a program to reduce energy consumption from lighting in the Senate. The lighting energy savings program consists of three main projects, installing compact fluorescent light bulbs, installing dimmable ballasts in Senate offices, and installing solar lighting in Senate parking lots.

*Light Bulbs*. Since 2006, the Senate has installed approximately 4,000 compact fluorescent light (CFL) bulbs to replace incandescent bulbs [69]. While CFLs are more energy efficient than incandescent light bulbs, the Senate is not switching all lights to CFLs. Committee hearing rooms have not been switched to CFLs because CFL bulbs cannot produce the light levels required for television broadcasting [70]. Incandescent bulbs replaced as part of the CFL replacement project are being recycled by the Senate [71].

The Senate has also undertaken lighting projects that are projected to reduce energy consumption by approximately one million kilowatt hours (kWh) per year. Table 2 lists the projects, provides a description, and lists the estimated kWh saved per year.

**Table 2. Senate Energy Saving Lighting Projects**

| Project | Description | kWh Saved Per Year |
|---|---|---|
| SHG 008 Storage Room | Motion sensor installed | 28,404 |
| Dirksen Cove Lighting | Controller installed to turn cove lights off at night and on weekends | 343,837 |
| Russell Rotunda Lighting | Controller installed to turn lights on only at night | 19,710 |
| Dirksen Cafeteria | Dimmer panel removed to allow 215 incandescent bulbs to be replaced with 26 watt CFLs | 289,664 |
| Russell Basement Lights | Controller installed to turn center corridor lights off at night | 2,982 |
| Dirksen and Russell Bathroom Exhaust Fans | Exhaust fans turned off at night | 149,175 |
| Senate Underground Garage | Motion sensors | 158,865 |
| Total | | 992,637 |

Source: Email exchange between the author and Scott Shapleigh, recycling program manager, Senate office buildings, Architect of the Capitol, Aug. 22, 2008.

*Dimmable Ballasts*. The Architect has installed a dimmable ballast lighting system in 11 Senate and committee offices in the Hart Senate Office Building.

Dimmable ballasts allow light levels to be networked and controlled from a central computer [72]. This allows light levels to be reduced on a per fixture basis, with a standard output of approximately 70% of available light. The Senate system includes daylight sensors near windows, occupancy sensors in conference rooms, and additional light switches for individual control in conference rooms [73]. The Architect estimates that the pilot program of 11 offices “typically saves 11,400 kilowatt hours per week or 40 percent of lighting energy used in an office suite. Over the first year, the pilot saved 692,000 kilowatt hours of electricity” [74]. With the completion of the pilot program, the Architect has begun to outfit an additional 10 offices in the Hart and Dirksen Senate Office Buildings with the dimmable ballast system. The Senate plans to install dimmable ballasts in all offices in the future.

*Solar Lighting in Parking Lots.* To reduce energy consumption in lighting the Senate parking lots, the Senate has selected a vendor to provide renewable, solar energy for lighting in parking lot 18. In testimony before the Senate Committee on Rules and Administration, acting Architect of the Capitol Stephen Ayers testified that the project is “[s]cheduled to be completed this fall [2008],” and that the “...new lights will save 1,825 kilowatt hours per year” [75].

*Water Savings Programs.* The Architect has developed a program to reduce water usage in the Senate. The water savings program consists of two main projects, installing dual flush valves in private restrooms and installing water cooling systems in offices that do not require plastic bottles.

*Dual Flush Valves.* The Architect is installing dual flush valve toilets in private bathrooms in Senate offices. These toilets provide more than one option of how much water is used to flush the system. Installation of the dual flush valves reduces the amount of water needed to flush a toilet. The Architect has chosen not to install dual flush valves in public restrooms for sanitary reasons [76].

*Water Coolers.* In 2008, the Senate Rules and Administration Committee approved the installation of bottle-less water filtration systems in Senate offices. Each individual office is responsible for selecting a vendor to supply the water cooler and filters. The Architect then facilitates the selection of appropriate cooler locations in an office, installs the necessary infrastructure to support bottle-less coolers through the plumbing office, regulates the types of systems that can be purchased or rented by offices, and connects the office to the existing building water supply [77]. Through September 2008, requests have been made for 80 coolers to be installed by Senate offices. The Architect’s office anticipates another 20 to 30 requests will be made [78].

*Steam Traps.* The Architect has replaced 147 steam traps [79] in the Hart Senate office building. The steam traps were replaced because when a steam trap fails, "it bleeds steam in to the air and wastes energy." The new traps have been placed on a preventative maintenance program and will be replaced or repaired as needed [80].

*Dirksen Green Roof.* A green roof is an alternative roofing option that places vegetation or solar panels on a building's roof to absorb heat and reduce rainwater runoff. The American Institute of Architects defines a green roof as·

> a roof of a building that is partially or completely covered with vegetation and soil, or a growing medium, planted over a waterproofing membrane. A green roof may also include additional layers such as a root barrier and drainage irrigation systems. Green roofs can be below, at , or above grade, but in all cases the plants are not planted in the "ground." The term "green roof" may also be used to refer to roofs that incorporate some form of green technology, such as solar panels or photovataic modules [81]

Pursuant to the passage of P.L. 109-58, the Energy Policy Act of 2005, [82] the Architect was asked by Congress "to evaluate the potential for converting some of the roof areas on Dirksen Senate Office Building to 'vegetated' roofs." [83] In the report, the Architect evaluated multiple roof designs, including replacing the existing roof with another copper roof, creating a roof with a public courtyard accessible by a pedestrian bridge from the Hart Senate Office Building, and creating a vegetative roof that would be inaccessible to staff. Table 3 lists the costs associated with the three proposals presented by the Architect.

Cost differences presented in Table 3 result from the type of vegetation used in each roof plan. For the publicly accessible roof, the Architect proposed adding small, shallow rooted plants on the roof of the interior courtyard, creating an area with trees and shrubs where tennis courts currently exist on the roof of Dirksen, and building a pedestrian bridge from the Hart building. For the non-publicly accessible roof, the Architect proposed a variety of plants on both the interior roof and in the tennis court area [84]. The Architect has not been authorized to begin construction on a green roof [85].

*Restaurants.* As noted earlier, as part of the search process for a food service vendor for the Capitol Visitors Center, the House and the Senate were provided the option of contracting with the vendor chosen by the Architect for House and Senate food services operations, respectively. The Senate has chosen to exercise this option and is negotiating a contract with Restaurant Associates.

Contracting with Restaurant Associates to operate the Senate restaurants would presumably allow the Senate to participate in many of the green programs currently established in the House restaurants. As part of the new contract, the Senate could require Restaurant Associates to operate its cafeterias in accordance with environmental considerations. This would position the Senate to receive many of the green benefits associated with the practices currently in place under the House contract.

**Table 3. Costs of Architect-Proposed Roof Replacement Options for Dirksen Senate Office Building**

| Replacement Option | Estimated Cost |
|---|---|
| Similar to Existing Roof | $1,636,823 |
| Inaccessible Green Roof | $5,121,531 |
| Publicly Accessible Green Roof | $6,653,098 |

Source: U.S. Congress, Architect of the Capitol, Dirksen Senate Office Building Facilities Condition Assessment Vegetative Roof Study Project No. SB06015, July 27, 2007, p. 1-1.

## CAPITOL COMPLEX

In addition to programs specifically designed to green aspects of the House or the Senate, the Architect of the Capitol also facilitates greening programs for the Capitol Complex. These programs affect all buildings in the Capitol Complex [86].

### Administration

Pursuant to Chapter 28 and Chapter 30 of Title 2 United States Code, the Architect of the Capitol is responsible for the maintenance and upkeep of the United States Capitol and the House and Senate Office Buildings. These responsibilities include "the mechanical and structural maintenance of the building, the upkeep and improvement of the Capitol grounds, and the arrangement of inaugural ceremonies and other ceremonies held in the building or on the grounds" [87]. The Architect also manages the energy usage of Capitol Complex buildings and the operation of the Capitol Power Plant [88].

## Greening Programs

Among the Architect of the Capitol's responsibilities are energy reduction and greening programs in the Capitol Complex. Capitol Complex greening programs can generally be classified into energy reduction initiatives and Capitol Power Plant modifications. Both energy saving programs impact operation for all Capitol Complex buildings.

*Energy Reduction*. The Architect of the Capitol is required by law to improve energy efficiency in the Capitol Complex. The Architect's energy reduction requirements are set forth in the Energy Policy Act of 2005 and the Energy Independence and Security Act of 2007.

*Energy Policy Act of 2005*. The Energy Policy Act of 2005 amended 42 U.S.C. § 8251, et seq., to require the Architect to "develop, update, and implement a cost-effective energy conservation and management plan. ..for all facilities administered by Congress...to meet the energy performance requirements for Federal buildings" [89].

In testimony before the Senate Committee on Rules and Administration, the Acting Architect of the Capitol, Stephen T. Ayers, testified that his office has exceeded the goals set out in the Energy Policy Act.

> The Energy Policy Act requires us to increasingly reduce energy consumption per gross square foot per year in fiscal years 2006 through 2015. The AOC exceeded the goal of 2 percent by reducing energy consumption by 6.5 percent in 2006. In addition, for 2007, we achieved a total cumulative reduction of 6.7 percent over the 2003 baseline [90].

*Energy Independence and Security Act of 2007*. The Energy Independence and Security Act of 2007 further requires the Architect to reduce energy consumption in the Capitol Complex. The Act allows the Architect to perform a feasibility study regarding construction of a photovoltaic roof for the Rayburn House office building; to, when practical, include energy efficiency measures, climate change mitigation measures, and other appropriate environmental measures in the Capitol Complex master plan; to operate the steam boilers and the chiller plant at the Capitol Power Plant in the most energy efficient manner possible to minimize carbon emissions and operating costs; and to install technologies for the capture and storage or use of carbon dioxide emitted from coal combustion in the Capitol Power Plant [91].

Additionally, the Act requires the use of Energy Star lighting products in all federal buildings and establishes an Office of High-Performance Green Buildings in the U.S. General Services Administration to promote green building technology and implementation in federal buildings [92].

*Energy Audits*. In an April 2007 report, the GAO recommended that the Architect of the Capitol conduct energy audits on Capitol Complex buildings to identify projects that could reduce energy usage and greenhouse gas emissions. In the report, the GAO summarized the importance of energy audits.

> A strategy for reducing emissions includes conducting energy audits to identify and evaluate energy-efficiency and renewable-energy projects, as well as evaluating other emissions reduction projects that may fall outside the scope of energy audits. The strategy would also involve developing an implementation plan that considers cost-effectiveness, the extent to which the projects reduce emissions, and funding options [93].

Following the GAO recommendations, the Architect has begun to conduct energy audits of Capitol Complex buildings. The Architect has already conducted an energy audit of the U.S. Capitol Police Buildings and Grounds and is planing to "use $400,000 of FY2008 funds to perform comprehensive energy audits of the Capitol Building and the Ford House Office Building." The Architect will also "direct any remaining FY2008 funds to an audit of the Hart Senate Office Building" [94]. The Architect is currently scheduling energy audits in other buildings, with a goal of performing "energy audits on all buildings on a five-year rotating schedule" [95].

*Environmental Services Performance Contracts*. The Architect of the Capitol has entered into environmental services performance contracts (ESPC) to help Congress increase energy efficiency. ESPCs are a "contracting vehicle that allows agencies to accomplish energy projects for their facilities without up-front capital costs and without special Congressional appropriations to pay for the improvements" [96]. The Architect has entered into ESPCs with two energy companies for a total of 55 projects in the Capitol Building, the Capitol Power Plant, the House Office Buildings, the Senate Office Buildings, the Library of Congress buildings, and on the Capitol Grounds. These projects will costs $154,781,000 to implement, with $149,882,000 paid for by the ESPC vendor and $4,899,000 paid for by the government. Overall, the ESPC contracts will reduce Capitol Complex energy consumption by 5.25% and are projected to save $20,700,000 annually [97].

*Solar Cells*. Pursuant to the passage of P.L. 109-58, the Energy Policy Act of 2005, [98] the Architect requested that the Department of Energy Solar America Initiative study solar energy opportunities for Congressional office buildings [99].

The Department of Energy completed the study in October 2007, and concluded that “there is potential for over 2 Megawatts of photovoltaics made up of numerous arrays on each building” [100]. The Department of Energy also calculated the number of possible photovotaic (PV) arrays, the total square feet required for the arrays, the size of the photovotaic cells, the initial cost of the project, the estimated annual energy generated, and the estimated annual utility cost savings. Table 4 presents the Department of Energy’s findings.

**Table 4. Department of Energy Photovaltaic (PV) Evaluation for the Capitol Complex**

| | House of Representatives | Library of Congress | Senate | Total |
|---|---|---|---|---|
| PV Arrays Evaluated | 31 | 14 | 14 | 59 |
| Sum of PV Array Areas (ft2) | 133,972 | 30,305 | 39,889 | 204,166 |
| Sum of PV Size (kW) | 1,547 | 352 | 461 | 2,360 |
| PV Initial Cost | $13,872,288 | $2,973,796 | $4,065,589 | $20,911,673 |
| PV Annual Energy Delivery (kWh/year) | 1,566,654 | 351,766 | 471,469 | 2,379,889 |
| PV Annual Utility Cost Savings ($/year) | $158,364 | $35,793 | $47,923 | $242,080 |

Source: U.S. Department of Energy, Assessment of the United States Capitol Complex for Application of Solar Energy Technologies, Oct. 2007, p. 3.

The Department of Energy also considered the installation of solar water heating systems for the House Page Dorm and the Senate daycare building. The study concluded that photovoltaic systems have long payback periods with high initial costs and that without local government incentives, solar systems are not cost effective. “[W]hile the Washington, DC government does offer incentives for photovoltaics, they are often awarded to low-income neighborhoods, hospitals, and other non- Federal entities. Without such incentives, the cost of photovoltaic systems is high and the payback is long.” However, the study also concluded that "[d]ue to week-long use and the lower cost of the technology, solar water heating on the House Page Dorm would be cost effective according to the criteria of 10CFR436" [101].

*Capitol Power Plant.* The Capitol Power Plant consists of a main plant (built in 191 0), [102] the east refrigeration plant (built in 1938), an operations building (built in 1978), the west refrigeration plant (built in 1978), the coal yard (transferred from the General Services Administration [GSA] in 1987), and the west refrigeration building expansion (built in 2007) [103]. Between 1909 and 1938, the Capitol Power Plant provided electricity and steam to the Capitol Complex buildings. In 1938, the east refrigeration plant was completed and the power plant began supplying chilled water in addition to electricity and steam. Since 1952, the power plant has only supplied steam and chilled water [104].

To generate steam, the power plant's steam generation plant "contains seven boilers that utilize a combination of three fuels (natural gas, low-sulfur coal, and fuel oil) to generate steam." [105] On average, the Capitol Power Plant historically uses a mixture of 43% natural gas, 47% coal, and 10% fuel oil to generate steam [106]. For 2009, the Capitol Power Plant projects the mixture of fuels to be 60% natural gas, 35% coal, and 5% fuel oil [107].

In FY2008, the Architect has spent $67,570,000 on utilities for the Capitol Power Plant. For FY2009, the Architect has requested $68,791,000 in appropriations for the purchase of natural gas, coal, fuel oil, and electricity to operate the power plant.108 As part of the "Green the Capitol" initiative, the House has estimated that 31% of the Capitol Power Plant output can be attributed to the House office space in the Capitol Complex [109]. The House has appropriated additional funds for the Architect to purchase additional natural gas, so that the proportion of steam supplied to the House will no longer be generated with coal and fuel oil. The Senate will continue to use a mixture of coal, natural gas, and electricity [110].

## CRITICISM OF GREENING PROGRAMS

Opposition to the "Green the Capitol" initiative has developed as the program has expanded. While no Members of Congress have gone on record against the goal of creating a more environmentally friendly and sustainable Capitol, there have been concerns expressed about how money has been spent, the process used to choose some vendors, and the manner in which greening goals have been pursued.

The ranking member of the Subcommittee on Economic Development, Public Buildings, and Emergency Management of the House Committee on Transportation and Infrastructure, summarized the position of those opposed to aspects of green programs for financial reasons during his opening statement at a hearing on greening Washington and the National Capitol Region. In reference to green initiatives, he said:

> They make a lot of sense when they result in improved efficiency and real energy reductions and are done in the most cost efficient way. However, when done without regard to the cost or real benefit to the environment, they can be completely illogical and a waste of taxpayer's money [111].

Those opposed to greening programs have primarily focused their attention on the purchase of carbon offsets and the awarding of the contract to re-light the Capitol Dome.

## Carbon Offsets

As discussed previously, the House purchased $90,550 worth of carbon offset credits on the Chicago Climate Exchange on November 2, 2007. [112] Members of the minority opposed to the carbon offset purchase have argued that using funds to purchase carbon credits is a waste of taxpayer money as "it accomplishes nothing, but makes you feel good about yourself" [113]

To illustrate the point, the minority leader referred to an article in the Washington Post that questioned the logic of purchasing carbon offsets and stated that the money the House spent may not have provided the perceived benefit [114]. The article traced where the House's money went in an effort to offset pollution.

> Some of the money went to farmers in North Dakota, for tilling practices that keep carbon buried in the soil. But some farmers were already doing this, for other reasons, before the House paid a cent.
>
> Other funds went to Iowa, where a power plant has been temporarily rejiggered to burn more cleanly. But that test project had ended more than a year before the money arrived [115].

The Washington Post also quotes the ranking member of the House Administration Committee, as saying "[t]his is just extra money in their pocket for something they're already doing." [116].

On January 14, 2008, the ranking Member of the House Committee on Energy and Commerce, and the ranking Member of the Subcommittee on Oversight and Investigations, sent a letter to Comptroller General David M. Walker requesting that GAO examine the carbon credits marketplace [117]. On January 31, in a follow up letter, the two ranking members further requested that "GAO, in the course of work on these matters, specifically examine and report the manner and means by which the House of Representatives made the purchases." [118]. The GAO report was released in summer 2008 [119].

On July 29, 2008, the House minority leader further criticized the purchase of carbon offsets. In a letter addressed to the Speaker, the minority leader requested that the Speaker "immediately relieve House Chief Administrative Officer Dan Beard of his duties..." in part because "Mr. Beard spent $90,000 to purchase carbon credits on the Chicago Climate Exchange, ignoring a reasonable and sensible request by a member of the House Committee on House Administration to wait for a Government Accountability Office study of carbon credits to determine if they were worthwhile and effective" [120].

Criticism of carbon offsets was also leveled by a Senator during a hearing before the Senate Committee on Rules and Administration on renewable energy and the Capitol complex:

> Yes, I am very skeptical about carbon offsets. I could put it pleasantly, but I might as well just put it bluntly. The opportunities for scamming that thing are huge, and the question I have been unable to get anybody to answer for me when we have gotten into that area is: How do you know that the person who plants a tree in order to provide the carbon offset would not have planted the tree anyway? And, indeed, I have heard from some farmers who have said, "You know, I just got an insight into a major new income stream for me, because as I was out planting trees, somebody came up and said, 'Can we buy the planting of your trees to sell as carbon offsets?'" And he said, "I would have planted the trees anyway, but now I can get some money for doing something that would have happened anyway." And when I raised that with some people, they say, "Oh, well, we are going to investigate that." We are going to have to be sure that there is, in fact, a real carbon offset rather than a scam [121].

## Capitol Dome

Opponents of the "Green the Capitol" initiative are also dissatisfied with the process used to solicit and evaluate proposals to relight the Capitol dome, the length of time required to realize energy savings as a result of dome lighting expenditures, and the necessity for a separate contract to install the lighting design. As discussed above under "Green the Capitol Programs," on October 19, 2007, the CAO issued a Request for Proposal (RFP) to design a lighting scheme for the Capitol Building dome [122] and on March 4, 2008, a contract for $671,900 was awarded to the Lighting Practice of Philadelphia to design a new configuration for the Capitol dome [123].

A representative addressed the Capitol Dome lighting project in a post on his personal blog.

> I agree that we have a responsibility to be good stewards of the environment, but it must be done in a consistent manner. Dan Beard, The House Chief Administrative Officer, said of this new lighting project: "We're not going to drastically cut our energy consumption..." If Speaker Pelosi would like to upgrade the Capitol's lighting system at such an exuberant cost, why doesn't she just come out and say it?
>
> Furthermore, it would take more than 45 years to recoup the money spent on the new "energy efficient" systems design.
>
> My question is this, if it is not going to significantly cut energy consumption, and it will actually cost more money in the long run, what is the goal of such a extensive and costly overhaul? [124]

The House minority leader also stated his opposition to the cost of the design contract when he was quoted in a Washington Post article. "Everyone supports making the Capitol more energy efficient, but we don't have to waste taxpayer dollars to do it: This is a ridiculous boondoggle" [125].

The House minority leader restated his opposition in his July 29, 2008 letter to the Speaker. In the letter, the minority leader refuted the CAO's claim that relighting the Capitol dome will save Congress money. "Mr. Beard claims that this effort will save money on lighting costs, but in reality it will take the House more than 50 years to generate enough energy savings to finally recoup the cost of Mr. Beard's misguided design effort. When multimillion dollar construction and installation costs are factored in, the payback period grows to well over a century" [126].

## OPTIONS FOR PROGRAM ADMINISTRATION

The "Green the Capitol" initiative has become a central piece of the 1 10th Congress's administrative policies and programs. However, the "Green the Capitol" initiative is a non-statutory program that is operated by the Chief

Administrative Officer at the request of the Speaker of the House. While the Speaker has the authority to create internal House programs, a number of policy options are potentially available to create an inter-chamber greening program on Capitol Hill [127]

## Formal House Greening Program

The current "Green the Capitol" initiative exists because of a request by the Speaker of the House, the majority leader, and the Committee on House Administration for the CAO to "undertake a 'Green the Capitol' initiative to ensure that the House institutes the most up-to-date industry and government standards for green building and green operating procedures" [128]. Because the "Green the Capitol" initiative operates under the authority of the Speaker, it is possible that should the current minority become the majority, or the current Speaker steps down, the program could be discontinued.

To ensure the program's continuation, the House has the option of passing a resolution creating a more formal greening initiative. The resolution could create a program that includes input from both the majority and minority and considers the critiques of the opponents and the goals of the proponents. Should a new majority or Speaker desire to alter or terminate the program once a resolution has been agreed to, a subsequent resolution could amend or terminate the program.

## "Green the Senate" Initiative

Senate greening programs are currently administered by the Architect of the Capitol under direction from the Committee on Rules and Administration. To augment the green programming taking place in the House of Representatives, the Senate could create its own "Green the Senate" initiative.

A "Green the Senate" initiative could allow the Senate to create energy and cost savings programs that cover administrative functions not typically covered by the Architect. Should the Senate consider its own green initiative, it could choose to place its implementation with the Architect, or could assign implementation to the Sergeant at Arms, the Secretary of the Senate, or a combination of the three officers. If the Senate followed this course, the same continuity issues raised by the current House initiative would also apply to the Senate.

## Independent Greening Commission

The Senate, the House, or both could create a greening commission to oversee greening efforts. Should the Senate or House choose to create a commission, it could be modeled after the commission on Congressional Mailing Standards, also known as the "Franking Commission" [129]. The franking commission "has a three fold mandate: (1) to issue regulations governing the proper use of the franking privilege; (2) to provide guidance in connection with mailings; (3) to act as a quasi-judicial body for the disposition of formal complaints against Members of Congress who have allegedly violated franking laws or regulations" [130].

A greening commission could serve a similar purpose in guiding the Architect and the CAO to coordinate greening activities within the Senate and the House and between the two chambers. The greening commission could provide long-term strategic guidance to the Architect and CAO, provide context to the Architect and CAO of Member intent and interest in new greening opportunities, and act as a liaison between the greening program and the committees of jurisdiction in the Senate and in the House.

## Capitol Complex-Wide Greening Program

Although the program created in March 2007 by the House is called the "Green the Capitol" initiative, the initiative only covers actions and opportunities in the House. By functioning in only one chamber, "Green the Capitol" does not have the authority to set policy in the Capitol as a whole. To maximize impact on the energy use and conservation of the Capitol, the House and the Senate could pass a concurrent resolution or a bill to create a Capitol-wide greening initiative.

The passage of either a concurrent resolution or bill could create a more formal, cooperative greening program that would encompass activities in the House and the Senate. Cooperation between chambers might encourage costs savings since purchasing services or goods in quantity often leads to lower prices. Additionally, the passage of a concurrent resolution or a bill would allow the House and Senate to addresses green programs for the entire Capitol complex, rather than creating programs that affect only a portion of the Capitol grounds.

Such legislation would need to determine who would administer a Capitol Hill- wide greening program. The House and the Senate could chose the Architect of the Capitol and expand Architect's jurisdiction to include all energy and green programs associated with building administration. The House and the Senate could also choose to designate officers within each chamber to coordinate Capitol

Hill-wide efforts, create a new officer of the Capitol for greening issues, or create a joint committee to facilitate and provide oversight to a combination of offices responsible for greening.

## Continued Case-by-Case Programming

The House and the Senate might determine the current system of operating greening programs is effective. Instead of creating a statutory House or Senate program, creating a "Green the Senate" Program, or creating a joint greening effort, the House and the Senate could continue to allow the CAO to operate the "Green the Capitol" initiative and allow the Architect of the Capitol to administer other greening and energy usage programs in the House and Senate. Expansion could continue on an as-needed basis, with minimal coordination between the Houses.

To provide oversight in the case-by-case system, the House and the Senate could rely on the existing committee system to guide green programs. In the House, the Committee on House Administration, the Committee on Transportation and Infrastructure, the Committee on Appropriations, and in the $110^{th}$ Congress the Select Committee on Energy Independence and Global Warming have jurisdiction. In the Senate, the Committee on Rules and Administration, the Energy and Natural Resources Committee, and the Environment and Public Works Committee, and the Committee on Appropriations maintain jurisdiction over current greening initiatives. Each of these committees could hold hearings, individually or jointly, to discuss greening programs and provide direction to the officers of Congress responsible for implementing energy reduction and greening.

# References

[1] U.S. Congress, Chief Administrative Officer of the House of Representatives, Executive Summary of Green the Capitol Initiative Preliminary Report, $110^{th}$ Cong., 1st sess., p. 4. [http://www.speaker.gov/pdf/GTCsummary.pdf], accessed Sept. 29, 2008. (Hereafter, Green the Capitol Preliminary Report Executive Summary.)

[2] U.S. Congress, Speaker of the House of Representatives, "*House Democrats Urge Greening of Capitol Complex*," press release, Mar. 2, 2007,

[http://www.speaker.gov/newsroom/pressreleases?id=0082], accessed Sept. 29, 2008.

[3] Green the Capitol Preliminary Report Executive Summary, p. 3.

[4] U.S. Congress, Chief Administrative Officer of the House of Representatives, Preliminary Report Green the Capitol Initiative, 110th Cong., 1s t sess. [http://www.speaker.gov/pdf/GTCreport.pdf], accessed Sept. 29, 2008, p. 4.

[5] Ibid., pp. 19-26.

[6] U.S. Congress, Chief Administrative Officer of the House of Representatives, *Green the Capitol Initiative Final Report Executive Summary,* 1 10th Cong., 1st sess. [http://speaker.gov/pdf/GTCI62 1 sum2.pdf], accessed Sept. 29, 2008, p. iv.

[7] U.S. Congress, Chief Administrative Officer of the House of Representatives, *Green the Capitol Initiative Final Report*, 110th Cong., 1st sess. [http://speaker.gov/pdf/GTCI62 1full2.pdf], accessed Sept. 29, 2008, p. 2.

[8] Webster's Dictionary defines "carbon neutral" as "emitting no carbon dioxide into the atmosphere; also, employing a technique to absorb carbon dioxide so it is not emitted." See, Webster's New Millennium Dictionary of English, Preview Edition, [http://dictionary.reference.com/browse/carbon neutral], accessed Sept. 29, 2008. Alternatively, the Oxford English Dictionary defines the term "carbon neutral" as "making no net release of carbon dioxide to the atmosphere, especially through offsetting emissions by planting trees." See, *Shorter Oxford English Dictionary*, vol. 1 (New York: Oxford University Press, 2007), p. 346.

[9] U.S. Congress, Speaker of the House of Representatives, "*Pelosi: As Part of 'Green the Capitol' Initiativ*e, House to Reduce Energy Consumption by 50 Percent in Just 10 Years," press release, June 21, 2007 [http://speaker.gov/newsroom/pressreleases?id=0222], accessed Sept. 29, 2008.

[10] U.S. Congress, House Chief Administrative Officer, Green the Capitol: Six Months of Progress, 110th Cong., 1st sess., Dec. 2007 [http://cao.house.gov/greenthecapitol/progress-booklet-2007dec.pdf], accessed, Sept. 29, 2008, p. 1. (Hereafter, Green the Capitol Six-Month Progress Report).

[11] Ibid, pp. 2-7.

[12] According to the Federal Acquisition Institute, a request for proposal (RFP) is a solicitation for offers under negotiation procedures. Federal Acquisition

Institute, *Glossary of Acquisition Terms*, FAC-97-09, Dec. 1998 [http://www.fai.gov/pdfs/glossary.pdf], p. 92, accessed Sept. 29, 2008.

[13] Green the Capitol Six-Month Progress Report, p. 2.

[14] U.S. Congress, Chief Administrative Officer of the House of Representatives, "*Comprehensive Lighting Design for the U.S. Capitol Building Dome*," Solicitation Number OPR080000004. A synopsis of the request for proposal can be found [https://www.fbo.gov/spg/House/HOCAO/HOCAOOP/OPR08000004/listing.html], accessed Sept. 29, 2008.

[15] U.S. Congress, Chief Administrative Officer of the House of Representatives, "*Plans to Relight Symbol of Democracy Taking Shape*," press release, March 4, 2008 [http://cao.house.gov/press/cao-20080305.shtml], accessed Sept. 29, 2008.

[16] U.S. Congress, House Committee on Appropriations, Subcommittee on Legislative Branch, Legislative Branch Appropriations for 2009: *Part 2 Fiscal Year 2009 Legislative Branch Appropriations Requests*, hearing, 1 10th Cong., 2nd sess. (Washington: GPO, 2008), pp. 576-577.

[17] U.S. Congress, Chief Administrative Officer of the House of Representatives, "*Plans to Relight Symbol of Democracy Taking Shape*," press release, March 4, 2008 [http://cao.house.gov/press/cao-20080305.shtml], accessed Sept. 29, 2008. For press accounts of the dome lighting project see "Seeing the Light," *The Washington Post*, Apr. 2, 2008, p. A8; Jordy Yager, "Who's Go the Brighter Lights? Capitol Dome vs. Memorials," The Hill, Mar. 5, 2008, p. 1, 8; "Editorial: Lightning Round," *The Philadelphia Inquirer*, Apr. 3, 2008, p. A14; and Linda Loyd, "Lighting Practice Caught Off-Guard by Furor," *The Philadelphia Inquirer*, Apr. 4, 2008, p. A1.

[18] For more information on compact fluorescent light bulbs see CRS Report RS22807, Compact Fluorescent Light Bulbs (CFLs): *Issues with Use and Disposal*, by Linda Luther.

[19] U.S. Congress, Chief Administrative Officer of the House of Representatives, *Six Months of Progress: A Report from the Green the Capitol Office*, "Checklist," [http://cao.house.gov/greenthecapitol/progress-report-2007dec.pdf], accessed Sept. 29, 2008. (Hereafter, Six Months of Progress Checklist).

[20] U.S. Congress, Chief Administrative Officer of the House of Representatives, "*Carpet Installation for the 111th Transition*," Solicitation Number: OPR08000028. A synopsis of the proposal can be found at [https://www.fbo.gov/spg/House/HOCAO/HOCAOOP/OPR08000028/listing.html], accessed Sept. 29, 2008.

[21] Volatile organic compounds (VOCs) are a class of chemicals that are commonly encountered by people as they go about their daily routines. Exposure to VOCs can occur from contact with chlorinated water, methane, smoking, paint, dry-cleaning, and gasoline. For more information about VOCs see David L. Ashley, Michael A. Bonin, Frederick L. Cardinali, Joan M. McGraw, and Joe V. Wooten, "Measurement of Volatile Organic Compounds in Human Blood," *Environmental Health Perspectives*, Vol. 104, Supp. 5 (Oct. 1996), pp. 87 1-877.

[22] Green the Capitol Six-Month Progress Report, p. 5.

[23] Eric C. Bettelheim and Gilonne d'Origny, "Carbon Sinks and Emissions Trading under the Kyoto Protocol: A Legal Analysis," *Philosophical Transactions: Mathematical, Physical and Engineering Sciences*, Vol. 360, No. 1797 (Aug. 15, 2002), p. 1843. For a discussion of carbon offsets see CRS Report RL34241, Voluntary Carbon Offsets: Overview and Assessment, by Jonathan L. Ramseur.

[24] For more information on the Chicago Climate Exchange and its operations see [http://www.chicagoclimatex.com], accessed Aug. 13, 2008.

[25] U.S. Congress, House of Representatives, Statement of Disbursements of the House: October 1, 2007 to December 31, 2007, 110th Cong., 2nd sess., Oct. 16, 2007, H.Doc. 110-87 (Washington: GPO, 2007), p. 35.

[26] U.S. Congress, Representative Rahm Emanuel, "Emanuel Announced Greening of the Capitol: U.S. Congress to Purchase Carbon Offsets from the Chicago Climate Exchange," press release, Nov. 5, 2007 [http://www.house.gov/apps/list/press/il05_emanuel/ capitolgreening.html], accessed, Sept. 29, 2008.

[27] U.S. Congress, House Committee on Appropriations, Subcommittee on Legislative Branch, Legislative Branch Appropriations for 2009: Part 2 Fiscal Year 2009 Legislative Branch Appropriations Requests, hearing, 110th Cong., 2nd sess. (Washington: GPO, 2008), p. 552.

[28] Six Months of Progress Checklist, p. 2.

[29] U.S. Government Accountability Office, Economic and Other Implications of Switching from Coal to Natural Gas at the Capitol Power Plant and at Electricity-Generating Units Nationwide, GAO-08-601R, May 1, 2008.

[30] U.S. Congress, House Committee on Transportation and Infrastructure, Administration Proposals on Climate Change and Energy Independence, hearing, 110th Cong., 1st sess., May 11 and 16, 2007, H.Hrg. 110-44 (Washington: GPO, 2007), p. 45.

[31] Rep. Jay Inslee, "Green the Capitol Initiative," *Congressional Record*, daily edition, vol. 153, no. 177(Nov. 15, 2007), p. H14074.

[32] U.S. Government Accountability Office, Economic and Other Implications of Switching from Coal to Natural Gas at the Capitol Power Plant and at Electricity-Generating Units Nationwide, GAO-08-601R, May 1, 2008, p. 2.

[33] Ibid., p. 6.

[34] U.S. Congress, Chief Administrative Officer of the House of Representatives, "House Car Sharing Pilot," [http://cao.house.gov /greenthecapitol/carshare.shtml], accessed Sept. 29,..34 2008.

[35] Six Months of Progress Checklist, p. 3.

[36] Zipcar, "How does Zipcar work? [http://www.zipcar.com/how/], accessed Aug. 19, 2008. For additional information on the car-sharing program, see Elizabeth Brotherton, "House Staff Get Zipcars, Flexcars," *Roll Call*, Oct. 29, 2007, posted at [http://cao.house.gov/press/rollcall-2007 1029.shtml], accessed Sept. 29, 2008.

[37] Rep. Earl Blumenhauer, "Green the Capitol Initiative," *Congressional Record*, daily edition, vol. 153, no. 177 (Nov. 15, 2007), p. H14073.

[38] U.S. Congress, House Committee on Appropriations, Subcommittee on Legislative Branch, Legislative Branch Appropriations for 2009: *Part 2 Fiscal Year 2009 Legislative Branch Appropriations Requests*, hearing, 1 10th Cong., 2nd sess. (Washington: GPO, 2008), p. 554.

[39] U.S. Congress, Chief Administrative Officer of the House of Representatives, "*House Bike Sharing Program*," Solicitation Number: OPR08000038. A synopsis of the proposal can be found at [https://www.fbo.gov/spg/House/HOCAO/HOCAOOP/OPR08000038/ listing.html], accessed Sept. 29, 2008.

[40] Dear-Colleague Letter from Representatives Earl Blumenauer and Thomas Petri, co- chairs, Congressional Bike Caucus, Aug. 6, 2008. To sign up for the bike-sharing program, House staff and employees need to bring their staff ID badge, a completed waiver form, and a completed participation form to the House Gym, located on level G2 of the Rayburn House Office Building between 11-2 Monday through Friday. Waiver and participation forms are available on Housenet, the House intranet, [https://housenet.house.gov/portal/server.pt?open=512&objID=372&&Page ID=36663&mode=2&in_hi_userid=2&cached= true], accessed Aug. 20, 2008, and are required to use the bike-sharing program. Housenet is available only to House offices.

[41] U.S. Congress, Chief Administrative Officer of the House of Representatives, "Wheels4Wellness Bike Sharing Pilot Program Rolls Out," [http://cao.house.gov/w4w.shtml], accessed July 17, 2008.

[42] Dear-Colleague Letter from Representatives Earl Blumenauer and Thomas Petri, co- chairs, *Congressional Bike Caucus*, Aug. 6, 2008.

[43] Dear-Colleague Letter from Representatives Earl Blumenauer and Thomas Petri, co- chairs, *Congressional Bike Caucus*, Sept. 5, 2008.

[44] U.S. Congress, House of Representatives, "Wheels 4 Wellness," Housenet [https://housenet.house.gov/portal/server.pt?open=512&objID=372&&PageID=36663&mode=2&in_hi_userid=2&cached=true], accessed Aug. 20, 2008.

[45] Testimony of Acting Architect of the Capitol Stephen T. Ayers, in U.S. Congress, House Committee on Transportation and Infrastructure, Regarding the Administrative Responses to Climate Change and Energy Independence, hearings, 110th Cong., 1st sess., May 11, 2007 [http://transportation.house.gov/hearings/Testimony.aspx?TID= 1131 &NewsID= 190], accessed Sept. 29, 2008, p. 4.

[46] For additional information on the Capitol Visitor Center, see CRS Report RL3 1121, The Capitol Visitor Center: An Overview, by Stephen W. Stathis.

[47] U.S. Congress, House of Representatives, Chief Administrative Officer, "House Cafeteria to Undergo Major Menu, Operational Changes in December," press release, Nov. 13, 2007 [http://cao.house.gov/press/cao-2007 1113 .shtml], accessed Feb. 4, 2008. Food service in the Ford Cafeteria is scheduled to transition from the current vendor, the Skenteris family, to Restaurant Associates in September 2008. U.S. Congress, House of Representatives, Chief Administrative Officer, "*CAO Allows Current Ford Cafeteria Vendor to Remain Until September 2008*," press release, Nov. 16, 2007 [http://cao.house.gov/press/cao-2007 11 16.shtml], accessed Sept. 29, 2008.

[48] Restaurant Associates, "*Sustainability*," House of Representatives Dining Services Website [http://go.compass-usa.com/house/content/sustainability.asp], accessed Sept. 29, 2008.

[49] Green the Capitol Six-Month Progress Report, p. 3.

[50] Rep. Sam Farr, "Green the Capitol Initiative," Congressional Record, daily edition, vol. 153, no. 177 (Nov. 15, 2007), p. H14077.

[51] For a discussion on composting see, George Tchobanoglous and Frank Kreith, *Handbook of Solid Waste Management* (New York: McGraw-Hill, 2002), pp. 1.9-1.11.

[52] U.S. Congress, Chief Administrative Officer of the House of Representatives, Green the Capitol Initiative, Green Team "Newsletter," vol. 1, 110th Cong., 2nd sess. Apr. 7, 2008 [http://cao.house.gov/

greenthecapitol/green-newsletter/greenteam0 1 .shtml], accessed Sept. 29, 2008.

[53] Testimony of Chief Administrative Office of the House of Representatives Daniel Beard, in U.S. Congress, House Select Committee on Energy Independence and Global Warming, Food for Thought: *A Primer on the Climate Consequences of Food Choices,* 110th Cong., 2nd sess., Feb. 26, 2008, [http://globalwarming.house.gov/tools/assets/files/0361.pdf], accessed Sept. 29, 2008.

[54] Testimony of Chief Administrative Office of the House of Representatives Daniel Beard, in U.S. Congress, House Committee on Transportation and Infrastructure, Subcommittee on Economic Development, Public Buildings, and Emergency Management, *A Growing Capitol Complex and Visitor Center: Needs for Transportation, Security, Greening, Energy, and Maintenance,* 110th Cong., 2nd sess., Apr. 1, 2008 [http://cao.house.gov/appearances/20080401_transportation.shtml], accessed Sept. 29, 2008.

[55] For information on how to request a compost bin for an office visit [http://cao.house.gov/greenthecapitol/recycle/faq.shtml], accessed Sept. 29, 2008.

[56] Section 4(c) of H.Res. 202, agreed to March 8, 2007, established the Select Committee on Energy Independence and Global Warming's jurisdiction. "The select committee shall not have legislative jurisdiction and shall have no authority to take legislative action on any bill or resolution. Its sole authority shall be to investigate, study, make findings, and develop recommendations on policies, strategies, technologies and other innovations, intended to reduce the dependence of the United States on foreign sources of energy and achieve substantial and permanent reductions in emissions and other activities that contribute to climate change and global warming." The select committee will expire at the end of the 110th Congress unless the House agrees to a resolution authorizing its continuance.

[57] H.Res. 104 (101st Congress), agreed to by voice vote, Aug. 1, 1989.

[58] For more information on the House recycling program see CRS Report RL34617, *Recycling Programs in Congress: Legislative Development and Architect of the Capitol Administration*, by Jacob R. Straus.

[59] Dear-Colleague Letter from Daniel Beard, Chief Administrative Officer of the House of Representatives, Dec. 12, 2007. See also, Elizabeth Brotherton, "Beard Details New Recycling Efforts," *Roll Call*, Feb. 27, 2008 [http://www.rollcall.com/issues/53_99/news/22279-1 .html], accessed Sept. 29, 2008.

[60] U.S. Congress, Committee on House Administration, "*Under Pressure? Proper Tire Inflation Save Energy, Money*," Dear Colleague Letter, July 28, 2008.

[61] For more information on Congressional Commissions see CRS Report RS22725, Congressional Advisory Commissions: An Overview, by Matthew Eric Glassman.

[62] H.R. 6474 (110th Congress), ordered reported from the Committee on House Administration, July 30, 2008.

[63] U.S. Congress, Committee on House Administration, Committee Meeting, markup of H.R. 6339, H.R. 6474, H.R. 6475, H.R. 6589, H.R. 998, H.R. 6608, H.Res. 1207, and committee resolutions 110-7 and 110-8, 1 10th Cong., 2nd sess., July 30, 2008.

[64] Statements of Representative Vernon, in U.S. Congress, House Committee on House Administration, Committee Meeting, markup of H.R. 6339, H.R. 6474, H.R. 6475, H.R. 6589, H.R. 998, H.R. 6608, H.Res. 1207, and committee resolutions 110-7 and 110-8, 110th Cong., 2nd sess., July 30, 2008.

[65] H.R. 6171 (110th Congress), introduced June 3, 2008.

[66] Based on CRS discussions with Scott Shapleigh, recycling program manager, Architect of the Capitol, and Michael Shirven, general engineer, Architect of the Capitol, Mar. 6, 2008.

[67] S.Res. 99 (101st Congress), agreed to by unanimous consent, Oct. 2, 1989.

[68] For more information on the House recycling program see CRS Report RL34617, Recycling Programs in Congress: Legislative Development and Architect of the Capitol Administration, by Jacob R. Straus.

[69] Testimony of Acting Architect of the Capitol Stephen T. Ayers, in U.S. Congress, Senate Committee on Rules and Administration, Improving Energy Efficiency, Increasing the Use of Renewable Sources of Energy, and Reducing the Carbon Footprint of the Capitol Complex, hearing, 110th Cong., 2nd sess., June 18, 2008 [http://rules.senate.gov/hearings/2008/06 1 8ayers.pdf], accessed Aug. 20, 2008. (Hereafter, Senate Rules Committee Energy Efficiency Hearing).

[70] Conversation between the author and Scott Shapleigh, recycling program manager, Senate office buildings, *Architect of the Capitol*, Sept. 10, 2008.

[71] Ibid., p. 17.

[72] Washington State University Cooperative Extension Energy Program, "Energy Efficiency Fact Sheet: Dimmable Compact Florescent Lamps" [http://www.energy.wsu.edu/documents/ building/light/compact_fluor.pdf], accessed Sept. 29, 2008.

[73] Conversation between the author and Scott Shapleigh, recycling program manager, Senate office buildings, Architect of the Capitol and Michael Shirven, general engineer, Senate office buildings, *Architect of the Capitol*, Mar. 6, 2008.

[74] Testimony of Acting Architect of the Capitol Stephen T. Ayers, Senate Rules Committee Energy Efficiency Hearing, p. 6.

[75] Ibid.

[76] Conversation between the author and Scott Shapleigh, recycling program manager, Senate office buildings, Architect of the Capitol and Michael Shirven, general engineer, Senate office buildings, Architect of the Capitol, Mar. 6, 2008.

[77] Email from Trent Wolfersberger, assistant superintendent, Senate Support Office, Architect of the Capitol, Sept. 11, 2008.

[78] Based on CRS conversations with Trent Wolfersberger, assistant superintendent, Senate Support Office, *Architect of the Capitol*, Sept. 11, 2008.

[79] "Steam traps are automatic valves that release condensed steam (condensate) from a steam space while preventing the loss of live steam. They also remove non-condensable gases from the steam space. Steam traps are designed to maintain steam energy efficiency for performing specific tasks such as heating a building or maintaining heat for process use. Once steam has transferred heat through a process and becomes hot water, it is removed by the trap from the steam side as condensate and either returned to the boiler via condensate return lines or discharged to the atmosphere, which is a wasteful practice." See, U.S. Department of Energy, Federal Energy Management Program, "FEMP Management and Maintenance: Steam Traps," [http://www 1.eere.energy.gov/femp/operations_maintenance/om_steamtraps.html], accessed Sept. 29, 2008.

[80] Email from Scott Shapleigh, recycling program manager, Senate office buildings, *Architect of the Capitol*, Aug. 22, 2008.

[81] The American Institute of Architects, 50 to 50 [http://www.aia.org/SiteObjects/files/50to50_2007 12 12.pdf], accessed Sept. 29, 2008. For more information about the benefits and drawbacks of green roofs see Erica Oberndorfer, Jeremy Lundholm, Brad Bass, Reid R. Coffman, Hitesh Doshi, Nigel Dunnett, Stuart Gaffin, Manfred Köhler, Karen K. Y. Liu, and Bradley Rowe, "Green Roofs as Urban Ecosystems: Ecological Structures, Functions, and Services," *Bioscience*, vol. 57, no. 10 (Nov. 2007), pp. 823-833.

[82] P.L. 109-58, 119 Stat. 1136-1137, Aug. 5, 2005. Section 1829 requires the Architect to carry out a study to explore the feasibility of installing energy and water conservation measures on the Dirksen Senate Office Building roof, including the area directly above the food service facilities in the center of the building.

[83] U.S. Congress, Architect of the Capitol, Dirksen Senate Office Building Facilities Condition Assessment Vegetative Roof Study Project No. SB06015, July 27, 2007, p. 1-1.

[84] Ibid. For additional information on green roofs see, Nancy Solomon, "Vegetation Systems Atop Buildings Yield Environmental Benefits: Roofing Technology Developed in Germany is Starting to Take Root in North America," Architectural Record, vol. 191, no. 3 (Mar. 1, 2003); and The American Institute of Architects, "*Green Roof Design*," AIA Best Practices, [http://www.aia.org/SiteObjects/files/bestpractice_18_1 8_02E.pdf], accessed Sept. 29, 2008.

[85] Conversation between the author and Scott Shapleigh, recycling program manager, Senate office buildings, Architect of the Capitol and Michael Shirven, general engineer, Senate office buildings, *Architect of the Capitol*, Mar. 6, 2008.

[86] The Capitol Complex includes the Capitol, the House Office Buildings (Cannon, Longworth, Rayburn, and Ford), Senate Office Buildings (Russell, Dirksen, and Hart), the U.S. Botanic Garden, the Capitol Grounds, the Library of Congress buildings (Jefferson, Adams, and Madison), the Supreme Court Building, the Thurgood Marshall Federal Judiciary Building, the Capitol Power Plant, the Capitol Visitors Center, and various support facilities. See U.S. Congress, Architect of the Capitol, "*Capitol Complex Overview*," [http://www.aoc.gov/cc/index.cfm], accessed Sept. 29, 2008.

[87] U.S. Congress, Architect of the Capitol, "*Responsibilities*," [http://www.aoc.gov/aoc/responsibilities/index.cfm]], accessed Sept. 29, 2008.

[88] 2 U.S.C. § 2162. For more information on the Architect of the Capitol, see CRS Report RL32820, *Architect of the Capitol: Appointment, Duties, and Current Issues*, by Mildred Amer.

[89] P.L. 109-58, 119 Stat. 605, Aug. 8, 2005. The act further required that the Architect's plan include: (1) a description of the life cycle cost analysis used to determine the cost-effectiveness of proposed energy efficiency projects; (2) a schedule of energy surveys to ensure complete surveys of all congressional buildings every five years to determine the cost and payback

period of energy and water conservation measures; (3) a strategy for installation of life cycle cost-effective energy and water conservation measures; (4) the results of a study of the costs and benefits of installation of sub-metering in congressional buildings; and (5) information packages and 'how-to' guides for each Member and employing authority of Congress that detail simple, cost-effective methods to save energy and taxpayer dollars in the workplace.

[90] Senate Rules Committee Energy Efficiency Hearing, p. 6.

[91] P.L. 110-140, 121 Stat. 1655-1658. For more information on the Energy Independence and Security Act of 2007, see CRS Report RL34294, Energy Independence and Security Act of 2007: A Summary of Major Provisions, coordinated by Fred Sissine.

[92] The White House, Executive Office of the President, "Fact Sheet: Energy Independence and Security Act of 2007," press release, Dec. 19, 2007 [http://whitehouse.gov/news/releases/2007/12/print/2007 1219-1 .html], accessed Sept. 29, 2008.

[93] U.S. Government Accountability Office, Energy Audits Are Key to Strategy for Reducing Greenhouse Gas Emissions, GAO-07-516, Apr. 2007, p. 4.

[94] U.S. Government Accountability Office, Architect of the Capitol: Progress in Improving Energy Efficiency and Options for Decreasing Greenhouse Gas Emissions, GAO-08-917T, June 18, 2008, p. 5.

[95] Testimony of Acting Architect of the Capitol Stephen T. Ayers, Senate Rules Committee Energy Efficiency Hearing, p. 7.

[96] U.S. Department of Energy, Federal Energy Management Program, Super Energy Savings Performance Contracts, [http://www 1.eere.energy.gov/femp/financing/superespcs.html], accessed Sept. 29, 2008.

[97] Based on CRS discussions with Charles Iliff, planning and project management project executive, *Architect of the Capitol*, Sept. 22, 2008.

[98] P.L. 109-58, 119 Stat. 1136-1137, Aug. 5, 2005.

[99] The Department of Energy studied the feasibility of installing solar panels on the Rayburn House Office Building (HOB), the Cannon HOB, the Ford HOB, the Longworth HOB, the House page dorm, and the House parking lot; the Dirksen Senate Office Building (SOB), the Hart SOB, the Russell SOB, and the Senate child care building; and the Adams and Madison Buildings of the Library of Congress.

[100] U.S. Department of Energy, Assessment of the United States Capitol *Complex for Application of Solar Energy Technologies*, Oct. 2007, p. 2.

[101] Ibid. 10 C.F.R. § 436 establishes the rules for Federal energy management and planning programs. These programs are designed to "reduce Federal energy consumption and to promote life cycle cost effective investments in building energy systems, building water systems and energy and water conservation measures for Federal buildings."

[102] P.L. 58-194, 33 Stat. 479, Apr. 26, 1904.

[103] U.S. Congress, Architect of the Capitol, Accountability Report 2003, [http://www.aoc.gov/aoc/cfo/upload/AOC-Financial-Report-2003 .pdf], accessed Sept. 29, 2008, p. 25.

[104] U.S. Government Accountability Office, Feasibility of Outsourcing the Management and Operation of the Capitol Power Plant, GAO-08-382R, Jan. 31, 2008, p. 4. Electricity for the Capitol Complex is purchased from Pepco.

[105] Testimony of Acting Architect of the Capitol Stephen T. Ayers, Senate Rules Committee Energy Efficiency Hearing, p. 8.

[106] U.S. Government Accountability Office, Economic and Other Implications of Switching from Coal and Natural Gas at the Capitol Power Plant and at Electricity-Generating Units Nationwide, GAO-08-601R, May 1, 2008, p. 2.

[107] Based on CRS discussions with Christopher Potter, deputy director, Capitol Power Plant, Sept. 5, 2008.

[108] Ibid., p. 510.

[109] U.S. Congress, Chief Administrative Officer of the House of Representatives, Preliminary Report Green the Capitol Initiative, 110th Cong., 1st sess. [http://www.speaker.gov/pdf/GTCreport.pdf], accessed Sept. 29, 2008, p. 11.

[110] U.S. Government Accountability Office, Economic and Other Implications of Switching from Coal to Natural Gas at the Capitol Power Plant and at Electricity-Generating Units Nationwide, GAO-08-601R, May 1, 2008, pp. 2-3.

[111] Statement of Ranking Member Sam Graves, in U.S. Congress, House Committee on Transportation and Infrastructure, Economic Development, Public Buildings and Emergency Management Subcommittee, Greening Washington and the National Capital Region, hearing, 1 10th Cong., 2nd sess. Apr. 17, 2008 [http://republicans.transportation.house.gov/news/PRArticle.aspx?NewsID=363], accessed Oct. 2, 2008.

[112] U.S. Congress, House of Representatives, Statement of Disbursements of the House: October 1, 2007 to December 31, 2007, 1 10th Cong., 2nd sess., Oct. 16, 2007, H.Doc. 110-87 (Washington: GPO, 2007), p. 35. For more information on the Chicago Climate Exchange see, [http://www.chicagoclimatex.com], accessed Sept. 29, 2008.

[113] U.S. Congress, Minority Leader of the House of Representatives, "Green Pork Update: Beard's 'Waste of Taxpayer Dollars' Now Under Examination by Government Auditors," press release, Feb. 6, 2008 [http://republicanleader.house.gov/News/ DocumentSingle.aspx?DocumentID=83264], accessed Sept. 29, 2008.

[114] Ibid.

[115] David A. Fahrenthold, "Value of U.S. House's Carbon Offsets Is Murky," The Washington Post, Jan. 28, 2008, p. A1.

[116] Ibid.

[117] Letter from Reps. Joe Barton and John Shimkus, to David M. Walker, Comptroller General of the United States, Jan. 14, 2008. A copy of the letter is available from the author.

[118] Letter from Reps. Joe Barton and John Shimkus, to David M. Walker, Comptroller General of the United States, Jan. 31, 2008. A copy of the letter is available from the author.

[119] U.S. Government Accountability Office, Carbon Offsets: The U.S. Voluntary Market Is Growing, but Quality Assurance Poses Challenges for Market Participants, GAO-08- 1048, August 29, 2008. For more information on the controversy surrounding the carbon offset market see Jonathan Weisman, "Capitol to Buy Offsets in Bid to Go Green," *The Washington Post*, Nov. 5, 2007, p. A6; David A. Fahrenthold, "Value of U.S. House's Carbon Offsets Is Murkey," *The Washington Post*, Jan. 28, 2008, p. A1.; and Jordy Yager, "CAO Would 'Welcome" Investigation into Carbon Offsets," The Hill, Feb. 6, 2008, p. 16.

[120] Letter from Minority Leader John Boehner to Speaker of the House of Representatives Nancy Pelosi, July 29, 2008.

[121] Senate Rules Committee Energy Efficiency Hearing, pp. 16-17.

[122] Green the Capitol Six-Month Progress Report, p. 2.

[123] U.S. Congress, Chief Administrative Officer of the House of Representatives, "*Plans to Relight Symbol of Democracy Taking Shape*," press release, March 4, 2008 [http://cao.house.gov/press/cao-20080305.shtml], accessed July 16, 2008.

[124] Representative John Campbell, "New Lights Over the Capitol," blog post [http://greeneyeshade.townhall.com/blog/g/e69697a1 - 1f2c-40ce-a1 ab-20a 17264ccab], accessed July 23, 2008.

[125] Christopher Lee, "Beacon or Boondoggle? New Lights For the Capitol: Update Would Conserve Energy, Democrats Say," *The Washington Post*, Apr. 2, 2008, p. A1.

[126] Letter from Minority Leader John Boehner to Speaker of the House of Representatives Nancy Pelosi, July 29, 2008. A copy of the letter is available from the author.

[127] CRS take no position on any of the options identified in this report.

[128] U.S. Congress, Speaker of the House of Representatives, "*House Democrats Urge Greening of Capitol Complex*," press release, Mar. 2, 2007, [http://www.speaker.gov/newsroom/ pressreleases?id=0082], accessed July 9, 2008.

[129] P.L. 93-191, 87 Stat. 737, Dec. 18, 1973. For more information on the Commission on Congressional Mailing Standards see CRS Report RL34274, Franking Privilege: Historical Development and Options for Change, by Matthew Eric Glassman; and CRS Report RS22771, Congressional Franking Privilege: Background and Current Legislation, by Matthew Eric Glassman.

[130] U.S. Congress, Committee on House Administration, "About Franking Commission," [http://cha.house.gov/franking_about.aspx], Sept. 23, 2008.

In: Recycling and Green Programs at the Capital... ISBN 978-1-60692-980-3
Editor: H. Y. Kim, pp. 105-150 

*Chapter 3*

# RECYCLING PROGRAMS IN CONGRESS: LEGISLATIVE DEVELOPMENT AND ARCHITECT OF THE CAPITOL ADMINISTRATION*

***Jacob R. Straus***

## ABSTRACT

The House of Representatives and the Senate created separate voluntary recycling programs in 1989, during the 101st Congress (1989-1991). Administered by the Architect of the Capitol, the recycling programs aimed to reduce the amount of material sent to landfills and establish the House and the Senate as leaders of the recycling movement.

The initial recycling programs in the House and Senate focused on the recycling of paper and the use of recycled paper, including white office paper, newspaper, and cardboard. While the program had modest beginnings, since 1992, when the General Services Administration (GSA) began managing the House and Senate recycling contracts, the House (9,939 tons) and the Senate (5,117 tons) have recycled a combined total of approximately 15,056 tons of paper.

At approximately the same time the House and Senate began recycling paper, they also began recycling bottles and cans. Since 1992, when GSA began managing the recycling of non-paper materials, the House (572 tons)

* Excerpted from CRS Report RL34617, dated August 13, 2008.

and the Senate (198 tons) have recycled a combined total of approximately 770 tons of bottles and cans. This number has fluctuated as the increased use of plastic instead of glass bottles has decreased the total weight of recycled bottles and cans.

In 2001, the House and the Senate began recycling e-waste (e.g., computers, printers, and toner cartridges), construction, and demolition waste products (e.g., carpet, concrete, ceiling tiles, and scrap metal). The additional categories of recycling have allowed the House (23,000 tons) and the Senate (15,700 tons) to recycle almost 39,000 tons of materials that were not part of the initial recycling efforts. Overall, the expansion of the recycling program in both the House and Senate has resulted in an increase of total tons recycled and a decrease in total tons of waste transferred to landfills.

Recently, the recycling program has expanded to include the recycling of cell phones and the composting of food waste in the House of Representatives. In the FY2009 budget justification, the Architect of the Capitol has proposed legislative language to amend Title 2, United States Code concerning the collection and sale of recycled materials and the use of proceeds. The new language, if enacted, would allow the Architect to offset the initial cost of new House recycling programs by using current proceeds. The Senate, by law, currently designates recycling proceeds to the Senate fitness center.

For further analysis of recycling programs beyond those in the House and Senate, see CRS Report RS22807, Compact Fluorescent Light Bulbs (CFLs): Issues with Use and Disposal, by Linda Luther; CRS Report RL34 147, Managing Electronic Waste: An Analysis of State E-Waste Legislation, by Linda Luther; and CRS Report RL3 1505, Recycling Computers and Electronic Equipment: Legislative and Regulatory Approaches for 'E-Waste,' by James E. McCarthy.

Recycling can have multiple meanings. "To some, it is the stacking of newspapers and separating of cans and bottles from the trash. To others, it is the program that collects those materials. And, to still others, it is just another waste disposal program." [1] Recycling programs in the House of Representatives and the Senate have taken two approaches: recycling of material as part of the overall congressional waste disposal program and purchasing products made from recycled materials. In each case, the House and the Senate encourage participation through educational outreach [2].

## Development of Recycling Programs

Formal recycling programs were created during the 101st Congress (1989-1991) through separate resolutions in the House and Senate [3]. Both the House and the Senate authorized the Architect of the Capitol (AOC) to "establish and implement a voluntary program for recycling paper" [4]. The recycling program has since expanded to include cardboard, toner cartridges, bottles, cans, and building materials.

In calendar year 2007, the AOC facilitated the recycling of more than 2,000 tons of materials by the House and Senate [5].

## HOUSE OF REPRESENTATIVES

While the first legislation to establish a recycling program in the House of Representatives was introduced in the 93rd Congress (1973-1975), a formal recycling program did not begin until the House agreed to H.Res. 104 in the 101st Congress. H.Res. 104 created a voluntary paper recycling program under the auspices of the Architect of the Capitol. The Architect, with guidance from the House Administration Committee and the Appropriations Committee's Subcommittee on Legislative Appropriations, has managed and expanded the recycling program. See Appendix A for a complete list of legislation introduced on House recycling programs.

Bills and Resolutions Prior to 1989. Initial attempts to create a recycling program occurred during the 93rd and 94th Congresses and focused on requiring the use of recycled paper to produce congressional documents. Initial legislation took one of three approaches:

1. amend Title 44 of the United States Code (12 bills and resolutions);
2. a concurrent resolution stating the government should use recycled paper (two resolutions); or
3. direct the General Services Administration (GSA) to issue regulations on the use of recycled paper products (two bills).

A total of 16 bills and resolutions were introduced using these three approaches. Each bill or resolution was referred to committee and did not receive further consideration.

*Establishing the House Recycling Program.* On March 7, 1989, Representative William Green introduced H.Res. 104, providing for a voluntary paper recycling program in the House of Representatives, administered by the Architect of the Capitol. Representative Green's resolution approached recycling differently than previous measures. Instead of amending Title 44, proposing a concurrent resolution, or directing the GSA to issue regulations, H.Res. 104

placed responsibility for recycling in the House with the Architect of the Capitol and made recycling a voluntary program.

> Resolved, That, not later than 6 months after this resolution is agreed to, the Architect of the Capitol shall establish and implement a voluntary program for recycling paper that is disposed of in the operation of the House of Representatives. Such program shall be designed to encourage separation of paper by type at the sources of the generation (including offices of Members of the House) and to sell such paper for the purpose of recycling [6].

H.Res. 104 was referred to the Committee on House Administration, where it was referred to the Subcommittee on Procurement and Printing.

The subcommittee, chaired by Representative Jim Bates, held hearings on July 19 and July 20, 1989 [7]. The hearings included testimony from the Office of Technology Assessment, the Architect of the Capitol, the General Services Administration, Waste Management Inc., and local governments with established recycling programs [8]

As a result of the hearings, the subcommittee supported the use of "source separation" techniques [9]. The Committee on House Administration issued a report that stated, "[s]ource separation makes sense both environmentally and economically. For example, the House currently receives $1 per ton for its recycled trash. Source separation would generate $80 per ton for Grade 1 paper and $40 per ton for Grade 2 paper." [10]

On July 25, the subcommittee recommended the approval of H.Res. 104 to the full committee [11]. On July 26, the full committee agreed to the resolution and reported the resolution favorably, without amendment. In its report, the committee raised concern that dividing paper into as many as five source separation categories could discourage staff and Member participation in the pilot program. As a result, the committee encouraged "the Architect to consider a phased-in approach, beginning with the separation of Grade 1 and Grade 2 paper." [12]

H.Res. 104 was debated on the House floor on August 1, 1989. During debate, Representative Bates stated that the resolution was the beginning of a larger recycling effort in the House. "Mr. Speaker, I think this is just the beginning of a much-needed recycling program here in the House of Representatives, and with that I hope this pilot program can be shortened from at least the 1-year period, but, if not, at least a 1-year period has been allowed." [13] H.Res. 104 was agreed to by voice vote.

*Subsequent House Legislation.* Following the passage of H.Res. 104, an additional 15 bills and resolutions were introduced between the 101st Congress (1989-1991) and the first session of the $110^{th}$ Congress (2007-2009) to expand the House recycling program. These bills and resolutions can be divided into two categories: efforts to create a more comprehensive paper recycling program in Congress and the inclusion of Congress in broader federal government recycling programs.

*Comprehensive Congressional Recycling Program.* Bills named "The Congressional Recycling Act" were introduced in the House during the 101st and 102nd Congresses [14]. For example, H.R. 4523 was introduced by Representative Glenn Anderson during the 101st Congress, with similar language to other bills [15] H.R. 4523 contained language mandating the recycled content of paper purchased by the Clerk of the House, the Secretary of the Senate, and the Public Printer. In his remarks accompanying the introduction of H.R. 4523, Representative Anderson summarized the bill's goals.

> This bill will require the House of Representatives and the Senate to use recycled paper and paper products to the greatest extent practical in their daily operations and increase their procurement of paper and paper products with the highest percentage of recycled content. This sends a clear message to the rest of the Nation that Congress is actively involved in addressing America's environmental concerns [16]

H.R. 4523 was referred to the Committee on House Administration and subsequently referred to the Subcommittee on Procurement and Printing. Hearings were conducted for H.R. 4523 in August 1990, but the measure was not subsequently reported by the committee [17].

*Federal Government Recycling Programs.* In addition to the Congressional Recycling Act legislation, two bills were introduced in the 101st and 102nd Congresses to create broader recycling in the federal government. Both bills aimed to clarify federal procurement standards for the purchase of recycled paper [18].

For example, Representative John Porter introduced H.R. 1201 during the 1 02nd Congress (1991-1993). In his remarks accompanying the introduction of H.R. 1201 Representative John Porter explained why he believed this legislation was necessary:

> My bill will amend the Resource Conservation and Recovery Act which currently requires the Federal purchasing agents to implement affirmative procurement programs for paper products containing recovered material. That is

> an interesting concept, but the truth of the matter is, Mr. Speaker, the act does not promote the use of paper with postconsumer-waste content; that is, paper which has already been used once, thrown away, and collected for recycling which would be deinked and put back into use. With no standard to include postconsumer waste paper, the affirmative procurement programs have not helped create a market in this country for separated paper and do nothing at all to help us solve the solid-waste problems plaguing the country [19]

Neither H.R. 1201 nor other bills creating a broader federal recycling program were reported by committee in any Congress.

## SENATE

The Senate recycling program was first proposed during the 101st Congress (1989-1991), and the introduction and passage of S.Res. 99 during that Congress created the basis for current Senate recycling efforts. See Appendix B for a complete list of legislation introduced on recycling in the Senate.

*Establishing the Senate Recycling Program.* In April 1989, Senator Rudy Boschwitz introduced S.Res. 99 to require the Architect of the Capitol to create a voluntary paper recycling program in the Senate. The resolution stated:

> Resolved, That, not later than 6 months after this resolution is agreed to, the Architect of the Capitol shall establish and implement a voluntary program for recycling paper that is disposed of in the operation of the Senate. Such program shall be designed to encourage separation of paper by type at the sources of generation (including the offices of Members of the Senate) and to sell such paper for the purpose of recycling [20].

The resolution was referred to the Committee on Rules and Administration.

In a floor speech in support of his resolution, Senator Boschwitz expressed his vision of the Senate as a leader of government recycling efforts. “Recycling is a cornerstone of the future plans of our municipalities and counties to ensure that necessary landfill space remains available. The Senate should serve as an example in the recycling efforts of the Government” [21].

Senator Boschwitz returned to the Senate floor on September 6, 1989 to encourage the inclusion of his resolution in the Legislative Branch Appropriations bill and to explain the potential environmental impact of recycling.

> While I am pleased to see the number of bills introduced in Congress to promote recycling, I feel that we as a Congress must set the example for the rest of the Nation. Capitol Hill currently produces 20,000 tons of trash every year, of which only 30 percent is recycled. To no one's surprise much of the Hill's trash is high-grade paper for which there is currently a large demand. Instead of paying people to dump our paper, along with wrappers, food, and other trash, in landfills, we could be responding to this market demand with recycled high-grade paper [22].

On September 27, the committee ordered S.Res. 99 to be reported without amendment. The next day, Senator Wendell Ford reported the resolution without a written report. On October 2, the Senate agreed to the resolution by unanimous consent.

*Subsequent Senate Legislation.* Following the passage of S.Res. 99, seven bills were introduced between the second session of the 101st Congress and the first session of the 1 10th Congress (2007-2009) to require broader recycling efforts in Congress. Again, these bills can be divided into two categories: efforts to create a more comprehensive paper recycling program in Congress and efforts to create a broader federal government paper recycling program.

*Comprehensive Congressional Recycling Program.* During the 101st and the 102nd Congresses, three bills, each called the "Congressional Recycling Act," were introduced in the Senate [23]. Each bill had identical language and attempted to place restrictions on the type of paper purchased by the Clerk of the House, the Secretary of the Senate, and the Public Printer [24]. In his remarks to accompany the introduction of S. 255, Senator Jeff Bingaman explained why he believed the Congress should purchase recycled paper. "Mr. President, I believe we must set the example on the use of recycled products. I hope my legislation and the reporting requirements contained therein will ensure that Congress does its fair share in the recycling effort" [25].

*Federal Government Paper Recycling Program.* During the 101st Congress, legislation was introduced to require all federal government agencies to use recycled paper. S. 2643 would have directed the Administrator of the Environmental Protection Agency (EPA) to announce regulations requiring the recycling of paper by agencies with more than 50 employees; required the Clerk of the House and the Secretary of the Senate to use source separation for recycling paper; required all procuring agencies to meet minimum content standards for recycled paper as set forth in 40 C.F.R. § 250.21; [26] required the Clerk of the House and the Secretary of the Senate to follow the same guidelines for recycled paper purchases as other federal agencies; required a study by the EPA to eliminate unnecessary packaging, to improve the ratio of product to packaging size, and to examine the use of non-toxic packaging; and required the Clerk of the House and Secretary of the Senate to ensure that the operations of the House of Representatives and the Senate, respectively, are minimizing their waste outputs [27].

S. 2643 was referred to the Committee on Environment and Public Works and did not receive further consideration.

## RECYCLING IN PRACTICE

Following the passage of H.Res. 104 and S.Res. 99 in the 101st Congress, the Architect of the Capitol established pilot, voluntary paper recycling programs in the House and Senate. In succeeding years, the Architect received direction for the operation of the House and Senate recycling programs through questions asked during appropriations hearings, in Legislative Branch Appropriations reports, in appropriations bills, and from the House Administration Committee and the Senate Rules and Administration Committee. While direction provided in appropriations bills could apply to both the House and the Senate, hearing questions, report language, and committee guidance has often been directed to either the House or the Senate program. As a result, the House and Senate recycling programs have developed somewhat separately since 1989.

### House of Representatives

The House of Representatives recycling program has expanded since it was established as a voluntary program in 1989. In 2007, the House recycled approximately 1,400 tons of paper and 21.5 tons of bottles and cans. This represents an increase of 595% for paper and 113% for bottles and cans since the House contracted with GSA for the removal of recycling waste in 1992. Since GSA began managing the contract for collecting House recycled paper, bottles, and cans in 1992, House recycling efforts have generated approximately $346,000 in proceeds. Figure 1 shows the amount of money generated per year under GSA contracts between calendar year 1996 and calendar year 2007. The Office of the House Superintendent of the Architect of the Capitol is responsible for managing the House's recycling program. The Architect, in general, has responsibility for implementing recycling initiatives. The Committee on House Administration and the House Appropriations Subcommittee on the Legislative Branch provide oversight for the program [28].

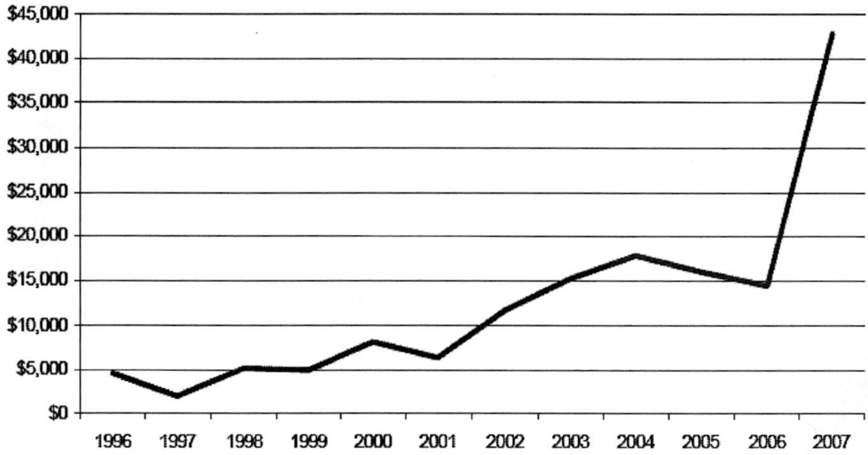


Source: U.S. General Services Administration.

Notes: All monetary figures are in nominal dollars. Proceeds between 1992 to 1995 were $107 or less per year and do not appear in Figure 1. In 1992, recycling proceeds were $10.84; in 1993, $106.20; in 1994, $100.98; and in 1995, $58.10. Proceeds were low because of contamination of potentially recycled materials. Figure 1 does not include proceeds from scrap metal recycling. Scrap metal is recycled through a non-GSA managed contractor and figures are available in fiscal year increments only. In FY2006, proceeds from scrap metal recycling were $1,352.38 and in FY2007 they were $11,992.57.

Figure 1. Proceeds from House Recycling, 1996-2007.

*Appropriations.* The House recycling program is not specified as a line item in the annual legislative branch appropriations bills. While funding to hire Architect of the Capitol staff, including those who administer the recycling program, is part of the Architect's annual budget request, funds to operate the program were first requested by the Architect for the recycling program beginning in fiscal years (FY) 1991 and 1992. According to the Architect, the request was made as the result of a downturn in the recycling market,29 which generated lower prices for recycled materials [30].

The following section provides an overview of the Appropriations Committee's use of the appropriations process to guide the Architect of the Capitol's operation of the House recycling program. While not a comprehensive list of every action by the Appropriations Committee, the fiscal years included provide a general outline of oversight activities through the appropriations process. Fiscal years not included did not have specific instructions or appropriations made by the Appropriations Committee for the House recycling program in requests, reports, or bills.

*FY1991.* For FY1991, the Architect of the Capitol, George White, requested $50,000 for waste recycling programs [31]. During the Architect's testimony on the budget request, Representative Lindy Boggs requested more information about the request and the use of the funds. In response to Representative Boggs, the Architect cited costs associated with the recycling pilot program, including the expense related to cardboard collection boxes that could be placed on an individual's desk. "We have asked for that because there is some cost associated with this pilot program. It costs $5 for the little cardboard device that is on people's desks" [32].

The Architect then continued by explaining the goal of making the recycling program self-supporting and reminding the committee that he was not able to ascertain whether an annual appropriations request would be made, but he hoped that eventually the committee would authorize the use of recycling proceeds to sustain future recycling efforts.

> In any event, the predicted savings in the sense of increased value for the recycling material is in the order of magnitude of a quarter million dollars. That is the amount we might get returned to us. This is all to be developed as part of the pilot program. Presumably, if those kinds of funds do become available, this committee could authorize us to recycle the money, as well as the other products, by our collecting that money and using it for the expenses associated with the recycling so that we could perhaps not expend appropriated funds annually, but end up with self supported recycling, which has another purpose entirely [33].

*FY1992.* In the Architect of the Capitol's budget justification for FY1992, a request was included for $180,000 for the disposal of waste paper. The funds were requested to offset costs associated with new contracts that required the House to pay a contractor to remove recyclable paper, instead of receiving proceeds from the sale of the paper.

In past years, the Architect of the Capitol has been able to dispose of recyclable paper through a contractor, who in turn has paid into the U.S. Treasury the market rate for mixed grade paper. This past year's Invitation for Bid for removal and disposal of mixed grade recyclable paper did not attract any bidders

> willing to provide the service at a profit to the Government. Rather, the bidders required payment for removing and disposing recyclable waste paper [34].

During hearings on the Legislative Branch Appropriations Bill, the Architect was asked questions about recycling and the separation of materials before pickup. In response, the Architect stated that,

> With the appropriate direction from the Committee of Jurisdiction and the Speaker of the House of Representatives as Chairman of the House Office Building Commission, we could begin the deployment of a complex-wide source separation program. Adequate funds are not currently available to implement a comprehensive complex-wide program of source separation as an expansion of the existing recycling program [35].

In the report to accompany the Legislative Branch Appropriations Act for 1992, the committee addressed the reduced market for recycled paper discussed in the Architect's testimony. The committee directed the Public Printer to review the technical requirements resulting from the purchase of paper containing post-consumer waste content.

> The Committee, therefore, directs the Public Printer to review technical printing requirements for individual print jobs such as business and committee calendars, wall calendars, committee prints, committee reports, document envelopes, business envelopes, blank paper and blank forms to study the feasibility of using paper with a 10 percent post-consumer waste content. The findings shall be published within 6 months of the enactment of this bill and should include a list of appropriate jobs which can employ the use of post-consumer waste paper [36].

*FY1993*. During testimony on the FY1993 Legislative Branch Appropriations Bill, the Architect updated the committee on the status of the House recycling program, the use of private contractors to remove recycled materials from the House, and the status of the expansion of the recycling program to all House offices. In summary, the Architect stated that "[t]he new and expanded recycling program is currently being incorporated in all buildings under schedules approved by the committees of jurisdictions." In addition, the Architect believed that the expanded recycling program would provide "recycling materials (recycling stations, informational materials, etc.) in accordance with the approved schedules which indicate full deployment by September 30, 1992."[37]

*FY1995*. For FY1995, the Architect of the Capitol included a request for $150,000 for the waste recycling program in his budget justification. The purpose for the request was not specified in the budget justification or during the

Architect's testimony. The request did not generate questions from committee members [38].

On October 20, 1993, President Bill Clinton issued Executive Order 12873, which among other things, required the use of paper with a minimum of 20% post consumer content when practicable [39]. In response, Senator Wendell Ford, chair of the Joint Committee on Printing (JCP), submitted a written statement to the House Legislative Branch Appropriations Subcommittee on the use of recycled paper in the legislative branch.

> After President Clinton issued his Executive Order on recycling in early October, the JCP immediately reviewed the requirements of on-going quarterly paper procurement and incorporated the 20 percent Post Consumer recycled fiber content provision wherever practical. As a result, most of the paper that will be shipped to GPO beginning in January 1994, will contain the desired 20 percent post consumer waste content. This was accomplished without an increase in the cost of paper [40].

John Chambers, staff director of the JCP, also testified on the use of recycled paper for the publication of the Federal Register and the Congressional Record. He stated, "[s]o the two biggest products that are produced at the Government Printing Office, the Federal Register and the Congressional Record are now on recycled, 100 percent post-consumer waste product" [41].

*FY1999.* As introduced, the Legislative Appropriations Bill for FY1999 did not contain provisions appropriating funds for the House recycling program. In a speech on the House floor, Representative Lloyd Doggett addressed what he perceived as the deficiencies in the recycling program and the need for better management and organization.

> Let me recite the facts: For 3 of the last 3 1/2 years that this House has been under Republican control, there has been no recycling coordinator in this Congress. Indeed there is no recycling coordinator today. As we debate today this bill, there is no recycling plan in place. As we debate this bill there is no recycling of mixed paper in this House; indeed that is zero, zip, nada, being done with reference to recycling of mixed paper.
>
> Why is that particularly important? Because since there is no recycling coordinator and no real recycling effort, most people even if they have the best of intent with regard to recycling, do not have correct information about how to recycle in a way that will be effective, and that is reflected in other facts. When the House did recycle, it earned 30 cents per ton on the paper it recycled. Compare that with the Department of Housing and Urban Development which earned $60 per ton because it did it properly [42].

Following Representative Doggett' s speech, Representative Sam Farr, introduced an amendment to H.R. 4112 to provide $100,000 from the Architect's House office building funds to address specifically the financial needs of the recycling program.

> For all necessary expenses for the maintenance, care and operation of the House office buildings, $42,139,000, of which $11,449,000 shall remain available until expended: Provided, That of the total amount provided under this heading, not less than $100,000 shall be used exclusively for waste recycling programs [43].

In his remarks, Representative Farr provided his rationale for the amendment. "The amendment, by earmarking specific funds for this program, sets recycling as a priority for the House. I offer this amendment because recycling is a program that has been neglected, and consequently has had very limited success." [44] The amendment was agreed to by voice vote, [45] was included in the conference report, [46] and was signed into law by President Clinton on October 21, 1998 [47].

*FY2000.* During hearings on the FY2000 Legislative Branch Appropriations Bill, Representative Steny Hoyer asked the Architect to provide a status report on the recycling program. Lynne Theiss, executive officer for the Architect, testified on efforts to improve the recycling program and make it self-sustaining.

> Currently the House complex sends about 2,200 tons of paper for recycling annually. The program has not been very successful, but during fiscal year 1998 it underwent a renovation in the House group. The Superintendent of the House introduced color coded bags for material separation that our custodial staff actually used each evening when they were removing the office recycle program materials [48].

Ms. Theiss then continued by discussing specific improvement made between 1997 and 1998.

> There was an improvement in the quality of the recycling effort as reflected in the funds received in 1998 versus 1997. In 1997, with 2,226 tons recycled, the value of the material was less than $2,000. In 1998, (with almost three months of "out of service" time) we recycled 1,532 tons but with a value of $25,483. (Had we been in operation for those other months, we anticipated a total tonnage of 2,770.) The object of the program is to increase the overall tonnage and, at the same time, insure that the quality (reduced contamination) is improved to increase the recyclability of the materials. While the program measures tonnage

and dollars it must also reflect the market value given to the tonnage so it is incumbent upon the program to have the cleanest recycling stream possible regardless of the tonnage measured [49].

Subsequently, the House report to accompany H.R. 1905 included four provisions on the House recycling program. These included (1) making participation in the recycling program mandatory for all Members and House officers, (2) directing the Architect to make collection of recyclables more efficient by providing a "convenient, clearly marked, user-friendly system for the collection of recyclable materials in each building," (3) requiring the Architect to make a semi-annual report to the Appropriations and House Administration Committees, and (4) in an effort to create an incentive for participation, directing that proceeds from the recycling program would contribute to the House Child Care Center [50].

*FY2001.* As part of the conference report on the FY2001 Legislative Branch Appropriations Bill, the conferees agreed to continue to allow proceeds from agency recycling programs to finance the cost of recycling and waste prevention programs.

> Section 607. The conferees agree to continue the provision allowing agencies to finance the costs of recycling and waste prevention programs with proceeds from the sale of materials recovered through such programs [51].

*FY2002.* In the report accompanying the FY2002 Legislative Branch appropriations bill, the committee directed the Architect to hire outside consultants to conduct a review of the House recycling program.

> Concerns have been raised about efforts to separate trash for recycling which, when collected, is ultimately dumped into the same receptacles destined for disposal. The Committee directs that the review should include recommendations to improve the program, establish a criteria for measuring compliance, and establish reasonable milestones for increasing the amount of material recycled [52].

*FY2003.* In the report accompanying the FY2003 Legislative Branch Appropriations Bill, the committee stated that the House should establish a more comprehensive recycling program comparable to the objectives of Executive Order 13101 [53]. The committee also directed the Chief Administrative Officer of the House to "develop a proposal that ensures that items composed of recovered materials are purchased to the maximum extent practicable" [54]

The committee addressed the progress by the Architect in reviewing the recycling program by stating that they were “encouraged by the progress being made on the review of the Architect of the Capitol’s recycling program.” The committee continued by directing the Architect to “implement and expand the recommendations of the best practices review as soon as practicable by developing a pilot project in the Capitol complex, which would address electronic equipment waste recycling. The Committee expects the Architect of the Capitol to provide quarterly reports on the recycling program both for traditional and electronic waste” [55].

*FY2009.* In the Architect’s budget justification for FY2009, the Architect has proposed legislative language to amend Title 2, United States Code on the collection and sale of recycled materials and how the proceeds can be utilized. The proposed language would allow the Architect to offset the initial cost of new recycling programs by using the proceeds generated by current House recycling initiatives. Currently, 2 U.S.C. § 1869 states,

> Advance Payments. — During fiscal year 2008 and each succeeding fiscal year, following notification of the Committees on Appropriations of the House of Representatives and the Senate, the Architect of the Capitol may make payments in advance for obligations of the Office of the Architect of the Capitol for subscription services if the Architect determines it to be more prompt, efficient, or economical to do so [56].

The proposed language would amend 2 U.S.C. § 1869 to say the following:

> § 1869. Collection and sale of recyclable materials; use of proceeds.
>
> (a) The Architect of the Capitol shall establish a program for the collection and sale of recyclable materials collected from or on Capitol Buildings and Grounds.
> (b) Any sale of recyclable materials by the Architect of the Capitol shall be in accordance with the procedures in the Federal Property and Administrative Services Act of 1949 (40 U.S.C. 551 et seq.) for the sale of surplus property.
> (c) Proceeds from the sale of recyclable materials shall be credited to funds available to the Architect of the Capitol for the improvement of the environment, energy savings, and to pay for the costs of the recycling program.
> (d) Any recycling program established by the Architect of the Capitol pursuant to this section shall not be in conflict with any other authorized recycling program on Capitol Buildings and Grounds including any

> recycling program undertaken pursuant to Section 121f of Title 2, United States Code [57].

If enacted, the proposed language would allow the Architect to use proceeds generated from the recycling program to offset the costs of the recycling program and other energy savings programs. The proposed language would specifically affect the House recycling program, as the Senate has previously designated their recycling proceeds to the Senate fitness center [58]

Committee on House Administration. The Committee on House Administration maintains oversight authority over the Architect of the Capitol and the House recycling program. In the past, the committee has been active in assisting the Architect in establishing the pilot program and with implementing general improvements mandated through the appropriations process. The following is a sample of the House recycling activities the Committee on House Administration has undertaken.

*101st Congress.* Following the passage of H.Res. 104, which established voluntary House recycling, the Committee on House Administration became active in the implementation and oversight of the pilot program. As part of the committee's general oversight activities, the committee held a series of meetings with recycling experts from Prince George's County Maryland, the General Services Administration, and San Diego County California to make recommendations to the Architect's office on establishing the pilot program. The committee also sent a "Dear Colleague" letter with a questionnaire for Member officers on the pilot program and congressional recycling, and held a forum for the Office Waste Recycling Pilot Program [59].

*103rd Congress.* The Committee on House Administration issued a "Dear Colleague" letter on July 17, 1993 discussing the impact of the Office of Waste Recycling Program, introduced in March of 1992, on recycling efforts in the House [60].

*105th Congress.* In May, June, and August 1998, the Committee on House Oversight [61] met with the staff of the Architect of the Capitol and the House Superintendent to discuss the recycling program. According to the committee's activity report, in each instance the discussion dealt with unspecified proposed improvements [62].

Since the 105th Congress, the House Administration Committee activity reports have not specified action taken by the committee concerning the recycling program. The committee continues to maintain its oversight responsibility for the House recycling program, but has not included its activities in reports.

*Current Recycling Efforts*. The House of Representatives currently recycles a number of products including paper, cans, bottles, and toner cartridges. In December 2007, the House also began to compost food waste, sugar cane-based food and beverage containers, and corn-based plastic forks, spoons, and knives used in the House restaurants. Additionally, the House created a recycling program for the personal cell phones of House staff members. These recycling efforts are ongoing and continue to expand as part of a new "Green the Capitol" Initiative under the direction of the Chief Administrative Officer (CAO) of the House.

Since 1992, the House has contracted with the General Services Administration (GSA) for recycled material pickup and disposal. GSA-managed contractors pick up House recycled materials at three locations: the Cannon House Office Building, the Rayburn House Office Building, and the Ford House Office Building [63]. Materials from the Longworth House Office Building, the House wing of the U.S. Capitol, the Capitol Power Plant, the Page dormitory, and the United States Botanical Gardens are transported to one of the three collection points.

*Paper*. While the House paper recycling program began in August 1989, data on the amount of paper recycled is only available since 1996. In 1996, GSA began managing the contracts for the collection of recycled materials in the House. Figure 2 shows the total volume of paper recycled by the House and compares it with the total volume of recycled materials collected by the House.

Figure 2 shows that recycled paper has become a larger percentage of total recycling in the House. In 1996, recycled paper was a modest 9.5% of the total recycled tons. Since 2004, paper has accounted for no less than 84% of total recycled tons, with a high of 85.3% in 2007. Between 1996 and 2007, paper has accounted for a total of 44.9% of total recycled tons in the House of Representatives. The overall figure represents the increase in construction and building materials recycled since 2001.

Since June 1, 1992, the *Congressional Record* has been printed on 100% recycled paper.[64] The first issue of the *Congressional Record* printed on paper with some recycled content on March 24, 1992 [65]. The next day, Representative Charlie Rose, chairman of the Joint Committee on Printing, spoke about the importance of printing the *Congressional Record* on recycled paper. "I am proud to say that the Congress is taking the lead in promoting efforts to increase the use of recycled materials in Federal Government printed products" [66].

*Bottles and Cans*. In addition to recycling paper, the House of Representatives has recycled bottles and cans since at least 1992. Figure 3 shows the volume of bottles and cans recycled by the House.

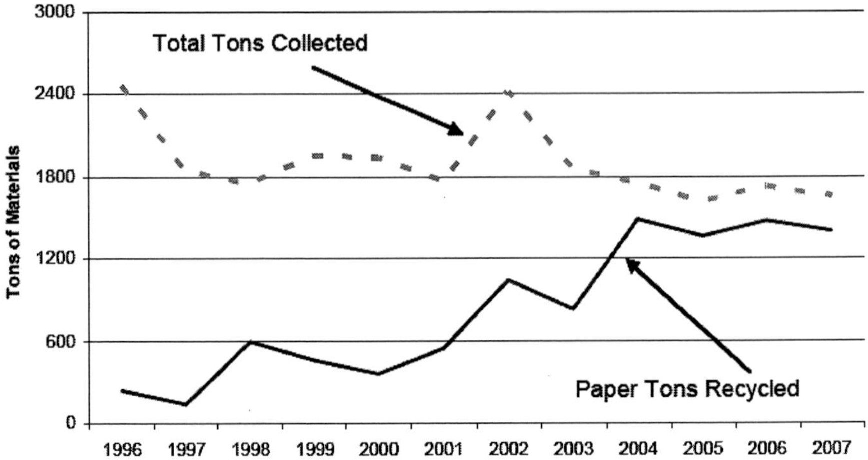


Source: U.S. General Services Administration and Office of the House Superintendent, Architect of the Capitol.

Figure 2. Total Tons and Paper Tons Recycled in the House, 1996-2007.

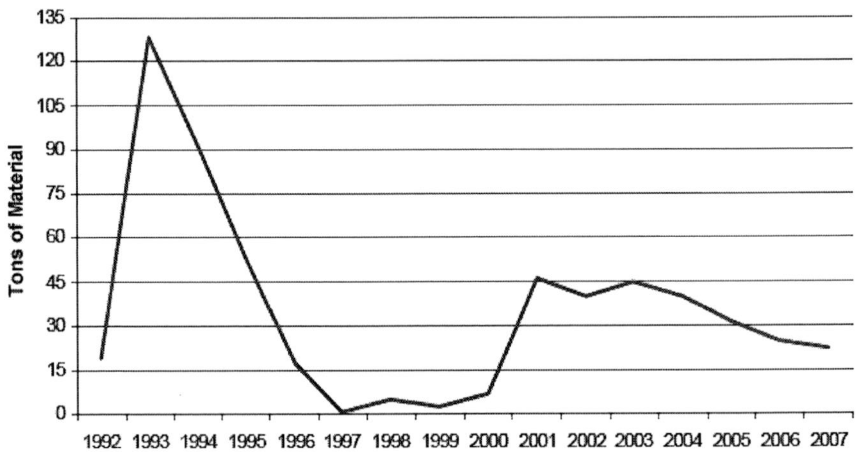


Source: U.S. General Services Administration.

Figure 3. Total Tons of Bottles and Cans, 1992-2007.

Figure 3 shows a drop in the volume of bottles and cans recycled following a peak in 1993 (128 tons). This drop is due in part to an increase in mixed recycled materials labeled as "commingled" by GSA. Beginning in 1994, commingled materials were divided after pickup by GSA. As a result the House was not credited with the volume for those materials individually [67]. The decrease in volume of recycled bottles and cans also coincides with the use of more plastic bottles and lighter aluminum cans that weigh less than the glass bottles previously in use [68]. Since 2004, the House has been dividing recyclables before GSA pickup.

*Other Materials.* In addition to paper, bottles, and cans, the House recycles scrap metal, toner cartridges, batteries, sawdust, e-waste, [69] plastic, pallets, ceiling tiles, carpet, and other building materials. The Architect of the Capitol's Superintendent of the House recycling office has tracked the volume of non-paper, non-bottle, and non-can recycled material since FY2004. Figure 4 shows the total volume of recycled material in each of these categories since FY2004. Some categories, such as masonry material, were only recycled in one year (2007) as the result of a particular project and have not been specifically recycled since.

*Green the Capitol Initiative.* In March 2007, Speaker Nancy Pelosi, Majority Leader Steny Hoyer, and the then chair of the Committee on House Administration, the late Representative Juanita Millender-McDonald, asked the CAO to provide an "environmentally responsible and healthy working environment for employees" [70]. The initiative created three goals for reducing the House of Representatives' environmental impact [71].

- Operate the House in a carbon-neutral manner by the end of the 1 10th Congress.
- Reduce the House's carbon footprint by cutting energy consumption by 50 percent in 10 years.
- Make House operations a model of sustainability [72]

From these goals, the Green the Capitol Initiative has worked to recycle materials not previously covered by the Architect's contact with the GSA. These items have included the composting of food waste, corn-based biodegradable forks, spoons, and knives, and sugar cane-based biodegradable carry out containers from the House restaurants, and the recycling of cell phones [73].

*Composting.* The House of Representatives began composting food waste in partnership with the House restaurant food vendor in December 2007 [74]. Between December 2007 and April 2008, the House has reduced the volume of materials sent to the landfill by 120 tons [75]. Food waste from the House cafeterias is transported to a composting facility in Crofton, Maryland [76].

In testimony before the Select Committee on Energy Independence and Global Warming on February 26, 2008, CAO Daniel Beard described the process for composting food service waste and its benefits for the reduction of transportation costs of waste materials.

> We send the compostable food service items along with all of the food waste from the front of the cafeteria and from the kitchens to a pulper. The pulper is like a giant garbage disposal that breaks down and dewaters the compost material. This reduces the volume of the compost material by a ratio of 10-1 and reduces the weight by as much as 4-1. The result is reduced hauling costs and reduced tipping fees by 60%-75%. [77].

In testimony before the House Committee on Transportation and Infrastructure's Subcommittee on Economic Development, Public Buildings, and Emergency Management, the CAO discussed the expansion of the composting program to Member's offices. "The House has completely revamped its paper recycling program to ensure compostable food waste is picked up from Member offices." [78] According to a press report, food waste compost bins are available for Member's offices who desire to recycle food waste and have it picked up with other recyclables to be composted [79].

*Cell Phones.* In December 2007, the House began a drive to recycle the personal cell phones of staff members. The drive lasted for a week and half and did not include government-issued equipment. In a "Dear-Colleague" letter, the CAO provided details of the recycling program and listed reasons why cell phones are an environmental concern, including that "[t]hey are made from valuable resources that can be recovered, such as precious metals, copper, gold, silver, palladium, plastics and glass — all of which require energy to mine and process[,]" and "[r]ecovering these materials through recycling conserves our natural resources and avoids air and water pollution as well as greenhouse gas emissions" [80]. In addition, the Green the Capitol Initiative website includes information on how Members can recycle cell phone in their districts or provide opportunities for constituents to recycle used cell phones [81].

## SENATE

The Senate recycling program has expanded since it was created as a voluntary program in 1989. In 2007, the Senate recycled approximately 700 tons of paper and 290 tons of other materials [82]. This represents an increase of 145% in the volume of paper recycled compared to 1992 and an increase of 1,154% in the volume of other materials recycled compared to 2001.

Since GSA began pickups for Senate recycled materials in 1992, the Senate has generated $149,452 in proceeds. Figure 5 shows the amount of money generated per year under GSA contracts between 1996 and 2007. In 2007, the proceeds almost tripled the previous year's level. The increase was the result of a new contract with a GSA vendor that included higher payments for recycled materials.

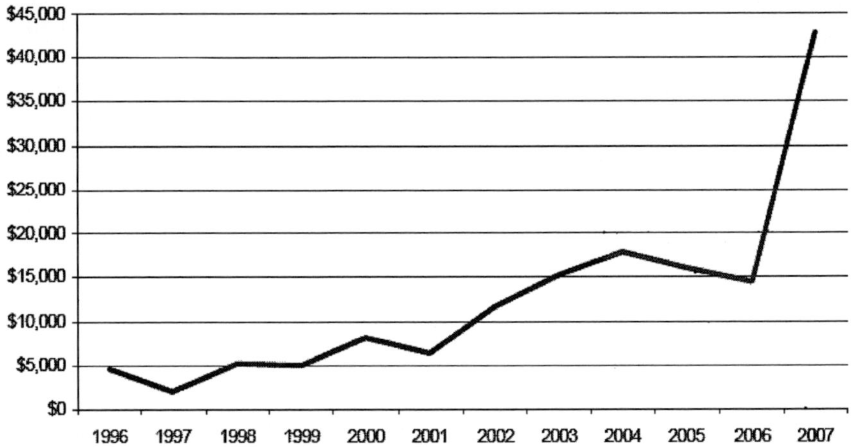


Source: U.S. General Services Administration.

Notes: All monetary figures are in nominal dollars. Proceeds for 1992 to 1995 were $17 or less per year and do not appear in Figure 5. In 1992 and 1994, the Senate did not receive recycling proceeds. In 1993, recycling proceeds were $1.08; and in 1995, $17.20.

Figure 5. Proceeds from Senate Recycling, 1996-2007.

The Office of the Senate Superintendent of the Architect of the Capitol is responsible for managing the Senate's recycling program. The Architect, in general, controls the implementation of recycling initiatives. The Senate Appropriations Committee and the Senate Committee on Rules and Administration provide oversight on the program. The subsequent sections outline examples of the oversight provided by the Appropriations Committee and discuss the current status of the Senate recycling program.

*Appropriations.* The Senate recycling program, in general, has not been specifically mentioned in the annual appropriations bills. The appropriations process utilizes report language and hearings to provide oversight to the recycling program. This section provides an overview of how the appropriations process has guided the Architect of the Capitol on the Senate recycling program. While not a comprehensive list of every appropriations request, hearing, bill, or report, the fiscal years selected provide examples of the use of the appropriations process and the occasional directions for programs provided by the committee Members.

*FY1991.* In testimony on the FY1991 budget request, the Architect discussed the status of the Office Waste Recycling Program in the Senate and requested $150,000 to hire a permanent recycling coordinator and provide for adequate recycling containers. The Architect also reported on the participation rate among Members and staff in the pilot program. "All of the offices (total of 23 member and Committee offices) on the fifth and sixth floors of the Hart SOB [Senate Office Building] are participating in the pilot program. Within these offices we estimate that approximately 80% of the staff are actively and cooperatively participating in the voluntary pilot program" [83].

*FY1992.* During Senate Appropriations Committee hearings on the FY1992 Legislative Branch Appropriations Bill, the Secretary of the Senate testified that the Senate Library "in cooperation with the Sergeant at Arms and the Architect, developed a pilot project for the Secretary's Office to test procedures for recycling paper and other matters" [84] Additionally, the Secretary reported that the stationery room began making recycled materials available, despite the cost of recycled goods being "7 to 10 percent higher in most instances" than non-recycled materials [85].

*FY1993.* During hearings on the FY1993 Legislative Branch Appropriations Bill, the committee asked the Architect to provide an update concerning five problem areas identified during the FY1992 hearings. The Architect responded that the problems had been resolved and that "[w]ith the anticipation of improved markets for recyclable materials, the focus of the expanded recycling program in years to come will be to improve the productivity and cost effectiveness of our waste material recycling systems" [86].

*FY1998.* In FY1998, Senator Daniel Akaka introduced S. 2368, [87] the Senate Day Care Center Recycling Funding Support Act. S. 2368 would have allowed the Architect of the Capitol to transfer Senate recycling proceeds to the Senate Day Care Center.

> Mr. President, my bill would authorize the Architect of the Capitol to receive Senate recycling funds and make them available for the payment of SECCC [Senate Employees Child Care Center] activities and expenses, through the annual appropriations process. This would achieve two mutually beneficial goals: first, to provide a small but important supplement to the day care center's operating budget; second, to improve the efficiency of the Senate recycling program by establishing an internal incentive to recycle [88].

During his remarks on the Senate floor, Senator Akaka also included a letter of support from the Board of Directors of the SECCC. The letter stated the SECCC's strong support of legislation "that would allow the SECCC to receive the proceeds from the Senate recycling and other waste prevention programs to support the operation and other expenses of the SECCC" [89]. S. 2368 was referred to the Senate Committee on Rules and Administration and did not receive further consideration.

*FY2001.* In the Senate report to accompany the FY2001 Legislative Appropriations Act, the Appropriations Committee stated that the Senate recycling program could be improved. The committee then provided recommendations.

> First, the Architect of the Capitol is directed to fill the position of Recycling Program Manager which has been vacant for approximately a year. Second, the Architect of the Capitol is directed to develop a program with the approval of the Senate Rules Committee to educate staff on how to properly recycle. Given the high turnover in staff on Capitol Hill, it is important that new employees are given every opportunity to learn and participate in recycling. This program should involve making recycling containers readily available in an esthetically pleasing and practical way [90].

In FY2001, the Senate also designated the proceeds from the Senate recycling program to supplement the Senate fitness center. The language designating the funds was enacted as part of the Consolidated Appropriations Act of 2001 [91]. The language, enacted as 2 U.S.C. § 121f, states the following:

> § 12 1f. Senate Staff Health and Fitness Facility Revolving Fund
>
> (a) Establishment - There is established in the Treasury of the United States a revolving fund to be known as the Senate Staff Health and Fitness Facility Revolving Fund ("the revolving fund").
> (b) Deposit of receipts - The Architect of the Capitol shall deposit in the revolving fund - (1) any amounts received as dues or other assessments for use of the Senate Staff Health and Fitness Facility, and (2) any amounts received from the operation of the Senate waste recycling program.
> (c) Availability of funds - Subject to the approval of the Committee on Appropriations of the Senate, amounts in the revolving fund shall be available to the Architect of the Capitol, without fiscal year limitation, for payment of costs of the Senate Staff Health and Fitness Facility.

Withdrawal of excess amounts - The Architect of the Capitol shall withdraw from the revolving fund and deposit in the Treasury of the United States as miscellaneous receipts all moneys in the revolving fund that the Architect

> determines are in excess of the current and reasonably foreseeable needs of the Senate Staff Health and Fitness Facility.
>
> (e) Regulations - The Committee on Rules and Administration of the Senate shall promulgate regulations pertaining to the operation and use of the Senate Staff Health and Fitness Facility [92].

*FY2002.* In the report to accompany the Legislative Branch Appropriations Act for FY2002, the Appropriations Committee requested that the Sergeant at Arms and the Secretary of the Senate jointly develop and implement in conjunction with the Architect, a recycling education program. The program would have required the approval of the Senate Committee on Rules and Administration [93].

In the same report, the committee also expressed its concern over the Senate recycling program.

> The Committee is troubled that the Senate Waste Recycling Program has not improved in the last year and prior-year report language on this program seemingly has been ignored. The Architect of the Capitol is directed to participate in a program being jointly developed and implemented by the Secretary of the Senate and the Senate Sergeant at Arms and Doorkeeper and approved by the Senate Committee on Rules and Administration to educate staff on how to properly recycle [94].

The Architect was also directed to contract with an outside vendor for a "best-practices review" of the recycling program and to submit quarterly reports to the committee.

*FY2004.* In the report to accompany the Legislative Branch Appropriations Act for FY2004, the Appropriations Committee directed the Architect to work with the Senate Sergeant at Arms to implement the recommendations of the "best-practices" review and to "continue implementation of a pilot program to address electronic equipment waste recycling." The committee also stated that they were "encouraged by the progress with the AOC's recycling program." [95].

*Current Recycling Efforts.* The Senate currently recycles a number of products and materials, including paper, cans, bottles, scrap metal, toner cartridges, batteries, sawdust, e-waste, plastic, pallets, ceiling tiles, concrete and brick, and carpet. Senate recycling efforts are managed by the Architect of the

Capitol through the recycling coordinator in the Office of the Superintendent of the Senate. The Senate contracts with the General Services Administration (GSA) for pickups at the Hart Senate Office Building for paper, bottles and cans. For other materials, the Senate uses additional vendors based on type of product.

*Paper.* While the Senate paper recycling program began in October 1989, data on the volume of paper recycled is not available prior to 1996. Between 1989 and 1995, GSA did not weigh paper separately from cans and bottles. Figure 6 shows the total volume of recycled materials and the total volume of paper recycled by the Senate since the GSA began weighing paper volume separately from other recycled materials in 1996.

Figure 6 shows that recycled paper has become a larger percentage of total recycling in the Senate. In 1996, recycled paper represented 29.7% of total recycled materials. This decreased in 1997 (17.2%), increased in 1998 (24.6%), and decreased again in 1999 (17.4%). Part of this fluctuation can be explained by election cycles. During election years, the total volume of recycled materials increases in the Senate as Senators leave office and clean their office space [96]. This effect is less pronounced since 2004, when paper became a greater percentage of total recycled materials in the Senate. Overall, paper accounted for 32.6% of total recycled materials in the Senate since 1996.

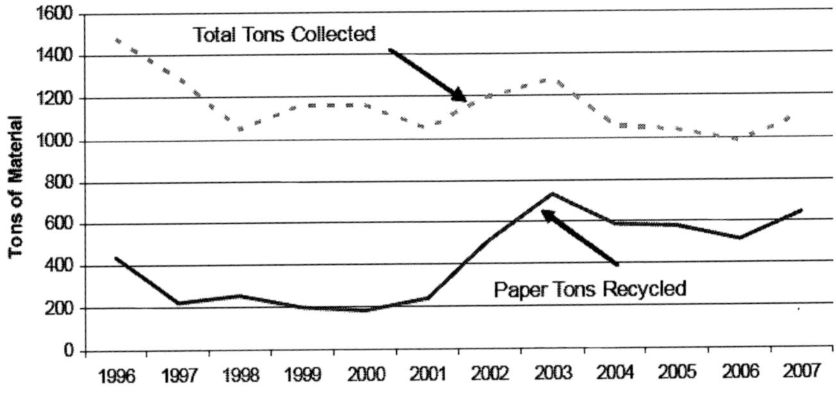


Source: U.S. General Services Administration and Office of the Senate Superintendent, Architect of the Capitol.

Figure 6. Total Tons and Paper Tons Recycled in the Senate, 1996-2007.

*Bottles and Cans.* The Senate has been recycling bottles and cans since at least 1992. Figure 7 shows the total volume of bottles and cans recycled by the Senate since GSA began pickups in 1992. Overall, the total volume of bottles and cans has been as low as two tons in 1997 and as high as 26.3 tons in 1993. On average, the Senate recycles 12 tons of bottles and cans per year. The decline in total tons of bottles and cans recycled following 1995 is due in large part to the use of plastic bottles. Prior to 1995, the Senate recycled a higher tonnage of bottles and cans as the result of the use of glass bottles, which have a greater weight [97].

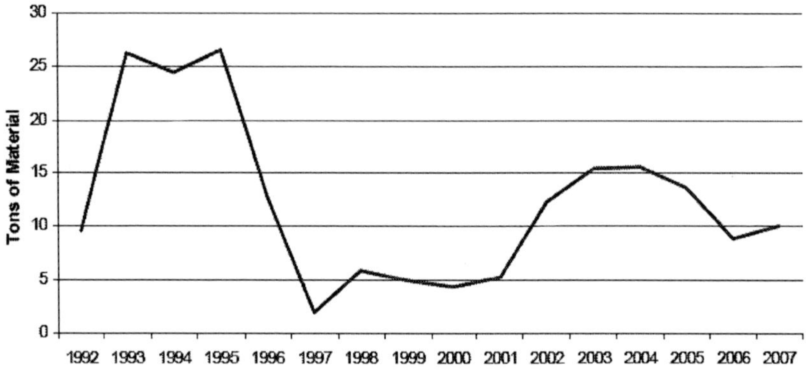


Source: U.S. General Services Administration.

Figure 7. Total Tons of Bottles and Cans Recycled in the Senate, 1992-2007.

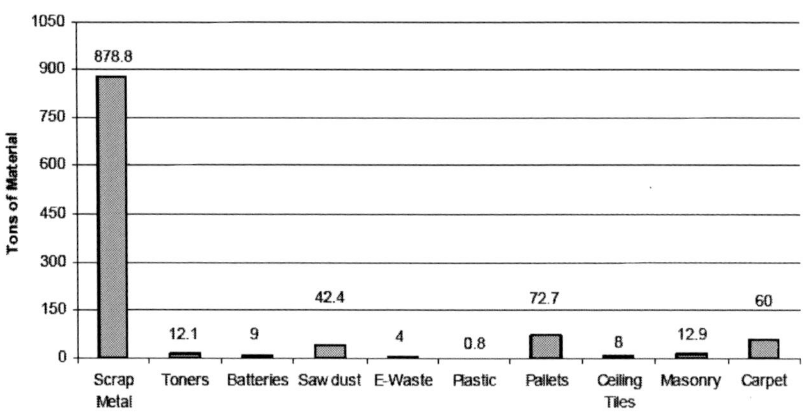


Source: Office of the Senate Superintendent, Architect of the Capitol.

Figure 8. Total Tons of Other Materials Recycled in the Senate, 2001-2007.

*Other Materials.* In addition to paper, bottles, and cans, the Senate recycles scrap metal, toner cartridges, batteries, sawdust, e-waste, plastic, pallets, ceiling tiles, concrete, brick, and carpet. The Architect of the Capitol's Superintendent of the Senate Recycling Office has tracked the volume of non-paper, non-bottle, and noncan recycled material since 2001. Figure 8 shows the total volume of other materials recycled in each non-paper, non-bottle, and non-can category since 2001. Some categories, such as ceiling tiles, were only recycled in one year (2004) as the result of a particular project.

## Options for Program Administration

Since 1989, recycling has been a formal program in the House and the Senate. Created as a voluntary program, the Architect of the Capitol has developed recycling from a program that handled a limited volume of material and a small number of products into a program that recycled almost 2,800 tons of materials and 12 different categories of materials in 2007. Even with this progress, there are potential legislative and administrative policy options available to expand congressional recycling programs.

### Legislative Options

There are several legislative options for the recycling program. Since current participation in the recycling program is voluntary, the House of Representatives and the Senate could each pass legislation to make recycling a mandatory program. Also, the House could address the Architect's proposed amendment to 2 U.S.C. § 1869 to use the proceeds from the recycling program to offset program costs.

*Creating a Mandatory Recycling Program.* Participation in the current recycling program is voluntary. To increase participation, the Architect of the Capitol could request that the Committee on House Administration and the Senate Committee on Rules and Administration consider passing resolutions to make participation in the House and Senate recycling programs mandatory for all member offices, committees, and support organizations.

In a nationwide survey conducted in 1989 and 1996, 158 cities reported switching from voluntary to mandatory community recycling programs. Overall, those cities that switched to mandatory recycling reported higher participation rates. Those cities that continued to offer voluntary programs, however, reported that offering curbside pickup (i.e., pickup in individual offices) "resulted in a much higher mean level of participation compared to those programs in which citizens could only drop off materials at recycling collection centers "[98].

As the result of greater participation, the benefits of a mandatory recycling program could include an increase in total volume of material recycled by individual, committee, and support organization offices. An increase in the volume of paper, bottles, and cans recycled from these offices, the most commonly recycled products, could result in greater proceeds. An increase in proceeds would benefit the Senate fitness center and, if passed, would allow the Architect to develop other recycling initiatives in the House [99].

On the other hand, it may prove difficult for the Architect to enforce participation. Some Member offices may object to mandatory participation. While incentives, such as an enhanced Senate fitness center, could increase participation, ultimately individuals decide whether they participate in a recycling program. Should an individual choose not to participate, enforcement of a mandatory program could be logistically difficult and costly. The nature of a penalty and its enforcement would further burden the Architect [100].

*Dedication of Recycling Proceeds*. The Architect of the Capitol has included in his budget justification for FY2009 legislative language to amend Title 2, United States Code concerning the collection and utilization of proceeds from the House recycling program. If enacted, the language would "allow that proceeds from AOC recycling program be applied to other environmentally friendly efforts such as energy conservation program and other efforts" [101]. Currently, the proceeds from the House recycling program are deposited in the United States Treasury, and are not returned to the House.

Proponents of the Architect's proposed legislation could argue that providing the House recycling program with a dedicated stream of funds might allow for a reduction in appropriations. Dedicating funds generated by the recycling program to energy conservation and recycling efforts could motivate additional participation in the recycling program. Dedicating funds would also mirror action previously taken by the Senate, which directs proceeds from the Senate recycling program to the Senate fitness center [102]. Opponents of allowing the Architect to retain proceeds from the House recycling program could argue that the current system meets the recycling program's needs. Other opponents could argue that dedicating the proceeds to the recycling program would not motivate additional participation, and that dedication of the funds to the House day care center or the House fitness center would be a better incentive [103].

## Administrative Options

Since the current recycling program is voluntary and administered by the Architect of the Capitol, there are three major administrative options available to expand the recycling program. The Architect, through the recycling coordinators in the House and Senate, could expand their educational programs to encourage staff to recycle, expand the number and placement of recycling containers, or continue to look for additional materials to recycle.

*Educational Programs.* During a hearing of the Senate Rules and Administration Committee, Chairwoman Senator Dianne Feinstein addressed the issue of staff education during her opening statement. She stated, "[a]nother avenue for change is educating the Senate community on how simple actions can make a big difference in lowering our energy usage. Creating a culture of 'energy consumption awareness' through educational seminars and emails might hold the key to further reduce our energy needs" [104]. To continue to raise awareness of the recycling program, the Architect, through the recycling coordinators in the House and Senate Superintendent's offices, could expand educational programs.

Both the House and the Senate maintain recycling webpages on the House and Senate Architect's websites and hold educational seminars to educate staff about what can and cannot be recycled [105]. To continue to educate House and Senate staff, the Architect could expand the educational offerings on recycling. These programs could range from single seminars on the recycling process and recyclable materials to in-depth programs on the short-term and long-term benefits of recycling on Capitol Hill. Research suggests that recycling increases with greater awareness and that "[s]uch awareness is achieved by educating the public about the urgency of waste stream reduction" [106] Additionally, the Architect could offer visits to individual offices to demonstrate recycling techniques or consultation on the placement and quantity of recycling bins.

*Recycling Containers.* To increase participation in the recycling program the House and the Senate could examine the number of recycling containers and the placement of the containers throughout the Capitol complex. Increasing the number of containers and the placement of containers could allow the Architect to collect greater volumes of recycled materials from individual Member and committee offices. Should individual Member and committee offices desire multiple containers, the containers could be placed strategically to facilitate greater staff participation. While increasing the number and the placement of the containers could increase staff participation, it could also make it more difficult for the Architect to collect recycled materials. More containers will increase the number of pickup points. This could make the collection of materials more time consuming and more difficult to monitor. The House or Senate could change how recycled items are collected by moving from having a few centralized locations for the drop-off of recyclables to creating a more decentralized with in-office collection of materials. In a decentralized pickup system, materials would be placed in recycling bins located within individual offices, picked up by the Architect and categorized at a central location. If individual staffers did not separate materials in their respective offices, such responsibility would remain with the Architect to ensure that the House and Senate receive maximum value for recycled materials.

*Recycling of Other Materials.* The House and the Senate currently recycle 12 different materials: paper, bottles and cans, wooden pallets, sawdust, ceiling tiles, batteries, carpet, e-waste, plastics, toner cartridges, masonry waste, and scrap metal. To ensure that the House and Senate recycling programs continue to recycle new materials, the Architect could continue to explore opportunities for expansion. New materials could include cell phone and personal data assistants (PDAs), the collection and composting of food materials from outside the House cafeterias, the creation of a recycling program for compact fluorescent light bulbs (CFLs) when they need to be replaced,107 and the continuation of construction and industrial waste recycling associated with maintenance and upgrade projects through Capitol Hill.

## CONCLUSION

Recycling in the House of Representatives and the Senate is an ongoing process that has been expanded during the 110$^{th}$ Congress. Under the combined supervision of the Architect and the CAO, the House continues to increase recycling options to include non-traditional material such as cell phones. Similarly, the Senate has created a flexible recycling program that responds to the needs of Members and staff. Both the House and the Senate continue to look for ways to augment recycling initiatives in a cost effective and environmentally conscious way. *Report RS22807, Compact Fluorescent Light Bulbs (CFLs): Issues with Use and Disposal,* by Linda Luther.

# APPENDIX

Since the 93rd Congress (1973-1975), 32 bills and resolutions have been introduced to create or refine the recycling program in the House of Representatives. While only one of these proposals was agreed to (H.Res. 104 in the 101st Congress), each attempted to create a modern recycling program in the House.

| Congress | Measure | Title | Sponsor | Introduced |
|---|---|---|---|---|
| 93rd (1973-1975) | H.R. 913 | A bill to amend Chapter 9 of Title 44, United States Code, to require the use of recycled paper in the printing of the Congressional Record | Peter Peyser (R-NY) | Jan. 3, 1973 |
| | H.R. 1812 | A bill to amend Chapter 9 of Title 44, United States Code, to require the use of recycled paper in the printing of the Congressional Record | William Lehman (D-FL) | Jan. 11, 1973 |
| | H.R. 2182 | A bill to amend Section 734 of Title 44, United States Code, to require the Public Printer to furnish recycled material for the official use of the Senate and the House of Representatives | Vernon Thomson (R-WI) | Jan. 15, 1973 |
| | H.R. 2183 | A bill to amend Chapter 9 of Title 44, United States Code, to require the use of recycled paper in the printing of the Congressional Record | Vernon Thomson (R-WI) | Jan. 15, 1973 |
| | H.Con.Res. 89 | Concurrent resolution expressing the sense of Congress that the Federal Government should use recycled paper products to the fullest extent possible | Jack Edwards (R-AL) | Jan. 22, 1973 |
| | H.R. 3846 | A bill to amend Chapter 9 of Title 44, United States Code, to require the use of recycled paper in the printing of the Congressional Record | Peter Peyser (R-NY) | Feb. 6, 1973 |

**Table (Continued)**

| Congress | Measure | Title | Sponsor | Introduced |
|---|---|---|---|---|
| | H.R. 3847 | A bill to amend Chapter 9 of Title 44, United States Code, to require the use of recycled paper in the printing of the Congressional Record | Peter Peyser (R-NY) | Feb. 6, 1973 |
| | H.R. 3952 | A bill to authorize and direct the Administrator of the General Services Administration to prescribe regulations with respect to the amount of recycled material contained in paper procured or used by the Federal Government or the District of Columbia | John Dingell (D-MI) | Feb. 7, 1973 |
| | H.R. 4015 | A bill to amend Chapter 9 of Title 44, United States Code, to require the use of recycled paper in the printing of the Congressional Record | William Lehman (D-FL) | Feb. 7, 1973 |
| | H.R. 5142 | A bill to amend Chapter 9 of Title 44, United States Code, to require the use of recycled paper in the printing of the Congressional Record | William Lehman (D-FL) | Mar. 5, 1973 |
| 94th (1975-1977) | H.R. 483 | A bill to amend Chapter 9 of Title 44, United States Code, to require the use of recycled paper in the printing of the Congressional Record | Kevin Hechler (D-WV) | Jan. 14, 1975 |
| | H.R. 404 | A bill to amend Chapter 9 of Title 44, United States Code, to require the use of recycled paper in the printing of the Congressional Record | Hamilton Fish, Jr. (R-NY) | Jan. 14, 1975 |
| | H.R. 595 | A bill to amend Chapter 9 of Title 44, United States Code, to require the use of recycled paper in the printing of the Congressional Record | William Lehman (D-FL) | Jan. 14, 1975 |

| Congress | Measure | Title | Sponsor | Introduced |
|---|---|---|---|---|
| | H.R. 594 | A bill to authorize and direct the Administrator of the General Services Administration to prescribe regulations with respect to the amount of recycled material contained in paper procured or used by the Federal Government or the District of Columbia | William Lehman (D-FL) | Jan. 14, 1975 |
| | H.R. 835 | A bill to amend Chapter 9 of Title 44, United States Code, to require the use of recycled paper in the printing of the Congressional Record | Peter Peyser (R-NY) | Jan. 14, 1975 |
| | H.Con.Res. 397 | Concurrent resolution expressing the sense of the Congress that the Federal Government should use recycled paper products to the fullest extent possible | Jack Edwards (R-AL) | Sept. 17, 1975 |
| 101st (1989-1991) | H.Res. 130 | Requiring that disposable trays, dishes, and beverage containers used in the food service operations of the House of Representatives be biodegradable | Claudine Schneider (R-RI) | Apr. 17, 1989 |
| | H.Con.Res. 304 | Congressional Recycled Paper Act | Barbara Boxer (D-CA) | Apr. 18, 1990 |
| | H.R. 4523 | Congressional Recycling Act of 1990 | Glenn Anderson (D-CA) | Apr. 18, 1990 |
| | H.Res. 385 | Providing for a mandatory recycling program for the House of Representatives | Bill Grant (R-FL) | Apr. 26, 1990 |
| | H.Res. 104 | Requiring the Architect of the Capitol to establish and implement a voluntary program for recycling paper disposed of in the operation of the House of Representatives | William Green (R-NY) | Mar. 7, 1989 |
| | H.Con.Res. 188 | Requiring the Architect of the Capitol to conduct a voluntary pilot program for recycling of expendable materials disposed of within the Capitol grounds | James Hayes (D-LA) | Aug. 4, 1989 |

**Table (Continued)**

| Congress | Measure | Title | Sponsor | Introduced |
|---|---|---|---|---|
| | H.R. 3463 | To require the Federal Government to recycle bottles, cans, paper, and plastics and to provide a price preference for the purchase by the Federal Government of goods made of recycled material | Douglas Owens (D-UT) | Oct. 11, 1989 |
| 102nd (1991-1993) | H.R. 242 | Congressional Recycling Act of 1991 | Glenn Anderson (D-CA) | Jan. 3, 1991 |
| | H.Res. 96 | To provide a comprehensive recycling program for the House of Representatives | Glenn Anderson (D-CA) | Feb. 28, 1991 |
| | H.R. 1201 | Recycled Paper Procurement Act of 1991 | John Porter (R-IL) | Feb. 28, 1991 |
| | H.Res. 128 | Applauding the Architect of the Capitol and the Committee on House Administration for developing an effective recycling program in the House office buildings, and supporting ongoing efforts to expand and update source separation and recycling in the House office buildings during the 102nd Congress | Dennis Hastert (R-IL) | Apr. 17, 1991 |
| | H.Res. 245 | Requiring the Clerk of the House to take such action as may be necessary to ensure that stationery used in the House of Representatives is made from recycled paper | Rick Santorum (R-PA) | Oct. 10, 1991 |
| | H.R. 3939 | Reduce, Reuse, and Recycle for America Act | Gerry Sikorski (D-MN) | Nov. 26, 1991 |
| 104th (1995-1997) | H.Res. 513 | Providing for the mandatory implementation of the Office Waste Recycling Program in the House of Representatives | Sam Farr (D-CA) | Aug. 2, 1996 |

| Congress | Measure | Title | Sponsor | Introduced |
|---|---|---|---|---|
| 105th (1997-1999) | H.Res. 119 | Providing for the mandatory implementation of the Office Waste Recycling Program in the House of Representatives | Sam Far (D-CA) | Apr. 16, 1997 |
| $109^{th}$ (2005-2007) | H.Con.Res. 299 | Expressing the sense of Congress that the leaders of Congress and other legislative branch offices should work together to establish and implement a coordinated effort for the reuse, recycling, and appropriate disposal of obsolete computers and other electronic equipment used by offices of the legislative branch | Mike Thompson (D-CA) | Nov. 15, 2005 |

Source: Library of Congress, (LIS) Legislative Information System of the U.S. Congress, [http://www.congress.gov].

# Appendix B. Bills and Resolutions Introduced for Senate Recycling

Since the 101st Congress (1989-1991), seven bills and resolutions have been introduced to create or refine the recycling program in the Senate. While only one of these proposals was agreed to (S.Res. 99 in the 101$^{st}$ Congress), each attempted to create a modern recycling program in the Senate.

| Congress | Measure | Title | Sponsor | Introduced |
|---|---|---|---|---|
| 101$^{st}$ (1989-1991) | S.Res. 99 | A resolution requiring the Architect of the Capitol to establish and implement a voluntary program for recycling paper disposed of in the operation of the Senate | Rudy Boschwitz (R-MN) | Apr. 11, 1989 |
| | S. 2513 | Congressional Recycling Act of 1990 | Rudy Boschwitz (R-MN) | Apr. 25, 1990 |
| | S. 2522 | Congressional Recycling Act of 1990 | Jeff Bingaman (D-NM) | Apr. 25, 1990 |
| | S. 2643 | Federal Paper Separation, Recycling, and Waste Source Reduction Act of 1990 | Richard Bryan (D-NV) | May 16, 1990 |
| | S.Res. 337 | A resolution to express the sense of the Senate to encourage the purchase of recycled paper and paper products to the greatest extent practicable | Rudy Boschwitz (R-MN) | Oct. 10, 1990 |
| 102$^{nd}$ (1991-1993) | S. 255 | Congressional Recycling Act of 1991 | Jeff Bingaman (D-NM) | Jan. 23, 1991 |
| | S. 976 | Resource Conservation and Recovery Act Amendments of 1992 | Max Baucus (D-MT) | Apr. 25, 1994 |
| 105$^{th}$ (1997-1999) | S. 2368 | Senate Day Care Center Recycling Funding Support Act | Daniel Akaka (D-HI) | July 29, 1998 |

Source: Library of Congress, (LIS) Legislative Information System of the U.S. Congress, [http://www.congress.gov].

# REFERENCES

[1] Robert Cowles Letcher and Mary T. Sheil, "Source Separation and Citizen Recycling," in William D. Robinson, ed., *The Solid Waste Handbook: A Practical Guide* (New York: John Wiley & Sons, 1986), p. 216.

[2] The House and the Senate chose to create voluntary recycling programs as compared to compulsory programs requiring all offices to recycle. For a comparison of voluntary and compulsory programs and their impact on recycling participation see, Ann E. Carlson, "Recycling Norms," *California Law Review,* vol. 89, no. 5 (Oct. 2001), pp. 123 1-1300.

[3] CRS does not address the distinct question of whether separately from these resolutions, a requirement that the Architect of the Capitol administer a recycling program in congressional offices could be derived from the federal Solid Waste Disposal Act. That act states that agencies of the legislative branch, presumably including the Architect of the Capitol, are subject to D.C. laws "respecting control and abatement of solid waste ... to the same extent ... as any person is subject to such requirements...." 42 U.S.C. § 6961(a).

[4] H.Res. 104 (101st Congress), agreed to by voice vote, Aug. 1, 1989; and S.Res. 99 (101st Congress), agreed to by unanimous consent, Oct. 2, 1989.

[5] U.S. General Services Administration, GSA National Capitol Region, National Capitol Region Recycling Program, [http://ncr.gsa.gov/Recycle/AL/Default.aspx], accessed July 15, 2008.

[6] H.Res. 104 (101st Congress), agreed to by voice vote, Aug. 1, 1989.

[7] U.S. Congress, Library of Congress, (LIS) Legislative Information System of the U.S. Congress, [http://www.congress.gov], accessed Apr. 18, 2008. To find information about the detailed status of H.Res. 104, search for the resolution under the advanced tab for the 101st Congress.

[8] U.S. Congress, Committee on House Administration, *Requiring the Architect of the Capitol to Establish and Implement a Voluntary Program for Recycling Paper Disposed of in the Operation of the House of Representatives,* report to accompany H.Res. 104, 10 1st Cong., 1st sess., H.Rept. 101-204 (Washington: GPO, 1989), p. 1.

[9] 40 C.F.R. § 246.101. See also, William D. Robinson, editor, *The Solid Waste Handbook: A Practical Guide* (New York, NY: John Wiley & Sons, 1986), p. 216. Source separation is an alternative to central disposal of waste. Instead of combining all waste materials prior to disposal, source separation divides the material, based on categories designed to maximize their reuse, prior to disposal.

[10] U.S. Congress, Committee on House Administration, *Requiring the Architect of the Capitol to Establish and Implement a Voluntary Program for Recycling Paper Disposed of in the Operation of the House of Representatives,* report to accompany H.Res. 104, 10 1st Cong., 1st sess., H.Rept. 101-204 (Washington: GPO, 1989), p. 2.
[11] U.S. Congress, Committee on House Administration, *Report on the Activities of the Committee on House Administration of the House of Representatives During the One Hundred and First Congress*, 101st Cong., 2nd sess., H.Rept. 101-1005 (Washington: GPO, 1991), p. 112.
[12] U.S. Congress, Committee on House Administration, *Requiring the Architect of the Capitol to Establish and Implement a Voluntary Program for Recycling Paper Disposed of in the Operation of the House of Representatives,* report to accompany H.Res. 104, 101st Cong., 1st sess., H.Rept. 101-204 (Washington: GPO, 1989), p. 2.
[13] Rep. Jim Bates, "*Requiring Architect of the Capitol to Establish Voluntary Program for Recycling Paper Disposed of by the House,*" Congressional Record, vol. 135, part 13 (Aug. 1, 1989), p. 17172.
[14] Companion bills were also introduced in the Senate. See S. 2513 (101st Congress), introduced Apr. 25, 1990; S. 2522 (101st Congress), introduced Apr. 25, 1990; and S. 255 (102nd Congress), introduced Jan. 23, 1991.
[15] H.R. 4523 (101st Congress), introduced Apr. 18, 1990.
[16] Rep. Glenn Anderson, "The Congressional Recycling Act of 1990," *Congressional Record*, vol. 136, part 5 (Apr. 18, 1990), p. 7278.
[17] U.S. Congress, Committee on House Administration, Report on the Activities of the Committee on House Administration of the House of Representatives During the One Hundred and First Congress, 101st Cong., 2nd sess., H.Rept. 101-1005 (Washington: GPO, 1991), p. 116. See also, U.S. Congress, Committee on House Administration, Subcommittee on Procurement and Printing, *Congressional Recycling Act of 1990*, hearing on H.R. 4523, 101st Cong., 2nd sess., Aug. 1 and Aug. 2, 1990 (Washington: GPO, 1990).
[18] H.R. 3463 (101st Congress), introduced Oct. 12, 1989 and H.R. 1201 (102nd Congress), introduced Feb. 28, 1991.
[19] "The Federal Government and Congress Should Buy Real Recycled Paper," *Congressional Record*, vol. 137, part 3 (Feb. 26, 1991), p. 4244.
[20] S.Res. 99 (101st Congress), agreed to by unanimous consent, Oct. 2, 1989.
[21] "Senate Resolution 99 — Relating to the Recycling of Paper in the Senate," *Congressional Record*, vol. 135, part 5 (Apr. 11, 1989), p. 6048.

[22] "Legislative Branch Appropriations, 1990," *Congressional Record*, vol. 135, part 14 (Sept. 6, 1989), p. 19607.

[23] A companion bill was also introduced in the House. See H.R. 4523 (101*st* Congress), introduced Apr. 18, 1990.

[24] S. 2513 (101st Congress), introduced Apr. 25, 1990; S. 2522 (101*st* Congress), introduced Apr. 25, 1990; and S. 255 (102*nd* Congress), introduced Jan. 23, 1991.

[25] "Purchase of Recycled Paper by Congress," *Congressional Record*, vol. 137, part 2 (Jan. 23, 1991), p. 2123.

[26] Four executive orders have been issued since 1993 to require executive branch agencies to purchase recycled paper. See Executive Order 12873, "Federal Acquisition, Recycling, and Waste Prevention," 58 *Federal Register* 54911, Oct. 22, 1993; Executive Order 12995, "Amendment to Executive Order No. 12873," 61 Federal Register 13645, Mar. 28, 1996; Executive Order 13101, "Greening the Government Through Waste Prevention, Recycling, and Federal Acquisition," 63 *Federal Register* 49641, Sept. 16, 1998; and Executive Order 13423, "Strengthening Federal Environmental, Energy, and Transportation Management," 72 *Federal Register* 3921, Jan. 26, 2007.

[27] S. 2643 (101st Congress), introduced May 16, 1990.

[28] The Committee on House Administration has oversight jurisdiction over measures relating to financial accounts of the House and over measures relating to administration of the House Office Buildings and the House Wing of the Capitol. Since recycling officially began in 1989, the House Administration Committee has not provided public guidance to the Architect on the operation of the recycling program. In the 104th and 105th Congresses, the committee was known as the Committee on House Oversight.

[29] For a further discussion of recycling markets see also John Pichtel, *Waste Management Practices: Municipal, Hazardous, and Industrial* (New York: Taylor and Francis, 2005), p. 130.

[30] U.S. Congress, House Committee on Appropriations, *Subcommittee on Legislative Appropriations, Legislative Branch Appropriations for 1992: Part 1 Justification of the Budget Estimates*, hearings, 102nd Cong., 1st sess. (Washington: GPO, 1991), pp. 608-609.

[31] U.S. Congress, House Committee on Appropriations, *Subcommittee on Legislative Appropriations, Legislative Branch Appropriations for 1991: Part 1 Justification of the Budget Estimates*, hearings, 101st Cong., 2nd sess. (Washington: GPO, 1990), p. 585.

[32] U.S. Congress, House Committee on Appropriations, Subcommittee on Legislative Appropriations, *Legislative Branch Appropriations for 1991: Part 2 Legislative Branch*, hearings, 101st Cong., 2nd sess. (Washington: GPO, 1990), p. 234.

[33] Ibid.

[34] U.S. Congress, House Committee on Appropriations, Subcommittee on Legislative Appropriations, *Legislative Branch Appropriations for 1992: Part 1 Justification of the Budget Estimates*, hearings, 102nd Cong., 1st sess. (Washington: GPO, 1991), pp. 608-609.

[35] U.S. Congress, House Committee on Appropriations, Subcommittee on Legislative Appropriations, *Legislative Branch Appropriations: Part 2 Fiscal Year 1991 Supplemental Request and Fiscal Year 1992 Legislative Branch Appropriations Request*, hearings, 102nd Cong., 1st sess. (Washington: GPO, 1991), p. 260.

[36] U.S. Congress, House Committee on Appropriations, *Legislative Branch Appropriations Bill, 1992*, report to accompany H.R. 2506, 102nd Cong., 1st sess., H.Rept. 102-82 (Washington: GPO, 1991), p. 23.

[37] U.S. Congress, House Committee on Appropriations, Subcommittee on Legislative Appropriations, *Legislative Branch Appropriations for 1993: Part 2 Fiscal Year 1992 Legislative Branch Appropriations Request*, hearings, 102nd Cong., 2nd sess. (Washington: GPO, 1992), pp. 708-709.

[38] U.S. Congress, House Committee on Appropriations, Subcommittee on Legislative Appropriations, *Legislative Branch Appropriations for 1995: Part 1 Justification of the Budget Estimates*, hearings, 103rd Cong., 2nd sess. (Washington: GPO, 1994), p. 713.

[39] Executive Order 12873, "Federal Acquisition, Recycling, and Waste Prevention," 58 *Federal Register* 5491 1, Oct. 22, 1993. Subsequently, three additional executive orders, two by President Bill Clinton and one by President George W. Bush, have been issued related to recycling. See, Executive Order 12995, "Amendment to Executive Order No. 12873," 61 *Federal Register* 13645, Mar. 28, 1996; Executive Order 13101, "Greening the Government Through Waste Prevention, Recycling, and Federal Acquisition," 63 Federal Register 49641, Sept. 16, 1998; and Executive Order 13423, "Strengthening Federal Environmental, Energy, and Transportation Management," 72 *Federal Register* 3917, Jan. 26, 2007.

[40] U.S. Congress, House Committee on Appropriations, Subcommittee on Legislative Appropriations, *Legislative Branch Appropriations for 1995: Part 1 Justification of the Budget Estimates*, hearings, 103rd Cong., 2nd sess. (Washington: GPO, 1994), pp. 280-281.

[41] U.S. Congress, House Committee on Appropriations, Subcommittee on Legislative Appropriations, *Legislative Branch Appropriations for 1995: Part 2 Fiscal Year 1995 Legislative Branch Appropriation Requests*, hearings, 103rd Cong., 2nd sess. (Washington: GPO, 1994), p. 341.

[42] "Legislative Branch Appropriations Act, 1999," *Congressional Record*, vol. 144, part 10 (June 25, 1998), p. 13955.

[43] P.L. 105-275, 112 Stat. 2443, Oct. 21, 1998.

[44] "Amendment No. 1 Offered by Mr. Farr of California," *Congressional Record,* vol. 144, part 10 (June 25, 1998), p. 13963.

[45] Ibid, p. 13964.

[46] U.S. Congress, Conference Committee, *Making Appropriations for the Legislative Branch for the Fiscal Year Ending September 30, 1999, and for Other Purposes*, conference report to accompany H.R. 4112, 105th Cong., 2nd sess., H.Rept. 105-734 (Washington: GPO, 1998), p. 15.

[47] P.L. 105-275, 112 Stat. 2443, Oct. 21, 1998.

[48] U.S. Congress, House Committee on Appropriations, Subcommittee on *Legislative, Legislative Branch Appropriations, 2000: Part 2 Fiscal Year 2000 Legislative Branch Appropriation Requests, hearings*, 106th Cong., 1st sess. (Washington: GPO, 1999), p. 450.

[49] Ibid, p. 452.

[50] U.S. Congress. House Committee on Appropriations, *Legislative Branch Appropriations Bill, 2000*, report to accompany H.R. 1905, 106th Cong., 1st sess., H.Rept. 106-156 (Washington, GPO, 1999), p. 22. For text of the Legislative Branch Appropriations Bill for FY2000 as enacted see P.L. 106-57, 113 Stat. 408, Sept. 29, 1999.

[51] U.S. Congress, Conference Committee, *Making Appropriations for the Legislative Branch for the Fiscal Year Ending September 30, 2001, and for Other Purposes,* conference report to accompany H.R. 4516, 106th Cong., 2nd sess., H.Rept. 106-796 (Washington: GPO, 2000), p. 118.

[52] U.S. Congress, House Committee on Appropriations, *Legislative Branch Appropriations Bill,* 2002, report to accompany H.R. 2647, 107th Cong., 1st sess., H.Rept. 107-169 (Washington: GPO, 2001), p. 20. For the text of the Legislative Branch Appropriations Bill for FY2002 see P.L. 107-68, 115 Stat. 560, Nov. 12, 2001.

[53] Executive Order 13101, "Greening the Government Through Waste Prevention, Recycling, and Federal Acquisition," 63 *Federal Register* 49641, Sept. 16, 1998. Executive Order 13 101mandates that the "head of each executive agency shall incorporate waste prevention and recycling in the agency's daily operations and work to increase and expand markets for

recovered materials through greater Federal Government preference and demand for such products." It was revoked by Executive Order 13423 on Jan. 24, 2007. See Executive Order 13423, "Strengthening Federal Environmental, Energy, and Transportation Management," 72 *Federal Register* 3917, Jan. 26, 2007.

[54] U.S. Congress, House Committee on Appropriations, *Legislative Branch Appropriations Bill, 2003*, report to accompany H.R. 5121, $107^{th}$ Cong., $2^{nd}$ sess., H.Rept. 107-576 (Washington: GPO, 2002), p. 9.

[55] Ibid, p. 16. For text of the Legislative Branch Appropriations Bill for FY2003 see P.L. 108-7, 117 Stat. 11, Feb. 20, 2003.

[56] P.L. 110-161, 121 Stat. 2242, Dec. 26, 2007.

[57] U.S. Congress, House Committee on Appropriations, Subcommittee on Legislative Branch, *Legislative Branch Appropriations for 2009: Part 1 Justification of Budget Estimates*, hearings, $110^{th}$ Cong., $2^{nd}$ sess. (Washington: GPO, 2008), p. 430.

[58] 2 U.S.C. § 12 1f.

[59] U.S. Congress, Committee on House Administration, *Report on the Activities of the Committee on House Administration of the House of Representatives During the One Hundred and First Congress*, $101^{st}$ Cong., $2^{nd}$ sess., H.Rept 101-1005 (Washington: GPO, 1991), pp. 117-118.

[60] U.S. Congress, Committee on House Administration, *Report on the Activities of the Committee on House Administration of the House of Representatives During the One Hundred Third Congress*, $103^{rd}$ Cong., $2^{nd}$ sess., H.Rept. 103-893 (Washington: GPO, 1995), p. 5.

[61] During the 104th Congress and the 105th Congress the Committee on House Administration was renamed the Committee on House Oversight.

[62] U.S. Congress, Committee on House Oversight, *Report on the Activities of the Committee on House Oversight of the House of Representatives During the One Hundred Fifth Congress Together With Minority and Additional Views*, 105th Cong., 2nd sess., H.Rept. 105- 850 (Washington: GPO, 1999), pp. 37-39.

[63] Recycled materials from the Ford House Office Building are currently picked up by a non- GSA managed vendor. Data on House recycling by GSA managed contractors includes pickups of office waste from the Ford House Office Building between Oct. 1992 and Jan. 1997. Since 1997, GSA managed contractors only pick up scrap metal from the Ford House Office Building.

[64] "Notice," *Congressional Record,* vol. 138, part 9 (June 1, 1992), p. 12907.

[65] "Notice," *Congressional Record*, vol. 138, part 5 (Mar. 24, 1992), p. 6509.

[66] "*Congressional Record* Printed on 100 Percent Recycled Newsprint," Congressional Record, vol. 138, part 5 (Mar. 25, 1992), p. 6875.

[67] Email between the author and Patrick Moran, recycling program manager, Architect of the Capitol, U.S. House of Representatives Superintendent's Office, Apr. 15, 2008.

[68] Phone conservation between the author and Patrick Moran, recycling program manager, Architect of the Capitol, U.S. House of Representatives Superintendent's Office, May 29, 2008.

[69] E-Waste includes all electronic equipment such as computers, computer peripherals, printers, televisions, and copy machines. For more information on e-waste and e-waste recycling see, [http://www.epa.gov/ecycling/], accessed July 15, 2008. See also CRS Report RL3 1505, *Recycling Computer and Electronic Equipment: Legislative and Regulatory Approaches for 'E-Waste,'* by James E. McCarthy.

[70] U.S. Congress, Chief Administrative Officer of the House of Representatives, *Green the Capitol Initiative Final Report*, 1 10th Cong., 1st sess. [http://cao.house.gov/greenthecapitol/ green-the-capitol-final-report.pdf], accessed July 15, 2008.

[71] U.S. Congress, Chief Administrative Officer of the House of Representatives, "Immediate Office," *CAO Semi-Annual Report*, 1 10th Cong., 1st sess. [http://cao.house.gov/report/ cao-io.shtml], accessed July 15, 2008.

[72] U.S. Congress, Chief Administrative Officer of the House of Representatives, *Green the Capitol Initiative Final Report*, 1 10th Cong., 1st sess. [http://cao.house.gov/greenthecapitol/ green-the-capitol-final-report.pdf], accessed July 15, 2008.

[73] Cell phone recycling had occurred before the "Green the Capitol" initiative in the 1 10th Congress, but it was not a formal program. "*Green the Capitol" expanded the program.*

[74] For a discussion on composting see, George Tchobanoglous and Frank Kreith, Handbook of Solid Waste Management (New York: McGraw-Hill, 2002), pp. 1.9-1.11.

[75] U.S. Congress, Chief Administrative Officer of the House of Representatives, Green the Capitol Initiative, Green Team "Newsletter," vol. 1, 110th Cong., 2nd sess. Apr. 7, 2008 [http://cao.house.gov/ greenthecapitol/green-newsletter/greenteam01.shtml], accessed July 15, 2008.

[76] U.S. Congress, Chief Administrative Officer of the House of Representatives, "*Composting Heaps Ending Government Waste*," press

release, Apr. 15, 2008, [http://cao.house.gov/greenthecapitol/news-composting200804 17.shtml], accessed July 21, 2008.

[77] Testimony of Chief Administrative Office of the House of Representatives Daniel Beard, in U.S. Congress, *House Select Committee on Energy Independence and Global Warming, Food for Thought: A Primer on the Climate Consequences of Food Choices*, $110^{th}$ Cong., $2^{nd}$ sess., Feb. 26, 2008 [http://globalwarming.house.gov/tools/assets/files/036 1 .pdf], accessed July 15, 2008.

[78] Testimony of Chief Administrative Office of the House of Representatives Daniel Beard, in U.S. Congress, House Committee on Transportation and Infrastructure, Subcommittee on Economic Development, *Public Buildings, and Emergency Management, A Growing Capitol Complex and Visitor Center: Needs for Transportation, Security, Greening, Energy, and Maintenance*, $110^{th}$ Cong., $2^{nd}$ sess., Apr. 1, 2008 [http://cao.house.gov/appearances/ 20080401_transportation.shtml], accessed July 15, 2008.

[79] Elizabeth Brotherton, "Beard Details New Recycling Efforts," Roll Call, Feb. 27, 2008 [http://www.rollcall.com/issues/53_99/news/22279-1 .html], accessed July 15, 2008.

[80] Dear-Colleague Letter from Daniel Beard, Chief Administrative Officer of the House of Representatives, Dec. 12, 2007.

[81] U.S. Congress, Chief Administrative Officer of the House of Representatives, Green the Capitol Initiative, "*Personal Cell Phone Collection Initiative*" [http://cao.house.gov/ greenthecapitol/news-bberry-recycle.shtml], accessed July 15, 2008.

[82] Other materials include bottles, cans, scrap metal, toners, batteries, sawdust, e-waste, plastic, pallets, concrete, brick, and carpet. GSA only collects bottles, cans, and paper for the Senate. Other materials is recycled through non-GSA vendors.

[83] U.S. Congress, Senate Committee on Appropriations, Legislative Branch *Appropriations for Fiscal Year 1991*, hearings, $101^{st}$ Cong., $2^{nd}$ sess., S.Hrg. 101-839 (Washington: GPO, 1990), p. 249.

[84] U.S. Congress, Senate Committee on Appropriations, Legislative Branch *Appropriations for Fiscal Year 1992*, hearings, 102nd Cong., 2nd sess., S.Hrg. 102-244 (Washington: GPO, 1991), p. 37.

[85] Ibid, p. 39.

[86] U.S. Congress, Senate Committee on Appropriations, Legislative Branch *Appropriations for Fiscal Year 1993*, hearings, 102nd Cong., 2nd sess., S.Hrg. 102-658 (Washington: GPO, 1992), p. 293.

[87] S. 2368 (105th Congress), introduced July 29, 1998.

[88] U.S. Congress, Office of Senator Daniel Akaka, "Senate Day Care Center Recycling Funding Support Act," press release, July 29, 1998. See also, "Senate Day Care Recycling Funding Support Act," *Congressional Record*, vol. 144, part 2 (July 29, 1998), pp. 17663- 17664.

[89] "Senate Day Care Recycling Funding Support Act," *Congressional Record*, vol. 144, part 2 (July 29, 1998), p. 17664.

[90] U.S. Congress, Senate Committee on Appropriations, *Legislative Branch Appropriations, 2001*, report to accompany S. 2603, 106th Cong., 2nd sess., S.Rept. 106-304 (Washington: GPO, 2000), p. 29.

[91] P.L. 106-554, 114 Stat. 2763A-96, Dec. 21, 2000.

[92] P.L. 106-554, 114 Stat. 2763, Dec. 21, 2000; and P.L. 108-7, 117 Stat. 375, Feb. 20, 2003.

[93] U.S. Congress, Senate Committee on Appropriations, *Legislative Branch Appropriations, 2002*, report to accompany S. 1172, 107th Cong., 1st sess., S.Hrg. 107-37 (Washington: GPO, 2001), p. 10.

[94] Ibid, p. 29.

[95] U.S. Congress, Senate Committee on Appropriations, *Legislative Branch Appropriations, 2004*, report to accompany S. 1383, 108th Cong., 1st sess., S.Rept. 108-88 (Washington: GPO, 2003), p. 28.

[96] Conversation between the author and Scott Shapleigh, recycling program manager, Senate Office Buildings, *Architect of the Capitol*, Apr. 22, 2008.

[97] Conversation between the author and Scott Shapleigh, recycling program manager, Senate Office Buildings, Architect of the Capitol, June 3, 2008.

[98] David H. Folz, "Municipal Recycling Performance: A Public Sector Environmental Success Story," *Public Administration Review*, vol. 59, no. 4 (July-Aug. 1999), p. 338.

[99] U.S. Congress, House Committee on Appropriations, Subcommittee on Legislative Branch, *Legislative Branch Appropriations for 2009: Part 1 Justification of Budget Estimates, hearings*, 110th Cong., 2nd sess. (Washington: GPO, 2008), p. 430.

[100] Other research studies suggest that solid waste removal fees based on volume of material removed from a property (i.e. more garbage collected equates with higher service fees) has motivated people to recycle. The House and Senate, collectively or individually, could create a system to charge offices for the volume of non-recyclable materials collected. See James D. Reschovsky and Sarah E. Stone, "Market Incentives to Encourage Household Waste Recycling: Paying for What You Throw Away," *Journal*

*of Policy Analysis and Management*, vol. 13, no. 1 (Winter 1994), pp. 120-139.

[101] U.S. Congress, House Committee on Appropriations, Subcommittee on Legislative Branch, *Legislative Branch Appropriations for 2009: Part 1 Justification of Budget Estimates, hearings*, 1 10th Cong., 2nd sess. (Washington: GPO, 2008), p. 430.

[102] 2 U.S.C. § 121f.

[103] In 1998, Senator Daniel Akaka introduced S. 2368 to dedicate proceeds from the Senate recycling program to the Senate Child Care Center. While S. 2368 was not enacted, Senate recycling proceeds were designated to offset the cost of the Senate fitness center by the Consolidated *Appropriations Act of 2001* (2. U.S.C. § 121f).

[104] Statement of Senator Dianne Feinstein, in U.S. Congress, Senate Committee on Rules and Administration, Improving Energy Efficiency, Increasing the Use of Renewable Sources of Energy, and Reducing the Carbon Footprint of the Capitol Complex, hearings, 1 10th Cong., 2nd sess., June 18, 2008 [http://rules.senate.gov/hearings/2008/06 1 808feinsteinopen.pdf], accessed July 15, 2008.

[105] The House Superintendent maintains a recycling brochure on its website [http://house.aoc.gov/upload/InHousePrintBrochure7.pdf], accessed July 15, 2008 and the Senate Superintendent maintains contact information for the recycling coordinator as well as a list of materials that can be recycled in an office on its website [http://senate.aoc.gov/ Senate-Services/Programs/ Programs-Recycling.cfm], accessed July 15, 2008.

[106] James D. Ward and Dennis W. Gleiber, "Citizen Response to Mandatory Recycling," *Public Productivity and Management Review*, vol. 16, no. 3 (Spring 1993), p. 241. See also, Joanne Vining and Angela Ebreo, "An Evaluation of the Public Response to a Community Recycling Education Program," Society and Natural Resources, vol. 2 (1989), pp. 23-36; and Joanne Vining and Angela Ebreo, "What Makes a Recycler? A Comparison of Recyclers and Nonrecyclers," *Environment and Behavior*, vol. 22, no. 1 (1990), pp. 55-73.

[107] For more information on Compact Fluorescent Light Bulbs see, CRS Report RS22807, Compact Fluorescent Light Bulbs (CFLs): *Issues with Use and Disposal*, by Linda Luther.

In: Recycling and Green Programs at the Capital… ISBN 978-1-60692-980-3
Editor: H. Y. Kim, pp. 151-162 

*Chapter 4*

# ARCHITECT OF THE CAPITOL: PROGRESS IN IMPROVING ENERGY EFFICIENCY AND OPTIONS FOR DECREASING GREENHOUSE GAS EMISSIONS*

***United States Government Accountability Office***

## WHY GAO DID THIS STUDY

In April 2007, GAO reported that 96 percent of the greenhouse gas emissions from the Capitol Hill Complex facilities—managed by the Architect of the Capitol (AOC)—resulted from electricity use throughout the complex and combustion of fossil fuels in the Capitol Power Plant. The report concluded that AOC and other legislative branch agencies could benefit from conducting energy audits to identify projects that would reduce greenhouse gas emissions. GAO also recommended that AOC and the other agencies establish a schedule for conducting these audits and implement selected projects as part of an overall plan that considers cost- effectiveness, the extent to which the projects reduce emissions, and funding options. AOC and the other agencies agreed with our recommendations.

This statement focuses on (1) the status of AOC's efforts to implement the recommendations in our April 2007 report and (2) opportunities for the Senate to

* Excerpted from GAO Report 08-917T, dated June 18, 2008.

decrease greenhouse gas emissions and associated environmental impacts. The statement is based on GAO's prior work, analysis of AOC documents, and discussions with AOC management.

## WHAT GAO FOUND

AOC has made some progress toward implementing the recommendations in GAO's April 2007 report, but opportunities remain. For example, AOC has prioritized a list of Capitol Hill buildings that need energy audits but has not developed a schedule for conducting the audits that explains the prioritization scheme or provides information on the anticipated costs. AOC prioritized the order of energy audits based on each building's energy use and has begun conducting the first of the audits. In addition, AOC has contracted with a private firm to conduct preliminary audits of the Senate office buildings that could lead to more targeted audits and eventually identify cost-effective projects that would decrease energy use and related greenhouse gas emissions. We believe that developing a more detailed schedule for future audits that includes an explanation of the prioritization scheme and cost estimates would assist the Congress in its appropriations decisions and facilitate the completion of additional audits. With respect to our recommendation that AOC implement selected projects as part of an overall plan to reduce emissions, AOC has implemented projects to reduce energy use and related emissions, but the projects were not identified through the processes we recommended. AOC could more fully respond to our recommendation by first completing the energy audits and then evaluating the cost-effectiveness and relative merits of projects that could further decrease the demand for energy.

The Senate's options for decreasing the greenhouse gas emissions and related environmental impacts associated with its operations fall into three main categories—implementing projects to decrease the demand for electricity and steam derived from fossil fuels, adjusting the Capitol Power Plant's fuel mix, and purchasing carbon offsets or renewable electricity from external providers. Of these options, efforts to decrease the demand for energy could lead to recurring cost savings through reductions in energy expenditures while the other options may prove less cost-effective and involve recurring expenses. However, a key challenge in identifying energy-saving opportunities results from limited data on the baseline level of energy use within each Senate building. Specifically, the meters for steam and chilled water no longer function or do not provide reliable data. In addition, the buildings are not equipped with submeters for electricity that, if installed, could enhance efforts to identify sections of the buildings that consume relatively high levels of energy. AOC has purchased but not installed new chilled water meters, is evaluating options for acquiring new steam meters, and plans to install submeters by February 2009.

Madam Chairman and Members of the Committee:

Thank you for the opportunity to participate in this hearing to discuss opportunities for enhancing energy efficiency and decreasing the carbon footprint of the Capitol Hill Complex. In April 2007, we reported that 96 percent of the greenhouse gas emissions from the Capitol Hill Complex resulted from purchased electricity (59 percent) and the combustion of fossil fuels in the Capitol Power Plant (37 percent) [1]. The Architect of the Capitol (AOC) has jurisdiction over the day-to-day operations of facilities located in the complex. Because the vast majority of greenhouse gas emissions from the Capitol Hill Complex stem from energy use, our April 2007 report recommended that AOC and other legislative branch agencies conduct energy audits to identify projects that would reduce greenhouse gas emissions. We also recommended that AOC and other legislative branch agencies establish a schedule for conducting these audits and implement selected projects as part of an overall plan that considers the cost-effectiveness of the projects, the extent to which they reduce emissions, and options for funding them. AOC and the other agencies agreed with our recommendations.

In addition to the work we did for our April 2007 report, we analyzed the potential costs of fuel-switching from coal to natural gas at the Capitol Power Plant, as directed by the Chief Administrative Officer of the House of Representatives in the Green the Capitol Initiative [2]. Specific actions outlined in the initiative included purchasing electricity generated by renewable sources, purchasing carbon offsets, and directing AOC to adjust the fuel mix of the Capitol Power Plant so that the portion of its output consumed by the House is derived entirely from natural gas [3]. In May 2008, we recommended that, before adjusting the plant's fuel mix beyond the level directed by the initiative, AOC consult with its oversight committees in the Congress and evaluate the economic and environmental tradeoffs associated with the use of each fuel at the plant.

My statement today will focus on (1) the status of AOC's efforts to implement the recommendations in our April 2007 report and, (2) opportunities for the Senate to decrease greenhouse gas emissions, including the cost-effectiveness of decreasing demand for energy relative to other options such as fuel switching at the Capitol Power Plant or purchasing renewable electricity and carbon offsets. Today's remarks are based on our prior work, analysis of documents provided by AOC on its progress in responding to recommendations in our April 2007 report, and related discussions with AOC management.

## SUMMARY

The Architect of the Capitol has made some progress toward implementing the recommendations in our April 2007 report but more opportunities remain. For example, AOC has prioritized a list of Capitol Hill buildings that need energy audits but has not developed a schedule for conducting the audits that explains the prioritization scheme or provides information on the anticipated costs. With respect to energy audits, AOC is conducting an energy audit of the U.S. Capitol Police Buildings and Grounds and plans to use $400,000 of fiscal year 2008 funds for energy audits of the Capitol Building and the Ford House Office Building. AOC has also requested $1.4 million for additional energy audits in its fiscal year 2009 budget request. In addition, AOC has contracted with a private firm to conduct preliminary audits of the Senate Office Buildings that could lead to more targeted audits and eventually identify cost-effective projects that would decrease energy use and related greenhouse gas emissions. To more fully implement this recommendation, AOC would need to enhance its prioritized list of audits by providing a more detailed schedule for completing the audits. AOC also has an opportunity to more fully address our recommendation that it implement selected projects as part of an overall plan to reduce emissions that considers cost-effectiveness, the extent to which the projects reduce emissions, and funding options. Specifically, AOC has implemented numerous energy efficiency projects throughout the Capitol Complex but has not identified these projects through the process we recommended of first conducting energy audits and then implementing selected projects based on cost- effectiveness and other considerations. Projects underway or completed include upgrading lighting systems, replacing steam system components, conducting education and outreach, purchasing energy-efficient equipment and appliances, and installing new windows in the Ford House Office Building.

The Senate's options for decreasing Capitol Hill greenhouse gas emissions and related environmental impacts associated with its operations fall into three main categories—(1) implementing projects to decrease the demand for electricity and steam, (2) adjusting the Capitol Power Plant's fuel mix, and (3) purchasing carbon offsets or renewable electricity from external providers. Of these options, efforts to decrease the demand for energy could lead to a reduction in the Capitol

Hill Complex carbon footprint and recurring cost savings through reductions in energy expenditures. On the other hand, the other options may involve recurring expenses which may be large enough to render them less cost-effective. If natural gas prices remain relatively high, fuel switching may prove particularly costly. As we reported in April 2007, a strategy for reducing emissions could include energy audits that identify and evaluate energy-efficiency and renewable- energy projects, and the evaluation of other projects that may fall outside the scope of energy audits, such as purchasing energy-efficient appliances and computers. Importantly, these steps could assist the Senate in addressing the largest sources of emissions—the consumption of purchased electricity and fossil fuel combustion in the Capitol Power Plant. However, a key challenge in identifying energy-saving projects for the Senate buildings results from limited data on the baseline level of energy use within each Senate building. Specifically, the Senate Office Buildings currently have meters provided by the local utility to track electricity use in each building, but the AOC-owned meters that track the consumption of steam and chilled water either no longer work or do not provide reliable data. In addition, the Senate buildings are not equipped with submeters for electricity that, if installed, could enhance efforts to identify sections of the buildings that consume relatively high levels of energy. AOC has purchased but not installed new chilled water meters, is evaluating options for acquiring new steam meters, and plans to install submeters by February 2009. In addition to decreasing the demand for energy, the Senate could require AOC to adjust the fuel mix at the Capitol Power Plant to rely more heavily on natural gas, which produces about half as much carbon dioxide as coal when burned but also costs about four times as much for a comparable amount of energy input. As we estimated in May 2008, meeting the House of Representative's fuel- switching requirement would cost between $1.0 and $1.8 million in fiscal year 2008 and between $4.7 and $8.3 million over a five-year period. While we have not analyzed the potential costs of fuel switching at the Capitol Power Plant to meet the needs of the Senate, our estimates for the House may provide some indication of the potential costs of such a directive. Additionally, fuel-switching requirements could impose a recurring cost on AOC and may prove less cost-effective than implementing projects that decrease the demand for energy. Finally, the Senate could pay for electricity derived from renewable sources or purchase carbon offsets. Such steps could encourage emissions reductions outside of the Capitol Complex but would also impose a recurring cost on the Senate and may be less cost effective than decreasing the demand for energy.

## BACKGROUND

Energy audits typically identify information on projects that could address the consumption of fossil fuel and electricity as well as projects that could reduce emissions from other sources, such as leaks in refrigeration equipment. Energy audits also include information on the cost- effectiveness of projects and on the extent to which the projects could reduce emissions. This information can then be used to evaluate and select projects. The audits generally fall into three categories— preliminary, targeted, and comprehensive—and are distinguished by the level of detail and analysis required. Preliminary audits are the least detailed and provide quick evaluations to determine a project's potential. These audits typically do not provide sufficiently detailed information to justify investments but may prove useful in identifying opportunities for more detailed evaluations. Targeted audits are detailed analyses of specific systems, such as lighting. Comprehensive audits are detailed analyses of all major energy-using systems. Both targeted and comprehensive audits provide sufficiently detailed information to justify investing in projects.

Energy-saving projects that fall outside the scope of energy audits include efforts to enhance outreach and education efforts to curtail energy use by building occupants and purchasing high-efficiency appliances. Outreach and education efforts include providing information on how employees can conserve energy, such as AOC's "how-to guides" that detail cost- effective methods to save energy in the workplace. Efforts to curtail energy use include purchasing energy-efficient computer equipment and appliances, using information available from the Environmental Protection

Agency's Energy Star program or the Federal Energy Management Program (FEMP). Energy Star-qualified and FEMP-designated products meet energy-efficiency guidelines set by the Environmental Protection Agency and the Department of Energy and, in general, represent the top 30 percent most energy-efficient products in their class of products. These products cover a wide range of categories, including appliances and office equipment. According to the Energy Star program, office products that have earned the Energy Star rating use about half as much electricity as standard equipment and generally cost the same as equipment that is not Energy Star qualified.

# AOC Has Made Some Progress toward Implementing GAO's Recommendations on Energy Audits and Implementing Projects that Decrease Emissions

AOC has made some progress toward implementing the two recommendations in our April 2007 report. First, AOC has taken steps to address our recommendation that it develop a schedule for routinely conducting energy audits by developing a prioritized list of buildings for which it plans to conduct comprehensive energy audits (see App. 1). Specifically, AOC is currently undertaking a comprehensive energy audit of the U.S. Capitol Police Buildings and Grounds and obtained a draft submission in May 2008 from the private contractor performing the audit. AOC also plans to use $400,000 of fiscal year 2008 funds to perform comprehensive energy audits of the Capitol Building and the Ford House Office Building, and says it will direct any remaining fiscal year 2008 funds to an audit of the Hart Senate Office Building [4] Additionally, AOC has contracted with a private firm to conduct a preliminary energy audit of the Senate Office Buildings that could prove useful in identifying opportunities for more comprehensive and targeted evaluations.

AOC officials said that they developed the prioritized list of buildings to audit by comparing the amount of energy used per square foot of space in each building (referred to as energy intensity) and then placing the buildings that use relatively higher levels of energy at the top of the list. However, AOC's prioritized list does not provide information on the energy intensity of each building, an explanation of its prioritization scheme, or cost estimates. Furthermore, AOC has not developed a schedule for routinely conducting audits as we recommended in our April 2007 report. AOC officials said that they cannot complete a more comprehensive schedule because of uncertainty about the extent to which AOC will receive future appropriations to conduct the audits. We believe that developing a more detailed schedule for future audits along with an explanation of its prioritization scheme and cost estimates would assist the Congress in its appropriations decisions and facilitate the completion of additional audits.

Second, AOC can do more to fully address the second recommendation in our April 2007 report that it implement selected projects as part of an overall plan to reduce emissions that considers cost-effectiveness, the extent to which the projects reduce emissions, and funding options. In recent years, AOC has undertaken numerous projects throughout the Capitol Hill Complex to reduce energy use and related emissions, but these projects were not identified through the process we recommended. Projects completed or underway include upgrading lighting systems, conducting education and outreach, purchasing energy-efficient equipment and appliances, and installing new windows in the Ford building. Examples of projects in Senate office buildings include upgrading the lighting in 11 offices with daylight and occupancy sensors, installing energy efficiency ceiling tiles in the Hart building, and replacing steam system components. According to AOC, these efforts have already decreased the energy intensity throughout the Capitol Hill Complex. Specifically, AOC said that it decreased its energy intensity—the amount of energy used per square foot of space within a facility—by 6.5 percent in fiscal year 2006 and 6.7 percent in fiscal year 2007.

As AOC moves forward with identifying and selecting projects that could decrease energy use and related emissions, it could further respond to our recommendation by developing a plan that identifies the potential benefits and costs of each option based on the results of energy audits. Such a plan could build on AOC's existing Sustainability Framework Plan and its Comprehensive Emissions Reduction Plan for the Capitol Complex, which identify measures that could lead to improvements in energy efficiency and reductions in greenhouse gas emissions. Complementing these plans with information on projects identified through energy audits would further assist AOC in using the resources devoted to energy efficiency enhancements as effectively as possible.

## Efforts to further Reduce Energy Consumption May Prove More Cost-Effective Than Other Measures in Decreasing Emissions

The Senate has three primary options for decreasing greenhouse gas emissions and related environmental impacts associated with its operations. These include (1) implementing additional projects to decrease the demand for electricity and steam derived from fossil fuel; (2) adjusting the Capitol Power Plant's fuel mix to rely more heavily on natural gas, which produces smaller quantities of greenhouse gas emissions for each unit of energy input than the coal and oil also burned in the plant; and (3) purchasing renewable electricity or carbon offsets from external providers. Each option involves economic and environmental tradeoffs and the first option is likely to be the most cost-effective because the projects could lead to recurring cost savings through reductions in energy expenditures.

Regarding the first option, as we reported in April 2007, conducting energy audits would assist AOC in addressing the largest sources of emissions because the audits would help identify cost-effective energy-efficiency projects. In general, energy projects are deemed cost-effective if it is determined through an energy audit that they will generate sufficient savings to pay for their capital costs. These projects may require up-front capital investments that the Senate could finance through direct appropriations or contracts with utility or energy service companies, under which the company initially pays for the work and the Senate later repays the company with the resulting savings. Until AOC exhausts its opportunities for identifying energy-efficiency projects that will pay for themselves over a reasonable time horizon, this option is likely to be more cost-effective than the second two options, both of which would involve recurring expenditures.

In pursuing energy audits, AOC faces a significant challenge collecting reliable data on the baseline level of energy use within each Senate office building. Such data would help identify inefficient systems and provide a baseline against which AOC could measure potential or actual energy- efficiency improvements. First, while AOC has meters that track electricity use in each building, the meters that track the steam and chilled water used by each building no longer work or provide unreliable data. AOC officials said that they have purchased but not installed new meters to track the use of chilled water and are evaluating options for acquiring new steam meters. Installing these meters and collecting reliable data would enhance any efforts to identify potential energy saving measures. Second, AOC does not have submeters within each building to track the electricity use within different sections of each building. Such submetering would further assist in targeting aspects of the Senate buildings' operations that consume relatively high quantities of energy.

AOC said that it plans to install submeters for electricity, chilled water, and steam by February 2009.

A second option for decreasing greenhouse gas emissions would involve directing AOC to further adjust the fuel mix at the Capitol Power Plant to rely more heavily on the combustion of natural gas in generating steam for space heating. The plant currently produces steam using a combination of seven boilers—two that primarily burn coal, but could also burn natural gas, and five boilers that burn fuel oil or natural gas. The total capacity of these boilers is over 40 percent higher than the maximum capacity required at any given time, and the plant has the flexibility to switch among the three fuels or burn a combination of fuels. The percentage of energy input from each fuel has varied from year to year, with an average fuel mix of 43 percent natural gas, 47 percent coal, and 10 percent fuel oil between 2001 and 2007.

In June 2007, the Chief Administrative Officer of the House of Representatives released the Green the Capitol Initiative, which directed AOC to operate the plant with natural gas instead of coal to meet the needs of the House. The House Appropriations Committee subsequently directed GAO to determine the expected increase in natural gas use for House operations and the associated costs at the power plant that would result from the initiative. In May 2008, we reported that the fuel-switching directive should lead to a 38 percent increase in natural gas use over the average annual quantity consumed between 2001 and 2007. We also estimated that the fuel switching should cost about $1.4 million in fiscal year 2008 and could range from between $1.0 and $1.8 million depending on actual fuel costs, among other factors [5]. We also estimated that the costs would range from between $4.7 million and $8.3 million over the 2008 through 2012 period, depending on fuel prices, the plant's output, and other factors. While we have not analyzed the potential costs of fuel switching at the Capitol Power Plant to meet the needs of the Senate, our estimates for the House may provide some indication of the potential costs of such a directive. Additionally, AOC officials said that further directives to increase its reliance on natural gas in the plant could require equipment upgrades and related capital expenditures.

Our May 2008 report also found that decreasing the plant's reliance on coal could decrease greenhouse gas emissions by about 9,970 metric tons per year at an average cost of $139 per ton and could yield other environmental and health benefits by decreasing emissions of nitrogen oxides, particulate matter, and pollutants that cause acid rain. While fuel switching could decrease emissions of carbon dioxide and other harmful substances, it would also impose recurring costs because natural gas costs about four times as much as coal for an equal amount of energy input. Thus, fuel switching may prove less cost-effective than decreasing the demand for energy.

Finally, a third option for the Senate to decrease greenhouse gas emissions and related environmental impacts includes purchasing electricity that is derived from renewable sources and paying external parties for carbon offsets. Neither of these activities would involve modifications to the Capitol Complex or its operations but could nonetheless lead to offsite reductions in emissions and related environmental impacts. Both options, if sustained, would result in recurring costs that should be considered in the context of other options for decreasing emissions that may prove more cost-effective.

Madam Chairman, this completes my prepared statement. I would be pleased to answer any questions that you or Members of the Committee may have.

# APPENDIX I: PRIORITIZED LIST OF BUILDINGS FOR COMPREHENSIVE ENERGY AUDITS

| Fiscal Year | Facility |
|---|---|
| 2008 | Capitol Building |
| | Rayburn House Office Building |
| | Hart Senate Office Building[a] |
| 2009 | Russell Senate Office Building |
| | Dirksen Senate Office Building |
| | Senate Underground Garage |
| | Senate Employees Child Care Center |
| | Webster Hall Page Dormitory |
| | Senate Furniture Warehouse |
| | Robert A. Taft Memorial |
| | CPP Boiler Plant |
| | CPP West Refrigeration Plant |
| | CPP Administration Building |
| | CPP Generator Building |
| | CPP East Refrigeration Plant |
| | CPP Storage (Butler) Building |
| 2010 | Ford House Office Building |
| | Longworth House Office Building |
| | East and West Underground Garages |
| | House Page Dormitory |
| | Cannon House Office Building |
| 2011 | Thomas Jefferson Building |
| | James Madison Memorial Building |
| | LOC Special Facilities Center |
| | Book Storage Modules |
| 2012 | Alternate Computer Facility |
| | U.S. Capitol Police Headquarters |
| | 67 K Street |
| | Canine Facility |
| | Capitol Police Courier Acceptance Site |
| | John Adams Building |
| | BG Conservatory |
| | BG Administration Building |
| | BG Production Facility (Greenhouse) |
| | Construction Management Division |
| | CG Vehicle Maintenance Garage |
| | Supreme Court Building |

Source: AOC. [a]Hart is third in order for fiscal year 2008, if funding permits.

# References

[1] GAO, Legislative Branch: Energy Audits Are Key to Strategy for Reducing Greenhouse Gas Emissions, GAO-07-516 (Washington, D.C.: Apr. 25, 2007). Major greenhouse gases include carbon dioxide, methane, nitrous oxide, and certain synthetic gases including hydrofluorocarbons emitted from refrigerants. Buildings within the Capitol Complex include the Senate Office buildings (Dirksen, Hart, and Russell), House Office Buildings (Cannon, Longworth, and Rayburn), U.S. Capitol Building and Grounds, the Capitol Power Plant, Library of Congress Buildings and Grounds, U.S. Capitol Police Buildings, and the U.S. Botanic Garden. The Capitol Power Plant provides steam and chilled water for heating and cooling the Capitol building and 23 surrounding facilities.

[2] GAO, Economic and Other Implications of Switching from Coal to Natural Gas at the Capitol Power Plant and at Electricity-Generating Units Nationwide, GAO-08-601R (Washington, D.C.: May 1, 2008).

[3] According to the Department of Energy's Energy Information Administration, for a comparable amount of energy input, the amount of carbon dioxide emitted from burning natural gas is about half that emitted from burning coal. Carbon offsets are a measurable reduction in greenhouse gas emissions from a project in one location that is used to compensate for emissions occurring elsewhere.

[4] AOC completed energy audits of the Capitol Building in 2001, and of the Rayburn and James Madison Buildings in May 2005. AOC has requested $1.4 million for energy audits in its fiscal year 2009 budget request.

[5] All of our cost estimates are in constant 2006 dollars.

In: Recycling and Green Programs at the Capital... ISBN 978-1-60692-980-3
Editor: H. Y. Kim, pp.163-189 

*Chapter 5*

# Economic and Other Implications of Switching from Coal to Natural Gas at the Capitol Power Plant and at Electricity-Generating Units Nationwide*

***United States Government Accountability Office***

The Honorable Mary L. Landrieu
Chair The Honorable Lamar Alexander Ranking Member
Subcommittee on Legislative Branch Committee on Appropriations
United States Senate

The Honorable Debbie Wasserman Schultz
Chair
The Honorable Tom Latham
Ranking Member
Subcommittee on Legislative Branch Committee on Appropriations
House of Representatives

Elevated concentrations of greenhouse gases—carbon dioxide, methane, nitrous oxide, and several synthetic chemicals—in the atmosphere resulting from

* Excerpted from GAO Report 08-601R, dated May 1, 2008.

the combustion of fossil fuels and other sources have the potential to cause significant changes in the earth's climate. These potential impacts include shifts in sea level and weather patterns and could pose threats to coastal and other infrastructure. Concerns about the potential impacts of climate change have led the Congress to consider legislation that would place binding, nationwide limits on greenhouse gas emissions, and the House of Representatives' leadership has initiated efforts to decrease emissions attributable to its operations. Nearly all of the greenhouse gas emissions from House operations consist of carbon dioxide and are associated with electricity purchased from utilities and the combustion of fossil fuels in the Capitol Power Plant (CPP), which provides steam and chilled water for heating and cooling the Capitol building and 23 surrounding facilities. The Architect of the Capitol (AOC) operates CPP.

In June 2007, the Chief Administrative Officer (CAO) of the House of Representatives released the Green the Capitol initiative (the initiative) at the direction of the Speaker and the Majority Leader [1]. Among other goals, the initiative calls for the House of Representatives to operate in a carbon-neutral manner by the end of the 1 10th Congress (December 2008). Carbon-neutral, as defined in the initiative, means that operations produce no net contribution to greenhouse gas emissions. The initiative outlines several strategies to achieve the goal of carbon neutrality, including operating CPP with natural gas instead of coal to meet the needs of the House. (Natural gas generates about half as much carbon dioxide as coal when burned but costs about four times more for a comparable amount of energy input.) [2]. Based on an AOC estimate, the House's share of the cost of achieving the fuel-switching goal would total $2.75 million in fiscal year 2008. The Omnibus Appropriations Act for that year appropriated $85.3 million for CPP. The House Appropriations Committee Explanatory Statement directs $3.27 million of this amount to the Green the Capitol initiative [3]

CPP produces steam using a combination of seven boilers—two boilers that primarily burn coal, but could also burn natural gas, and five boilers that burn fuel oil or natural gas. These boilers burn fuel to convert water to steam that, in turn, provides energy primarily for space heating but they do not generate electricity [4]. The total capacity of these boilers is over 40 percent higher than the maximum capacity required at any given time, and the plant has the flexibility to switch among the three different fuels or burn a combination of fuels. The percentage of energy input from each fuel has varied from year to year, with an average fuel mix of 43 percent natural gas, 47 percent coal, and 10 percent fuel oil between 2001 and 2007. The overall amount of steam required depends on numerous factors, including weather, the adoption of voluntary and federally mandated energy-efficiency and conservation measures, and the addition of new buildings (such as the Capitol Visitor Center, scheduled to open in late 2008).

In addition to the House's efforts to implement the Green the Capitol initiative, the Congress is considering proposals that would create nationwide limits on greenhouse gas emissions from electricity-generating units and other sectors of the economy. Many of these proposals would involve the use of mechanisms that create an economic incentive for emitters to decrease their emissions by limiting the overall allowable quantity of emissions or by placing a direct price on each unit of emissions. Because the combustion of fossil fuels results in greenhouse gas emissions, efforts to limit emissions could lead to overall shifts in the prices and demand for different types of fuels. For example, the Department of Energy has projected that limits on greenhouse gases would shift the nation's demand for fossil fuels by decreasing the demand for coal and increasing the demand for natural gas. In 2006, production of electricity from coal totaled 49 percent of the nation's net generation, followed by 20 percent from natural gas, 19 percent from nuclear power, and 7 percent from hydroelectric power, with lesser quantities produced from other renewable sources, petroleum, and other fuels. These percentages have remained relatively stable in recent years with a slight increase in natural gas generation and a slight decrease in generation from coal. In principle, all coal units could be physically switched from coal to natural gas with varying degrees of modification. It would also be possible to build new gas-fired power plants to replace coal-fired power plants. These modifications or replacements would require different amounts of investment in the power plants themselves, as well as related infrastructure. Legislative proposals that would impose limits on greenhouse gas emissions from the electricity sector raise important questions about the potential supply and demand for different fuels under different scenarios, as well as about the ability of existing generating units to switch from burning high-emitting fuels, such as coal, to lower-emitting fuels, such as natural gas. Moreover, such proposals prompt questions about the overall economic benefits and costs that would accrue.

Within this context, the House Committee on Appropriations directed us to determine, in consultation with the Department of Energy, (1) the expected increase in natural gas use for House operations and the associated costs at CPP that would result from the Green the Capitol initiative, and (2) the ability of existing U.S. coal- burning, electricity-generating units to switch to burning natural gas and the associated economic implications.

To respond to the first objective, we first reviewed two studies prepared for the House CAO. One study was an analysis prepared by AOC that served as the basis for the fuel-switching funding estimate in the Green the Capitol initiative presented by CAO to the House leadership. The other study was a subsequent analysis prepared by the Department of Energy's Lawrence Berkeley National Laboratory (LBNL). We then determined the average annual quantity of each fuel (measured in British thermal units or Btu) consumed by the plant between 2001 and 2007. Next, we calculated the proportion of the plant's steam output consumed by buildings operated by the House of Representatives, which we estimated was 29 percent based on the total square footage of buildings served by the plant. We assumed that the fuel- switching approach outlined in the initiative required that this proportion of the plant's output be derived entirely from natural gas. The remaining 71 percent would continue to reflect the plant's historical average of 43 percent natural gas, 47 percent coal, and 10 percent fuel oil. We did not assume a change in the quantity of fuel oil that would be burned by the plant because of technical considerations at the plant that require the use of fuel oil as a back-up fuel. We then calculated the incremental cost of achieving an adjusted fuel mix. We made this calculation assuming that, beginning in 2008, the demand for the plant's output would decrease by 1 percent annually from the 2001 through 2007 baseline due to energy efficiency legislation and additions to the Capitol complex. We then estimated future CPP cost per unit of fuel for the period from 2008 through 2012 using historical data on AOC's fuel expenditures and projections of fuel prices for the industrial sector from the Annual Energy Outlook of the Energy Information Administration (EIA) within the Department of Energy. We adjusted EIA's projected fuel prices to account for historical differences in the average prices paid by industrial users of these fuels and the prices paid by AOC. All of our cost estimates are in constant 2006 dollars.

In preparing our estimates, we consulted with AOC staff, officials representing the House CAO, and the Department of Energy (including LBNL and EIA). We also reviewed relevant studies prepared by these agencies.

To respond to the second objective, we analyzed available data from the Department of Energy and other sources. We also obtained information from key stakeholders identified in discussions with the department that represent the electricity generation, natural gas, and coal industries using written interview questions.

Enclosure I provides a more detailed description of our scope and methodology. We conducted our audit work between October 2007 and April 2008 in accordance with generally accepted government auditing standards. Those standards require that we plan and perform the audit to obtain sufficient, appropriate evidence to provide a reasonable basis for our findings and conclusions based on our audit objectives. We believe that the evidence obtained provides a reasonable basis for our findings and conclusions based on our audit objectives.

## SUMMARY

According to our analysis, implementing the Green the Capitol initiative's fuel- switching directive to decrease carbon dioxide emissions from the CPP should lead to a 38 percent increase in natural gas use over the average annual quantity consumed between 2001 and 2007. We estimated that the fuel switching should cost about $1.4 million in fiscal year 2008 and could range from between $1.0 and $1.8 million depending on actual fuel costs, among other factors. Our cost estimates are less than the $2.75 million AOC budgeted for this purpose in fiscal year 2008, largely because we employed a different methodology than AOC when it prepared its estimates and maintained certain assumptions that AOC did not. Specifically, AOC based its estimates on a scenario in which the plant would eliminate its use of coal altogether and burn natural gas exclusively, for a total cost of $7.78 million. Of this total cost, AOC estimated that $2.75 million represented the portion that could be applied to the House, based on the number of square feet of building space served by the plant. In its estimate, AOC also did not account for the fact that the Ford House Office Building obtains steam from the General Services Administration rather than from CPP. As a result, AOC's plans to fulfill the Green the Capitol initiative involve increasing natural gas use by 48 percent, an increase that far exceeds the initiative's fuel-switching recommendation. In contrast, our analysis focused on estimating the incremental cost of adjusting the plant's fuel mix such that the portion of its output that serves buildings operated by the House (about 29 percent on a square footage basis) would consist entirely of natural gas. This equates to increasing the level of natural gas from 43 percent to 60 percent of the historical fuel mix, a net difference of 17 percentage points and a 38 percent increase in overall natural gas consumption. Importantly, the plant's existing natural gas boilers have the capacity to accommodate this increase in natural gas use and CPP would not have to eliminate its use of coal altogether. Looking ahead, we estimate that the incremental cost of maintaining the adjusted fuel mix will range between $4.7 million and $8.3 million over the 2008 through 2012 time period, depending on fuel prices, the plant's output, and other factors. However, an important uncertainty with our estimates stems from the fact that AOC does not have complete, reliable information on the efficiency of its seven boilers in converting fuel into steam or on the full costs associated with the use of each fuel, taking into account factors such as fuel transportation and handling, and fuel-specific pollution control devices. As a result, AOC does not have all the information it needs to make fully informed decisions about operating the plant as efficiently or cost-effectively as possible. While the increased use of natural gas and decreased use of coal will increase costs above a business-as-usual baseline scenario, the initiative would likely generate other important benefits. These benefits include decreased emissions of carbon dioxide and pollutants that cause smog and acid rain, as well as potential reductions in the plant's operating costs associated with the transportation, storage, handling, and treatment of coal and related waste streams.

With regard to the ability of U.S. coal-burning, electricity-generating units to switch to natural gas, according to available data and key stakeholders, the ability of these units to switch is limited by high natural gas prices, supply constraints, and existing infrastructure. In addition, increasing the nation's use of natural gas for electricity generation could result in adverse economic consequences. Natural gas currently costs about four times more than coal per British thermal unit and has shown a relatively higher rate of price increases and volatility over time relative to coal, according to EIA.

In addition to higher fuel costs, supply constraints limit the practicality of replacing electricity generated from coal with natural gas. The United States has limited capability to meet the growing demand for natural gas with domestic production and would need to become increasingly dependent on international supplies of natural gas if there was widespread switching to natural gas from coal. Even taking imported natural gas into account, key stakeholders doubted whether natural gas supply could meet the demand if plant operators decided to pursue fuel switching. Fuel switching to natural gas also poses challenges related to existing infrastructure, including limited pipeline and storage capacity and technical and regulatory barriers to the conversion of existing coal plants. Large-scale fuel switching would require substantial investments in pipeline and storage capacity and new terminals to process imported natural gas—all of which would require regulatory approval. With respect to the conversion of existing coal-burning plants, stakeholders said that it would be more feasible and cost-effective to construct new natural gas units or dispatch excess capacity at existing natural gas units than to convert a coal plant because of technical and economic factors, among other reasons.

For example, retrofitting an existing coal unit to burn natural gas would require significant capital expenditures, while also potentially decreasing the unit's overall efficiency in converting fuel input into electricity. Because of these technical and other issues, large-scale shifting demand for electricity production from coal to natural gas would increase electricity prices, residential and commercial heating costs, and fuel costs for certain industries that consume large quantities of natural gas, including chemical and fertilizer manufacturers. Because of these and other concerns, key stakeholders said that switching coal plants to natural gas has occurred infrequently in the past and is not likely to occur in the future.

We are recommending that, before adjusting the Capitol Power Plant's fuel mix beyond the level directed by the Green the Capitol initiative, the Acting Architect of the Capitol consult with AOC's oversight committees in the Congress and evaluate the economic and environmental tradeoffs associated with the use of each fuel at the plant, taking into account the efficiency of the plant's boilers, related fuel supply systems, and pollution control equipment.

We provided a draft copy of this report to the Acting Architect of the Capitol for review and comment. AOC provided comments via electronic mail. AOC officials said that they agreed with our cost estimate under the high fuel price scenario but expressed concerns about the potential level of resources that would be required to respond to our recommendation.

We subsequently met with AOC officials who said that they were concerned that implementing our recommendation would require them to collect exact information on the efficiency of its boilers and fuel supply systems. Based on this discussion, we adjusted the wording of the recommendation to clarify that this was not our intent. AOC also provided a number of technical clarifications regarding the plant's operation and their cost estimates for fuel switching, which we incorporated into our report as appropriate.

## Fuel Switching at the Capitol Power Plant Is Expected to Require a 38 Percent Increase in Natural Gas Use at a Cost of about $1.4 Million in Fiscal Year 2008

Based on available data and key assumptions about the plant's operation and future fuel costs, we estimated that fulfilling the Green the Capitol initiative's fuel-switching directive would require the plant to increase its natural gas use by 38 percent relative to its baseline level of fuel consumption between 2001 and 2007. As a portion of the plant's total fuel mix, natural gas would increase from about 43 percent of overall energy input to about 60 percent of input. Using information from the AOC on its fuel expenditures and fuel price projections from ETA, we estimate that implementing the fuel-switching directive could range in cost from $1.0 to $1.8 million in fiscal year 2008.

Because our calculations involve projections and assumptions about key variables, the estimates are inherently uncertain and actual expenditures may vary depending on changes to these variables. Key variables and assumptions underlying our estimates include the following:

- *Baseline fuel consumption and steam production.* We estimated the quantity of additional natural gas required to fulfill the initiative's fuel-switching goal for the year 2008. We assumed that the fuel-switching approach outlined in the initiative required that 29 percent of the plant's output be derived entirely from natural gas. The 29 percent figure is based on an estimate of the House's share of the total square footage of buildings served by the plant. The remaining 71 percent would continue to reflect the average fuel mix over the 2001 to 2007 time period [ 5]. Using an average, as opposed to a single year's level of production, provides a more realistic picture of the plant's historical operation. We held the amount of fuel oil constant because of technical considerations at the plant that require using oil as a backup fuel.
- *Boiler efficiency.* We assumed that each of the seven boilers at the power plant converts fuel into steam with equal efficiency. We made this assumption based on research conducted by an independent consultant to GAO, a previous analysis conducted by Ross Associates (a consultant to AOC), and discussions with AOC staff. Overall, we found that AOC does not have complete, reliable information on the efficiency of its seven boilers in converting fuel into steam or on the full costs associated with the use of each fuel, taking into account factors such as transportation, handling, and pollution control. As a result, AOC does not have all the information it needs to make fully informed decisions about operating the plant as efficiently or cost-effectively as possible. While the available data suggests that our assumption is reasonable, the lack of complete, reliable data on efficiency of each of the boilers and related fuel supply equipment represents an important uncertainty with our analysis.
- *Fuel costs.* To estimate the cost of each fuel in fiscal year 2008, we used fuel price projections from EIA' s Annual Energy Outlook 2008, which we then adjusted to account for historical differences in the prices paid by AOC versus the average price paid by industrial consumers [6].

## Our Estimates Are Substantially Lower than Previous Estimates and the Level of Funding AOC Budgeted for Fuel Switching at the Plant

Our estimated costs of increasing natural gas use at CPP to meet the initiative's fuel- switching directive fall well below a previous estimate prepared by AOC.

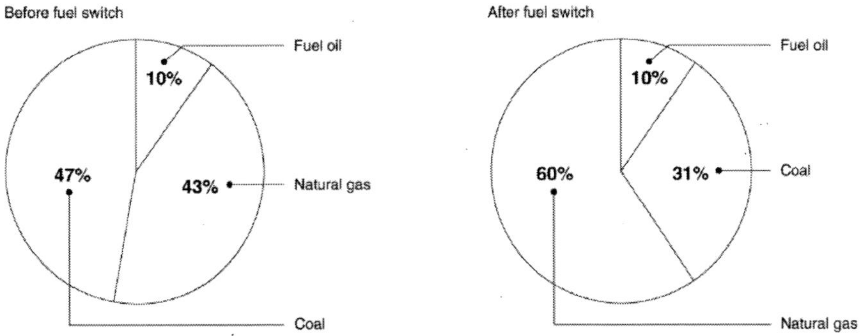


Note: Due to rounding, percentages do not add up to 100 percent in both charts.

Figure 1. Projected Change in CPP Fuel Use.

Specifically, AOC estimated that the cost in fiscal year 2008 would total about \$2.75 million. In fiscal year 2009, AOC is requesting a much lower amount—1.22 million—to complete the fuel switch. In its own analysis, LBNL estimated the total cost for fiscal year 2008 at about \$1.88 million.

The discrepancy between our estimates and those developed by AOC and LBNL stems from variations in the methodologies each party employed. Specifically, AOC's analysis involved a scenario in which the plant would burn only natural gas and eliminate the use of coal and fuel oil altogether. This analysis estimated that switching the entire plant to natural gas would cost a total of about \$7.8 million in fiscal year 2008.

Based on this analysis, AOC then estimated that the cost of fuel switching under the initiative would equal approximately 35 percent of the total cost of switching the entire plant. The 35 percent figure was based on the assumption that the House consumed that proportion of the plant's total output, based on the number of square feet of building space served by the plant. This yielded an estimate of \$2.75 million to switch fuels in fiscal year 2008.

To fulfill the initiative's fuel switching directive, AOC officials said that they planned to increase natural gas use from 42 percent of fuel use to 62 percent.

According to our analysis, this would increase natural gas use beyond the initiative's goals.

The analysis conducted by LBNL estimated the total cost at $1.88 million in 2008, a substantially lower figure than the previous estimate developed by AOC. Key differences between our methodology and the methodologies employed by AOC and LBNL follow:

- We based our cost estimates on EIA fuel price projections for fiscal year 2008 and used AOC historical cost data from 2001 through 2007 to estimate the actual cost of the fuel after delivery. In contrast, AOC's analysis used an average of their natural gas costs from 2005 through 2007, which may have inflated the cost estimates, since there were some very high natural gas price spikes during these years. LBNL used natural gas prices from fiscal year 2007.
- We assumed that House buildings use approximately 29 percent of the steam generated by the plant, based on data from AOC's 2006 Annual Report to Congress. We excluded the Ford House Office building from our analysis because it obtains steam from General Services Administration rather than from the plant. In contrast, AOC and LBNL included the Ford Building, which resulted in estimates of 31 percent and 35 percent, respectively.

## Estimated Annual Fuel-Switching Costs Are Expected to Range from $1.2 to $1.4 Million between 2008 and 2012

In addition to estimating the costs for fiscal year 2008, we projected the costs of maintaining the adjusted fuel mix over the 2008 through 2012 time period. Specifically, we estimated that CPP would spend roughly $1.2 to $1.4 million per year over the next 5 years. This amount could run as high as $1.8 million in fiscal year 2009 or as low as $823,000 in 2012, depending on fuel prices.

Table 1 summarizes the potential future costs of maintaining an adjusted fuel mix at CPP and, because of uncertainties about fuel price projections, includes low and high fuel price scenarios.

**Table 1. Projected Cost of Maintaining Adjusted Fuel Mix, 2008 through 2012**

| 2012 Fiscal year | Low fuel price scenario | B aseline scenario | High fuel price scenario |
|---|---|---|---|
| 2008 | $1,002,632 | $1,385,488 | $1,768,343 |
| 2009 | 1,045,606 | 1,435,660 | 1,825,714 |
| 2010 | 952,500 | 1,316,872 | 1,681,244 |
| 2011 | 868,061 | 1,210,391 | 1,552,721 |
| 2012 | 823,029 | 1,151,236 | 1,479,443 |
| Totals | $4,691,828 | $6,499,647 | $8,307,465 |

Similar to our fiscal year 2008 estimate, these projections rely on a number of assumptions which, if changed, would substantially affect the overall cost. In addition to the assumptions cited above, the following factors and assumptions could affect the accuracy of our estimates:

- *Fuel demand.* We estimated that the demand for the plant's steam would decline by 1 percent annually relative to a baseline level of demand equal to that we derived by averaging the annual demand for fiscal years 2001 through 2007. We based the 1 percent annual decline in demand on two important and partially offsetting considerations:
  - Additions to the Capitol Complex, including the Capitol Visitor Center, are expected to increase the plant's steam demand by 1 percent each year through 2025.
  - The Energy Policy Act of 2005 requires a 2 percent reduction in energy use per year for federal buildings. Because over a quarter of House energy use is for heating, the act's implementation may significantly reduce steam demand over time.
- *Fuel costs.* We used fuel price projections for the U.S. industrial sector from EIA fo r the years 2008 through 2012 and adjusted them to reflect our estimat e of the historical difference between these prices and the AOC per- unit cost of each fuel. Because of the uncertainty of fuel price projections, we constructed a low-price scenario and a high-price scenario for the years 2008 through 2012 based on measures of variability in the historical prices of these fuels.

Of these variables and assumptions, those associated with future fuel prices pose the greatest uncertainty. As we have previously reported, prices may depend on a variety of factors, such as supply, demand, available infrastructure, market conditions, and severe weather events [7]. Since 1999, market conditions generally have fostered an upward natural gas prices according to EIA, will continue until 2009. Starting in 2010, EIA expects natural gas prices to decline until approximately 2016.

Other important considerations can affect demand for the plant's services, including planned or future investments in energy efficiency, weather, and changes in energy or environmental legislation. Because of the uncertain and potentially offsetting effects of these factors on demand for the plant's services, we did not address them in our estimates.

## Fuel Switching Would Reduce Carbon Dioxide Emissions at an Average Cost of about $139 per Ton; Other Benefits May Also Accrue

Based on our cost projections for fiscal year 2008, we estimate that the fuel switch would yield carbon dioxide reductions of about 9,970 metric tons [8] per year at an average cost of $139 per ton. We developed this estimate using our $1.4 million cost estimate as a base price and applying EIA's carbon dioxide conversion factors for coal and natural gas. (The world's largest carbon market, the European Union's Emissions Trading Scheme, currently prices a metric ton of carbon at approximately $37.) Additional information on the cost-effectiveness of the fuel-switching strategy relative to other carbon dioxide abatement options would help inform future decision making on fuel switching and related investments intended to decrease emissions.

In April 2007, we recommended that legislative branch agencies establish a schedule for conducting energy audits and implement selected projects as part of a plan to reduce emissions [9]. Such audits have the potential to identify projects that compare favorably to fuel switching.

In addition to reducing carbon dioxide emissions, decreasing the plant's reliance on coal may yield other environmental and health benefits. While coal currently costs less than natural gas, coal's combustion generally produces more carbon dioxide and air pollutants compared to natural gas. These pollutants, in turn, pose a variety of adverse health effects. For example, nitrogen oxides may exacerbate existing conditions such as asthma, and particulate matter has been linked to heart attacks and chronic bronchitis.

Furthermore, acid rain may occur when the sulfur dioxide produced in the combustion of coal at the plant reacts with other chemicals in the atmosphere to form sulfuric acid. Burning less coal may also help Washington, D.C., and neighboring jurisdictions in their efforts to achieve compliance with federal air quality standards. Currently, the city is noncompliant for ground-level ozone and fine particulate matter.

Finally, fuel switching has the potential to reduce costs associated with the transportation, storage, and handling of coal and related waste streams. In addition, coal storage, handling, and related air pollution abatement require the use of electricity, a major source of carbon dioxide, nitrogen oxide, and mercury. As a result, increasing the plant's reliance on natural gas may also yield reductions in such emissions from the power plant and the electricity generating units that provide the plant with electricity.

## THE ABILITY OF U.S. ELECTRICITY-GENERATING UNITS TO SWITCH FROM COAL TO NATURAL GAS IS LIMITED, AND FUEL SWITCHING COULD CAUSE ADVERSE ECONOMIC CONSEQUENCES

### Relatively High Natural Gas Prices Limit the Potential for Fuel Switching from Coal

According to industry stakeholders, switching from coal to natural gas for electricity generation is generally not economically feasible due to the relatively high price of natural gas comp ared to coal, as illustrated in figure 2.

Currently, natural gas costs about four times more than coal per British thermal unit. Due to its higher cost, substituting natural gas for coal would increase operating costs for electricity-generating units. Natural gas fuels about 20 percent of electricity production in the United States and, according to one stakeholder, accounts for 55 percent of the electric utility industry's entire fuel expense ($50 billion out of $91 billion). In addition, natural gas has shown a higher rate of price increases over time relative to coal, according to EIA, and as illustrated in figure 3, natural gas prices have been volatile in recent years.

The market for natural gas has been susceptible to extreme price swings when unexpected changes occur in the market, such as weather-related spikes in demand or supply constraints caused by hurricane damage.

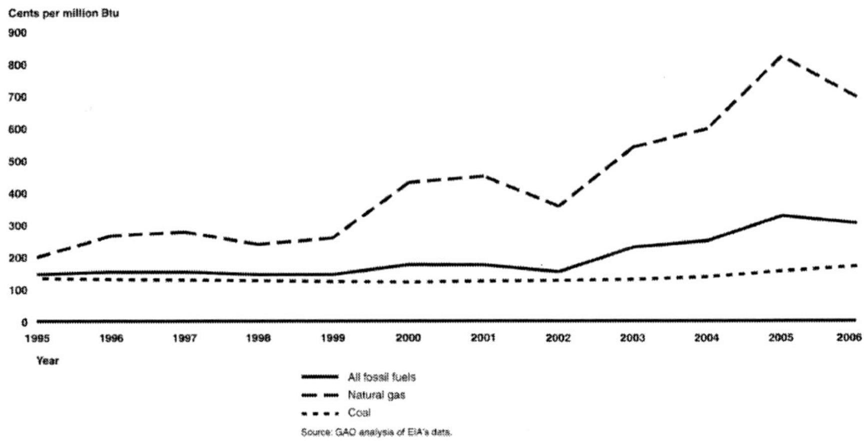


Note: Average cost is not adjusted for inflation.

Figure 2: Average Cost of Fuels for the Electric Power Industry, 1995 through 2006.

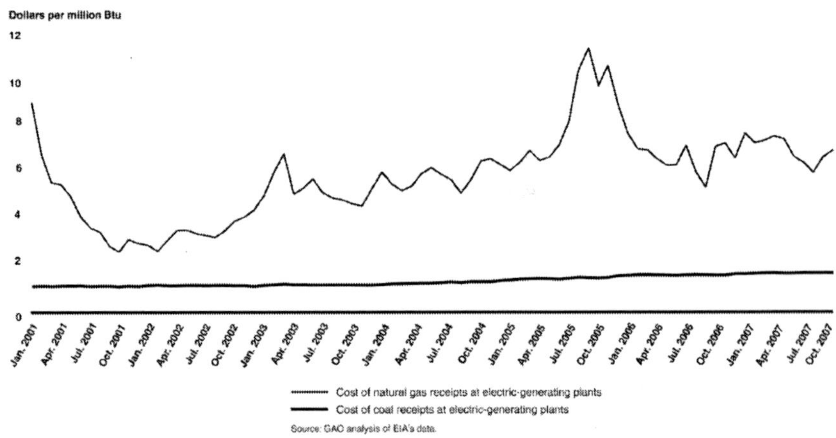


Figure 3. Natural Gas and Coal Costs at U.S. Electric-Generating Plants, 2001 through 2007.

## Constrained Natural Gas Supply Limits Fuel Switching from Coal

In addition to the relatively high price of natural gas, the ability of coal-fired, electricity-generating units to switch fuels is constrained by the available supply of natural gas. According to industry stakeholders, the United States already faces serious supply problems without a potential increase in demand due to fuel switching. According to industry stakeholders and available EIA data, U.S.

natural gas production peaked in 1973, and the average productivity of natural gas wells in the United States has declined for the past 35 years due to diminishing output of older wells and lower yields and higher depletion rates from more recent discoveries. EIA projects that natural gas production will not increase in the lower 48 U.S. states over the next 20 years. According to industry stakeholders, the United States has already found and used its easily recoverable natural gas and finding new gas requires drilling deeper and in more inaccessible locations, raising production costs. One stakeholder said that it is increasingly difficult to keep output constant because about one-third of U.S. natural gas production has to be replaced every year. Thus, the United States has limited capability to meet growing demand for natural gas with domestic production.

Consequently, widespread fuel switching at electricity-generating units would increase demand for natural gas beyond the capabilities of existing and projected supply. Stakeholders noted that the United States would require nearly twice as much natural gas supply by 2030, as currently projected by EIA, if the United States were to replace all coal-fired plants with natural gas. According to one stakeholder, replacing even one-half of coal-fired generation after 2015 with natural gas would lead to an overwhelming demand. Industry stakeholders said it is not possible to increase supplies by this magnitude, especially in light of a trend toward increas ed global demand and consumption.

Because of limited domestic supplies, meeting additional demand would require imports from Canada, pipelines from Alaska, or liquefied natural gas (LNG) from overseas suppliers. [10]. According to one stakeholder, imports, primarily from Canada, have steadily grown to comprise about 10 to 15 percent of U.S. supply. However, Canadian exports are declining as a result of decreased drilling and increased domestic demand. EIA identifies this as a significant problem facing the U.S. natural gas market, according to one stakeholder. In addition, prospects for an Alaskan pipeline and other pipelines are unclear, creating further supply concerns for the U.S. market.

With widespread fuel switching, the United States would be more dependent on imported LNG, according to industry stakeholders. The EIA's Annual Energy Outlook 2007 projected major increases in LNG imports into the United States. According to one stakeholder, all of the natural gas required by large-scale fuel switching with LNG by 2015 would require more than 50 percent of the global supply. Another stakeholder estimated that LNG supplies would be insufficient for the United States to fully switch from coal to natural gas unless the United States captured at least 90 percent of the world LNG market, which seems highly unlikely because of the significant projected growth in natural gas demand in the rest of the world.

## Fuel Switching for Electricity-Generating Units Would Require Investment in New and Existing Infrastructure

Switching from coal to natural gas would require investment in new infrastructure and changes to existing infrastructure, including pipeline and storage capacity and generation technologies employed at existing coal plants. In theory, all coal units can be physically switched from coal to natural gas, but stakeholders said this practice would not occur broadly due, in part, to inadequate existing distribution networks and storage capacity, including pipelines.

According to stakeholders, burning natural gas at an existing coal plant would require a pipeline with the ability to meet the plant's fuel supply requirements. If not, a new gas pipeline would have to be sited, permitted, designed, and constructed. Almost all coal-fired boilers use some natural gas to ignite and regulate combustion, but they require relatively small amounts of natural gas with correspondingly small supply pipelines. Thus, existing coal-fired units would have to enhance their supply pipelines to switch to natural gas. As a result, according to stakeholders, a major fuel-switching program would require a nationwide natural gas infrastructure construction program. This would require expansion of interstate and intrastate pipelines to transport increased volumes of natural gas. Furthermore, existing plants and local natural gas distribution systems would have to increase their storage capacity. Local storage can help buffer variations in demand, and addressing local storage requirements could pose challenges, according to stakeholders. Increased reliance on natural gas would also require other new infrastructure, such as LNG terminals.

Even with sufficient supply and storage capacity, stakeholders said that it would be more feasible and cost-effective to construct new natural gas units or dispatch excess capacity at existing natural gas units instead of fuel switching. Converting a coal- burning plant to natural gas would involve significant capital costs and result in a less efficient plant with higher operating costs. At a minimum, an existing boiler designed for coal would need a new combustion system and a new heating surface to account for the differences between coal and gas combustion, according to stakeholders. Because a gas-fired steam generator is designed differently from a coal-fired boiler, burning natural gas in a coal-fired boiler would result in a loss of efficiency, which could decrease the amount of electricity produced by the unit. According to one stakeholder, a decrease in capacity of 10 to 12 percent is a reasonable estimate. As a result, certain stakeholders said that it would be more economically efficient in terms of capital and fuel costs to tear down an existing coal unit and build a new natural gas unit instead of retrofitting an existing coal unit to burn natural gas. In addition, industry stakeholders said that some coal-fired units cannot switch fuels because natural gas is not available, existing technology cannot be modified, or the system reserve is so low in the area that shutting down the coal plant for conversion to natural gas would result in brownouts or blackouts. One stakeholder stated that modifying a coal unit to burn natural gas would take the unit out of service for 4 to 6 months.

In the few instances in which the industry has switched from coal to gas, existing plants have not been retrofitted to burn gas; instead, existing gas-fired units have displaced generation from marginally cost-effective coal-fired units rather than retrofitting existing plants to burn gas. Industry stakeholders said that many natural gas-fired power plants were constructed in the late 1990s and early 2000s, leading to a large amount of underutilized capacity at plants constructed during this boom. According to one stakeholder, it is likely that, instead of fuel switching at coal plants, utilities would dispatch these underutilized natural gas units and run coal units less aggressively. EIA data describing the average capacity factors of different generation options demonstrate that significant excess capacity exists at natural-gas-fired plants. Capacity factor, in general terms, measures how intensely and frequently a generating unit is run [11]. According to EIA, the average capacity factor for natural gas units is much lower than capacity factors for other generation options, such as nuclear and coal. As illustrated in figure 4, nuclear and coal-fired generation have the highest average capacity factors for 2006 at 89.6 percent and 72.6 percent, respectively.

As a result, coal and nuclear capacity serve base load energy requirements [12]. In 2006, average capacity factors for natural gas units ranged from 38.5 to 10.7 percent, depending upon the specific type of natural gas unit. Accordingly, there is potential to increase the utilization of existing natural gas units. Furthermore, the fact that there is excess capacity at existing natural gas units demonstrates the economic and other barriers to using natural gas for electricity production.

In the event that the owners or operators of a plant decided to switch from coal to natural gas, changes to infrastructure, including pipelines and individual electricity- generating units, would require regulatory approval, which can be costly and time- consuming to obtain. Certain stakeholders said that it may take years to complete all of the mandatory permitting requirements before constructing pipelines.

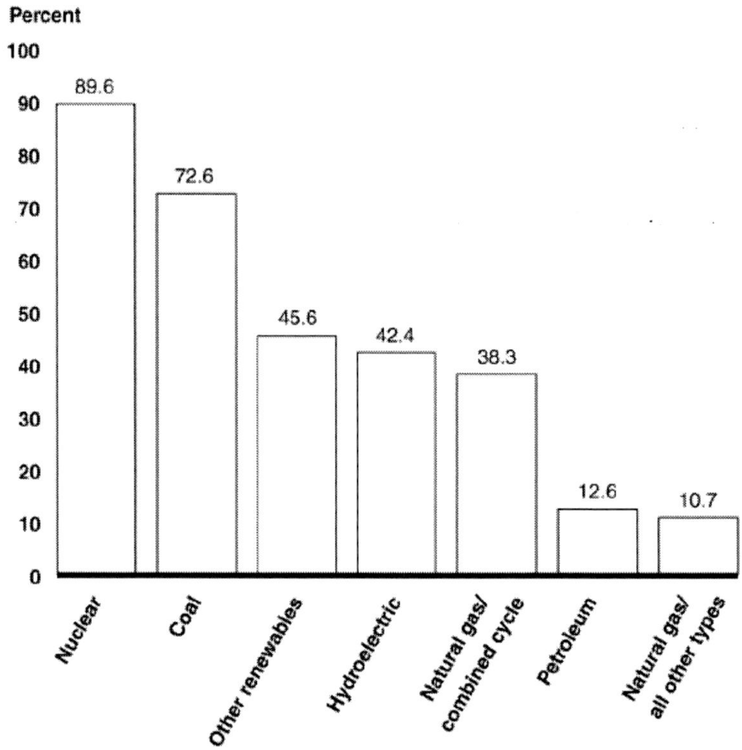


Source: Energy Information Administration, Form EIA-860, "Annual Electrci Generator Report" From EIA-906, "Power Plant Report" and Form EIA-920, "Combined Heat and Power Plant Report"

Figure 4. Average Capacity Factor by Energy Source, 2006.

One stakeholder had significant reservations about whether the industry could obtain the required permits and rights-of-way for such an undertaking. However, this stakeholder also said that the natural gas industry may acquire rights-of-way by eminent domain rights, which could help address pipeline-siting and construction challenges. Stakeholders also identified air quality issues as a concern in retrofitting a coal plant to burn natural gas. Modifying the equipment at an existing coal plant could trigger permitting requirements and necessitate the purchase of additional air pollution control technologies. Several stakeholders said that modifying air permits would not be difficult, but that it would take time for the regulatory agencies to review the applications and issue revised permits.

## Fuel Costs and Electricity Prices Could Increase As a Result of Fuel Switching, among Other Adverse Economic Consequences

Fuel switching and related pressure on available natural gas supplies could increase the price of natural gas, increasing energy costs for residential, commercial, and industrial consumers for both natural gas and electricity. Because energy costs account for a relatively large share of overall costs or because they are heavily dependent on natural gas, for some residential and industrial consumers, any price increases can present significant difficulties. According to industry stakeholders, higher natural gas prices would affect millions of residential consumers who cook and heat their homes and water with natural gas. In 2006, we reported that the effect of higher wholesale natural gas prices on consumers depends largely on the degree to which the consumers or their suppliers may have purchased gas on the spot market— which reflects current wholesale prices—or may have taken steps to reduce their exposure to these prices [13]. The effect of higher prices also depends on the consumer's sensitivity to price changes. Some consumers, such as low-income residents and certain high-energy intensive industries, are more sensitive to price changes than others and appear likely to experience the greatest impact.

As we reported in 2006, high natural gas prices adversely affected industrial consumers. In particular, industries that rely on natural gas, such as chemical and fertilizer manufacturers, could face increased fuel costs. Other affected industries could include iron, steel, automobile manufacturing, glass, aluminum, plastics, paper and machinery, according to industry stakeholders. High fuel costs could make these industries less competitive internationally, according to stakeholders. Recent high natural gas prices forced some industrial consumers to shut down production facilities, and further cutbacks could occur if prices are high in the future.

According to industry stakeholders, increases in the price of natural gas could also lead to electricity price increases. In the late 1990s and early 2000s, the combination of low gas prices and the fact that natural gas produces less air pollution than coal led to the construction of many new natural gas plants. However, these plants are currently underutilized because gas prices have risen substantially in recent years. Requirements to utilize these plants instead of coal plants could lead to higher electricity costs for consumers because some producers would be able to pass on their increased operating costs to consumers.

### Potential Benefits of Fuel Switching Include Reductions in Emissions and in Some Operation and Maintenance Costs, and Improvements in Local Environmental Benefits

Switching from coal to natural gas could decrease airborne emissions of carbon dioxide and air pollutants that cause adverse health effects, including nitrous oxide, sulfur dioxide, and particulates. Natural gas is the cleanest fossil fuel to burn in terms of air quality and carbon emissions, emitting up to 60 percent less carbon dioxide than coal when burned, according to industry stakeholders. However, stakeholders said that the magnitude of these benefits would depend on the source of the natural gas and other factors, such as plant efficiency.

For example, one stakeholder said that increased reliance on LNG would result in smaller carbon dioxide emission reductions relative to coal than those through production and consumption of domestic natural gas because of the carbon dioxide emissions associated with the processing and transportation of imported LNG. In addition, utilities switching from coal to natural gas could gain public relations benefits from emission reductions, as well as a potential advantage associated with early action toward compliance with any future emissions reductions policies.

Fuel switching from coal to natural gas could also decrease some operations and maintenance costs, in addition to lessening the physical impact on the surrounding environment. For example, fuel switching to natural gas would decrease the costs of storing coal on site and grinding it in preparation for combustion. In addition, according to one stakeholder, natural gas infrastructure has less of an impact on the surrounding environment because plants are modular and have smaller footprints than coal-burning facilities. Also, natural gas is delivered by pipelines, which are less visible than the infrastructure required for transporting and storing coal, particularly in urban areas, because they are often buried.

## CONCLUSIONS

Burning natural gas instead of coal at CPP and at electricity-generating units nationwide as part of efforts to reduce greenhouse gas emissions involves important tradeoffs related to economic, environmental, infrastructure, and fuel supply considerations. While CPP can adjust its fuel mix to burn more natural gas, doing so at existing electricity-generating units nationwide poses substantial challenges because of fuel supply constraints, infrastructure that would require modification, and economic considerations.

With respect to fuel switching at CPP, AOC's plans to purchase more natural gas than necessary under the Green the Capitol initiative raises questions about the efficient use of appropriated funds. Specifically, we estimated that fuel switching at the plant should cost between $1.0 and $1.8 million in 2008, well below the $2.75 million budgeted for this purpose. Key uncertainties with our estimates include the future price of each fossil fuel burned at the plant and the lack of complete, reliable information on the overall efficiency of the plant or its seven boilers. Based on our estimates, substituting natural gas for a portion of the coal used at the plant would achieve reductions in carbon dioxide emissions at a cost of about $139 per ton of emissions. We believe that any decisions to exceed the level of fuel switching called for by the initiative should take into consideration the sense of the Congress with respect to achieving greenhouse gas reductions at the plant, as well as the economic and environmental tradeoffs associated with the use of each fuel.

## Recommendation for Executive Action

We are recommending that, before adjusting the Capitol Power Plant's fuel mix beyond the level directed by the Green the Capitol initiative, the Acting Architect of the Capitol consult with AOC's oversight committees in the Congress and evaluate the economic and environmental trade-offs associated with the use of each fuel at the plant, taking into account the efficiency of the plant's boilers, related fuel supply systems, and pollution control equipment.

## Agency Comments and Our Evaluation

We provided a draft copy of this report to the Acting Architect of the Capitol for review and comment. AOC provided comments via electronic mail. AOC officials said that they agreed with our cost estimate under the high fuel price scenario but that they were concerned about the potential level of resources that would be required to respond to our recommendation. We subsequently met with AOC officials who said that they were concerned that implementing our recommendation would require them to collect exact information on the efficiency of its boilers and fuel supply systems. Based on this discussion, we adjusted the wording of the recommendation to clarify that this was not our intent. AOC also provided a number of technical clarifications regarding the plant's operation and their cost estimates for fuel switching, which we incorporated into our report as appropriate. We are sending copies of this report to the appropriate congressional committees. We are also sending this report to the Architect of the Capitol and the Department of Energy. We will make copies available to others upon request. In addition, this report will be available at no cost on the GAO Web site at http://www.gao.gov.

If you or your staffs have any questions about this report, please contact Terrell Dorn at (202) 512-6923 or dornt@gao.gov or Frank Rusco at (202) 512-3841 or ruscof@gao.gov. Contact points for our Offices of Congressional Relations and Public Affairs may be found on the last page of this report. GAO staff who made major contributions to this report are listed in enclosure II.

Terrell Dorn, Director Physical Infrastructure Issues

Frank Rusco, Director, National Resources And Environment
Enclosures

## Enclosure I: Scope and Methodology

To respond to the first objective, we reviewed two analyses prepared for the House of Representatives' Chief Administrative Officer (CAO), including an analysis prepared by the Architect of the Capitol (AOC) that served as the basis for the fuel-switching funding in the Capitol Power Plant's (CPP) fiscal year 2008 appropriation, and a subsequent analysis prepared by the Department of Energy's Lawrence Berkeley National Laboratory (LBNL). We then developed our own analysis based on data provided by AOC and U.S. Energy Information Administration (EIA). Part of our analysis was consistent with LBNL's approach. The primary differences are that we extended LBNL's analysis to future years based on projections of fuel use and prices.

In conducting our analysis, we relied on fuel input data from AOC that had been provided to LBNL via AOC's "Utilities Guru" database. In its analysis, LBNL had converted the fuel quantities from physical units to thermal units (expressed in millions of British thermal units). Next, we estimated the portion of steam produced by CPP that is used to heat House buildings. To do this, we divided the total square footage of House buildings by the total square footage served by the plant, based on data from the AOC's 2006 Report to Congress [14 ].We excluded the Ford House Office Building from our analysis because its steam is supplied by General Services Administration, not CPP. The resulting calculation indicated that approximately 29 percent of the plant's steam output is attributable to the House of Representatives.

Because the initiative recommends that CPP use natural gas to meet the energy needs of the House, we assumed that the House's 29 percent of steam would be provided by natural gas only. We added to this an amount of natural gas equivalent to 71 percent of the total natural gas used had the fuel switching not occurred. This last step ensures that the amount of natural gas is "additional" to what would have occurred in a business-as-usual scenario. We based our business-as-usual scenario on the plant's historical average of 43 percent natural gas, 47 percent coal, and 10 percent fuel oil over the period from 2001 through 2007. We left the amount of fuel oil used unchanged because the plant's operations require the use of fuel oil as a back-up fuel. These calculations enabled us to approximate the level of natural gas required to meet the initiative's directive in fiscal year 2008.

To calculate the incremental cost of the new fuel mix in fiscal year 2008, we estimated the total cost of fuel under the Green the Capital scenario and subtracted our estimate of fuel cost under the business-as-usual scenario. For both scenarios, we multiplied the quantities of fuels needed by our estimates of the average cost of fuel per unit. We based our estimates of the average cost per unit for each fuel on fiscal year 2008 price projections from EIA. We escalated the EIA-projected prices by percentage "premiums" based on estimated relationships between average U.S. fuel prices in the industrial sector, as reported by EIA, and AOC's annual average fuel costs per unit over the period from 2001 through 2007.

We assumed that each boiler at the plant converts fuel into steam with equal efficiency based on a review of available data from an independent consultant to GAO and from Ross Associates, a consultant to AOC. We also requested information from AOC on the efficiency of its boilers on three occasions between November 2007 and January 2008. In January 2008, AOC referred us to the Ross Associates analysis. In April 2008, AOC provided data on the combustion efficiency of its coal boilers and two of the four boilers that can burn oil or natural gas, which it collected during February 2008. Because AOC did not make us aware of this analysis or provide any results until after we had completed our work, time constraints precluded us from assessing its reliability or including it in our analysis. A review of the data suggests that it would not have made a material difference in our cost estimates.

As part of our analysis, we projected the AOC's per unit costs of natural gas, coal, and fuel oil for CPP for the period from 2008 through 2012. To estimate a baseline level of fuel consumption for the years 2008 through 2012, we started with the average fuel consumption by CPP during fiscal years 2001 through 2007. We then applied a 1 percent decline in demand each year, beginning in 2008. The 1 percent estimate is based on two partially offsetting factors:

- Additions to the Capitol Complex, including the Capitol Visitor Center, are expected to increase the plant's steam demand by 1 percent each year through 2025. This estimate was obtained from a 2004 report developed by an AOC consultant.
- The Energy Policy Act of 2005 requires a 2 percent reduction in energy use per year for federal buildings. Because over one-quarter of House energy use is for heating, the act's implementation may significantly reduce steam demand over time.

Next, we estimated the incremental cost of the fuel mix under a Green the Capitol scenario over what the cost would be without a policy change, for each year between 2008 through 2012. To do so, we used EIA-projected fuel prices for the industrial sector escalated with our estimated AOC cost premiums. These calculations produced a baseline cost scenario for each year, ranging from a high of $1.44 million in fiscal year 2009 to a low of $1.15 million in fiscal year 2012.

We also conducted sensitivity analyses around our baseline estimates using a low- price and a high-price scenario for fiscal years 2008 to 2012. EIA has not yet published new low- and high-price projections because of their recent revision of the Annual Energy Outlook 2008. To estimate low- and high-price projections, we adjusted the EIA projections of fuel prices for the industrial sector using measures of variability of these prices in the last few years. Specifically, we calculated the coefficient of variation [15] of monthly prices of coal, natural gas, and distillate oil in the U.S. industrial sector over the period of December 2003 through November 2007 [16]. The coefficient of variation for the monthly prices for this period were: 18.2 percent for the price of natural gas, 6.5 percent for coal, and 17.2 percent for fuel oil. For the- low price scenario, we reduced EIA's price projections for each of the three fuels by the corresponding percentage, while for the high-price scenario, we escalated the price projections by the same percentages.

All of our cost estimates are in constant 2006 dollar values. In preparing our estimates, we consulted with AOC staff, officials representing the House CAO, and the Department of Energy (including LBNL and EIA). We also reviewed relevant studies prepared by these agencies.

To respond to the second objective, we analyzed available data from the Department of Energy and other sources. We also obtained information from key stakeholders identified in discussions with the department that represent the electricity generation, natural gas, and coal industries using written interview questions. These key stakeholders included the American Gas Association (AGA), Edison Electric Institute (EEI), Electric Power Research Institute (EPRI), Interstate Natural Gas Association of America (INGAA), National Coal Council (NCC), National Mining Association (NMA), and Natural Gas Supply Association (NGSA). We conducted our work between October 2007 and April 2008 in accordance with generally accepted government auditing standards. Those standards require that we plan and perform the audit to obtain sufficient, appropriate evidence to provide a reasonable basis for our findings and conclusions based on our audit objectives. We believe that the evidence obtained provides a reasonable basis for our findings and conclusions based on our audit objectives.

# REFERENCES

[1] Chief Administrative Officer of the House of Representatives, Final Report, Green the Capitol Initiative (June 21, 2007). The Green the Capitol initiative establishes the goal of carbon neutrality for the House of Representatives only, whereas CPP also serves the Senate and additional congressional buildings.

[2] According to the Department of Energy's Energy Information Administration, the amount of carbon dioxide emitted from burning pipeline natural gas is 117.08 pounds per million British thermal units (Btu) of energy. The amount generated from burning coal ranges from 205.3 pounds to 227.4 pounds per million Btu and depends on the specific type of coal burned.

[3] Consolidated Appropriations Act, 2008, Committee Print of the House Committee on Appropriations on H.R. 2764/Public Law 110-161 (Legislative Text and Explanatory Statement), 153 *Cong. Rec.* H15479,

H15741 (Dec. 17, 2007). According to a House Appropriations Committee summary of the initial House-passed legislative branch appropriations bill, the Green the Capitol initiative funding in the earlier bill included "...$2.7 million to shift from coal to cleaner burning natural gas for heating needs, $520,000 to switch to 100 percent renewable wind power for electrical needs, $500,000 for an ethanol gas station for House automobiles, and $100,000 for energy efficient compact florescent light bulbs." (See http://appropriations.house.gov/press_releases_2007.aspx, follow link under "August.")

[4] In addition to space heating, these boilers provide energy for other minor services, including humidification and food services. The House of Representatives purchases electricity from an external provider.

[5] The plant's coal boilers underwent a number of renovations and repairs, including a grate replacement, in 2005 and 2006. This may have decreased the amount of coal that the plant would have otherwise burned in those years, leading to a lower average baseline level of coal use.

[6] The difference between AOC's per unit cost of a given fuel and the corresponding average U.S. price of the same fuel in the industrial sector can be due to various factors, including transportation costs.

[7] GAO, *Natural Gas: Factors Affecting Prices and Potential Impacts on Consumers*, GAO-06-420T (Washington, D.C.: Feb. 13, 2006).

[8] A metric ton is equal to 2,205 pounds, while a short ton, a measurement used in the United States is equal to 2,000 pounds.

[9] GAO, Legislative Branch: *Energy Audits Are Key to Strategy for Reducing Greenhouse Gas Emissions*, GAO-07-516 (Washington, D.C.: Apr. 25, 2007).

[10] EIA defines LNG as natural gas (primarily methane) that has been liquefied by reducing its temperature to -260 degrees Fahrenheit at atmospheric pressure. LNG and other liquefied petroleum gases are liquefied through pressurization for convenience of transportation.

[11] The EIA definition of capacity factor is "the ratio of the electrical energy produced by a generating unit for the period of time considered to be the electrical energy that could have been produced at continuous full power operation during the same period."

[12] EIA defines base load capacity as the generating equipment normally operated to serve loads on an around-the-clock basis. According to EIA, a base load plant usually houses high-efficiency, steam- electric units, which are normally operated to take all or part of the minimum load of a system, and which consequently produce electricity at an essentially constant rate

and run continuously. These units are operated to maximize system mechanical and thermal efficiency and minimize system operating costs.

[13] GAO, *Natural Gas: Factors Affecting Prices and Potential Impacts on Consumers*, GAO-06-420T (Washington, D.C.: Feb. 13, 2006).

[14] The buildings used by the House of Representatives that were included in our analysis are: Cannon House Office Building, Longworth House Office Building, Rayburn House Office Building, East and West underground garages, and the House Page Dorm. Our analysis also includes 50 percent of the U.S. Capitol building and CPP.

[15] The coefficient of variation is defined as the standard deviation divided by the mean.

[16] At the time of writing, December 2007 was the last month for which prices of these fuels were available from EIA.

In: Recycling and Green Programs at the Capital… ISBN 978-1-60692-980-3
Editor: H. Y. Kim, pp. 191-201 

*Chapter 6*

# STATEMENT OF BRENDAN OWENS OF THE U.S. GREEN BUILDING COUNCIL BEFORE THE SENATE COMMITTEE ON RULES AND ADMINISTRATION ON IMPROVING ENERGY EFFICIENCY, INCREASING THE USE OF RENEWABLE SOURCES OF ENERGY, AND REDUCING THE CARBON FOOTPRINT OF THE CAPITOL COMPLEX JUNE 18, 2008

## EXECUTIVE SUMMARY

Buildings are responsible for 39% of U.S. CO2 emissions per year. In addition, buildings annually account for 39% of U.S. primary energy use; use 12.2% of all potable water or 15 trillion gallons per year; and consume 40% of raw materials globally. Green buildings create opportunities to mitigate these environmental impacts and also to generate financial savings. As an integral part of the physical and cultural fabric of communities, historic buildings play a critical role in this green revolution, inspiring civic engagement, enabling dense development near public transportation, and attracting integrated public services, among other amenities.

# THE ROLE OF EXISTING BUILDINGS

Through its LEED rating system, the U.S. Green Building Council (USGBC)--a national nonprofit organization of 15,700 member organizations dedicated to transforming the built environment to sustainability--is engaged in improving the environmental and operational performance of both new buildings as well as existing facilities. LEED is a voluntary, third- party certification system for green buildings that was developed to provide the building community with a measurable consensus definition of leadership in energy and environmental design. Originally launched in 2001 for new commercial projects, LEED now includes rating systems for operations and maintenance, commercial interiors, schools, and residences, with additional systems in the pilot stage.

LEED for Existing Buildings: Operations & Maintenance (O & M) provides building owners and managers with a set of sustainable guidelines that address all aspects of building operations, highlighting opportunities to use less energy, water and natural resources; improve the indoor environment; and uncover operating inefficiencies. A key aspect of the program is the owner's development of an integrated plan for reporting, inspecting, and reviewing building operations and maintenance practices to ensure optimal performance throughout the building's life.

Government projects throughout the country, including Colorado's initiatives to green its Capitol complex, are now demonstrating the intrinsic linkages between historic preservation and sustainability. Through an initiative involving more than $23 million in system upgrades and retrofits to 18 state buildings, four of which are involved in LEED, Colorado expects to achieve guaranteed utility budget savings of more than $1 million annually. Colorado project staff report that while some measures may present financial and other challenges to historic projects, L EED certification is a very attainable goal for historic structures.

The federal Capitol complex, which includes many treasured buildings and serves as the heart of the federal government, puts Congress in a position to demonstrate leadership in improving energy efficiency and reducing greenhouse gas emissions. LEED for Existing Buildings: O & M provides a meaningful framework for identifying areas of concentration that have the potential to yield notable improvements to overall environmental impact, while at the same time creating significant financial savings. While USGBC is unable to make specific recommendations for improvements to the Capitol complex without further study of building plans and components, we would be honored to convene a forum of policymakers, architects, designers, and facility managers with authority over the

Capitol complex to identify and generate next steps for improving the energy efficiency and environmental performance of these facilities.

On behalf of the U.S. Green Building Council's (USGBC) 15,700 organizational members and 77 local chapters, I would like to thank Chairman Feinstein and Ranking Member Bennett for the opportunity to testify about the role that green building can play in improving the energy efficiency and sustai nabi lity of the Capitol complex. My name is Brendan Owens, and I am a Vice President with the U.S. Green Building Council.

## INTRODUCTION

The U.S. Green Building Council is a national nonprofit organization working to address current climate and energy challenges by advancing more environmentally responsible, healthy and profitable buildings. Green buildings are an essential element of a climate change mitigation strategy: they reduce greenhouse gas emissions and owners' utility bills, and they have a positive and increasingly well-understood impact on health and well-being. While new buildings offer the potential to integrate innovative green technologies and practices from the start, existing buildings offer an unparalleled opportunity to transform the built environment on a massive scale. As an integral part of the physical and cultural fabric of communities, historic buildings play a critical role in this green revolution, inspiring civic engagement, enabling dense development near public transportation, and attracting integrated public services, among other amenities.

We commend the Committee for its leadership in convening this important hearing to explore opportunities for reducing the environmental impact of the Capitol Complex, which includes several of the nation's most beloved and widely recognized structures.

## THE IMPACT OF THE BUILT ENVIRONMENT

On the aggregate, buildings are responsible for 39% of U.S. CO2 emissions per year [1]. In addition, buildings annually account for 39% of U.S. primary energy use; [2] use 12.2% of all potable water or 15 trillion gallons per year; [3] and consume 40% of raw materials globally (3 billion tons annually) [4]. The EPA estimates that 136 million tons of building-related construction and demolition debris are generated in the U.S. in a single year [5]. (By way of comparison, the U.S. creates 209.7 million tons of municipal solid waste per year [6]) It is clear that we must act quickly to reduce the impact of the built environment on our planet.

Policymakers and building owners alike are now embracing green building as one of the most effective strategies for meeting the challenges of energy consumption and climate change. By addressing the whole building, from construction materials to cleaning supplies, green building generates opportunities to reduce emissions and environmental impact throughout the supply chain and the complete building lifecycle, targeting:

- reduced energy consumption through the use of energy-efficient heating and cooling systems, renewable power, and building commissioning
- reduced water consumption through the use of low-flow fixtures and appliances, and the on-site treatment of storm water
- reduced waste and improved environmental performance through the use of salvaged, recycled, and local materials, and the development of plans for managing construction waste, and
- reduced emissions and environmental impact by promoting the location of facilities near public transportation, the use of hybrid or electric cars, and the use of alternative means of transportation, such as bicycles and walking

Importantly, the technology to make substantial reductions in energy use and CO2 emissions in buildings already exists; modest investments in energy-saving and other climate-friendly technologies can yield buildings and communities that are significantly less carbon intensive, and are also more profitable and healthy places to live and work. In its December 2007 report evaluating potential solutions for reducing greenhouse gas emissions, McKinsey & Company highlighted improvements to the energy efficiency of buildings and appliances as a “negative-cost” option, suggesting that investments of this kind would yield positive financial returns over the course of their life cycle [7].

## The Role of Existing Buildings

Existing buildings can play an important role in reducing greenhouse gas emissions and improving energy efficiency. Through its LEED (Leadership in Energy and Environmental Design) rating system, USGBC is engaged in improving the environmental and operational performance of both new green commercial buildings as well as existing facilities.

LEED is a voluntary, third-party certification system for green buildings that was developed by USGBC to provide the building community with a measurable consensus definition of leadership in energy and environmental design. First launched publicly in 2001, LEED seeks to set a high bar for environmental and energy performance, and challenges market leaders to meet it, building momentum for best practices and moving the whole market forward as these best practices enter the mainstream.

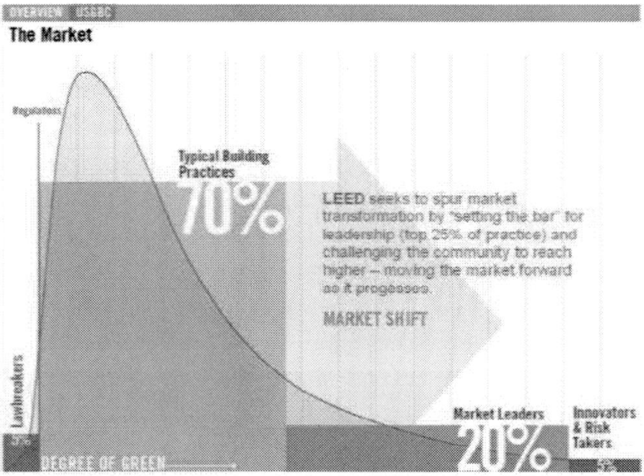


As USGBC's primary tool for advancing market transformation to sustainability, LEED must be continuously improved – seeking to make obsolete its greatest triumphs. Originally launched in 2001 for new commercial construction projects, LEED has completed a series of improvement cycles to respond to market demand and technical innovation. USGBC released rating systems for the operations and maintenance and commercial interiors markets in 2006, and for the schools and residential sectors in 2007. USGBC is also pilot-testing and nearing completion of rating systems for neighborhood developments, healthcare facilities, retail spaces, labs, and campuses.

Earlier this year, USGBC launched LEED for Existing Buildings: Operations and Maintenance, a revised and streamlined version of its rating system for existing facilities.

## LEED for Existing Buildings: Operations and Maintenance

Inefficient buildings are costly for both the environment and building owners. LEED for Existing Buildings: Operations & Maintenance (O&M) provides building owners and managers with an outline for improving and operating their facilities in a sustainable and efficient manner over time. To facilitate this effort, the rating system provides a set of sustainable guidelines that address all aspects of building operations, highlighting opportunities to use less energy, water and natural resources; improve the indoor environment; and uncover operating inefficiencies. A key aspect of the program is the owner's development of an integrated plan for reporting, inspecting, and reviewing building operations and maintenance practices to ensure optimal performance throughout the building's life.

To be awarded certification under LEED for Existing Buildings: O&M, a project must comply with certain minimum requirements (or "prerequisites") and earn a minimum point total, achieved through the owner's selection of additional optional credits. In contrast to the other LEED rating systems, which focus on the design and construction phases, LEED for Existing Buildings: O & M evaluates how buildings are operated on a day-to-day basis once completed and occupied. To this end, projects are required to submit actual performance data as part of the certification process to demonstrate that they are achieving the indicated performance measures. Once submitted, certification documentation is evaluated by third-party reviewers, and USGBC awards a project one of four progressive levels of LEED certification (Certified, Silver, Gold or Platinum) to reflect the number of credits achieved.

Please see the attached LEED for Existing Buildings: Operations & Maintenance checklist for additional specifics about rating system requirements and credits.

# LEED and the Government Sector

Governments at all levels have been highly influential in the growth of green building, both by requiring LEED for their own buildings and by creating incentives for LEED for the private sector. Currently, 12 federal agencies or departments, 28 states, 120+ local governments, 13 public school jurisdictions and 36 higher education institutions have made various policy commitments to use or encourage LEED.

In 2006, the U.S. General Services Administration (GSA)--the nation's largest civilian landlord--submitted a report to Congress evaluating the applicability, stability, objectivity, and availability of five different sustainable building rating systems [8]. Based on this study, GSA concluded that L EED "continues to be the most appropriate and credible sustainable building rating system available for evaluation of GSA projects" [9]. In particular, GSA noted that LEED "[i]s applicable to all GSA project types; [t]racks the quantifiable aspects of sustainable design and building performance; [i]s verified by trained professionals; [h]as a well-defined system for incorporating updates; and [i]s the most widely used rating system in the U.S. market." [10] GSA currently requires its new construction projects and substantial renovations to achieve L EED certification [11].

Government projects throughout the country, including Colorado's initiatives to green its Capitol complex, are now demonstrating the intrinsic linkages between historic preservation and sustainability.

## Colorado State Capitol Complex

Since 2003, Colorado has been engaged in a performance contracting project that leverages guaranteed utility savings from facility upgrades to finance facility improvements, including heating and cooling system upgrades, water conservation retrofits, lighting upgrades, and green purchasing programs, among other measures. The initiative involves more than $23 million in upgrades to 18 state buildings, including the historic State Capitol Building. Colorado reports guaranteed utility budget savings of more than $1 million each year from these projects.

The State Capitol Building, at 320,000 square feet in size and more than 100 years in age, is the fourth state facility in Colorado to apply for certification under LEED for Existing Buildings. The successes and challenges experienced by the Capitol project are instructive in evaluating potential improvements to the federal Capitol complex.

Staff attribute their success in implementing improvements to the Capitol complex in part to Governor Bill Ritter's "Greening of State Government" Executive Order, which outlines sustainability goals to be achieved by 2012 and adds both "justification and accountability" to their sustainability initiatives. The project has also benefited from the participation and growing experience of Capitol operations and maintenance staff, who have implemented and gained an understanding of the value of high performance operations and maintenance practices. Staff also report that LEED for Existing Buildings, which requires projects to verify their energy use and the proper functioning of their equipment, has generated increased attention to the "measurement and verification" of utility savings in state facilities.

Staff report that while certification under LEED for Existing Buildings is a very attainable goal for historic structures, it is not without some challenges. For example, the restoration of Capitol windows was identified as a conservation measure to be pursued, but was not cost effective, and thus, was not performed. Improvements to the facility's insulation also proved financially infeasible due to the cost of restoring plaster and stone walls. Staff report that they hope to revisit these improvements when funding permits.

### Howard M. Metzenbaum U.S. Courthouse

Large-scale renovations of historic structures have also been certified under LEED for New Construction. Among these projects is the historic Howard M. Metzenbaum U.S. Courthouse in downtown Cleveland, Ohio. In 2005, GSA completed a $44.6 million renovation of the 1910 facility, which spans more than 235,000 square feet. The Beaux-Arts style-building was awarded points for its sustainable site, owing to its location within 1/4 mile of six bus lines, its abatement of hazardous materials throughout the building, and its development in an area with high density. Marrying sustainability and preservation, the project also diverted more than 50% of construction waste through a waste management plan, maintained more than 50% of the building's interior elements, and preserved more than 90% of the building's existing structural shell. Points were also awarded for the project's achievement of a 15% reduction in energy use below the baseline code referenced in LEED and its more than 32% reduction in water use, among other measures.

## Opportunities for the Capitol Complex

As the above case studies demonstrate, sustainable design and historic preservation principles are very much in harmony when considering opportunities to reduce the environmental impact of existing structures. The Capitol complex, which includes many treasured buildings and serves as the heart of the federal government, puts Congress in a position to demonstrate leadership in improving energy efficiency and reducing greenhouse gas emissions.

LEED for Existing Buildings: O&M provides a meaningful framework for identifying areas of concentration that have the potential to yield notable improvements to overall environmental impact, while at the same time creating significant financial savings. Through the development of an integrated plan that coordinates operations and maintenance activities for the years and decades ahead, the federal government can maximize cost savings and lead by example in addressing current and future climate and energy needs. While USGBC is unable to make specific recommendations for improvements to the Capitol complex without further study of building plans and components, we would be honored to convene a forum of policymakers, architects, designers, and facility managers with authority over the Capitol complex to identify and generate next steps for improving the energy efficiency and environmental performance of these facilities.

## About the U.S. Green Building Council

USGBC is a 501(c) (3) nonprofit membership organization working to transform the way buildings and communities are designed, built and operated, enabling an environmentally and socially responsible, healthy, and prosperous environment that improves the quality of life. Our 15,700 member organizations and 91,000 active volunteers include leading corporations and real estate developers, architects, engineers, builders, schools and universities, nonprofits, trade associations and government agencies at the federal, state and local levels.

The organization is governed by a diverse, 31-member Board of Directors that is elected by the USGBC membership. Volunteer committees representing users, service providers, manufacturers, and other stakeholders steward and develop all USGBC programs, including the LEED (Leadership in Energy and Environmental Design) rating system, through well-documented consensus processes.

A staff of more than 140 professionals administers an extensive roster of educational and informational programs that support the LEED Rating System in addition to broad-based support of green building. USGBC's LEED Professional Accreditation program, workshops, green building publications, and the annual Greenbuild conference provide green building education for professionals and consumers worldwide. USGBC has trained more than 50,000 professionals through its green building workshops, and attracted more than 22,000 attendees from around the globe to its most recent Greenbuild conference.

Educational programs are delivered locally through USGBC's more than 70 Chapters and Affiliates, through the Web, and at conferences and events all over the world.

Brendan Owens,
LEED AP, P.E. Vice-President, LEED Technical Development

As the Vice President of LEED® Technical Development at the U.S. Green Building Council, Brendan Owens collaborates with volunteer technical committees to refine and evolve the USGBC's LEED Green Building Rating System. During his time at USGBC, Brendan has led development activities for LEED for New Construction, LEED for Existing Buildings, LEED for Core and Shell and several market specific LEED Application Guides including retail, healthcare facilities and laboratories. Brendan is currently focused on creating the framework for LEED Version 3, a system that promises to be technically more robust and easier to implement.

Brendan is a member of the ASHRAE/USGBC/IESNA committee developing Standard 189.1 – Standard for High-Performance Green Buildings and is a delegate to the United Nations Environmental Programme Sustainable Buildings & Construction Initiative (UNEP/SBCI) Think Tank on Benchmarking Sustainable Buildings. He represents USGBC on the steering committee for the Advanced Energy Design Guide series and the Green Guideline for Healthcare. Prior to joining USGBC, Brendan worked designing and implementing performance contract based energy conservation projects in existing buildings. Brendan also managed the energy conservation program for a 100+ building campus.

Brendan is a LEED Accredited Professional and a licensed Professional Engineer. He received his Bachelor's of Science in Engineering from Purdue University in West Lafayette, IN.

## REFERENCES

[1] EIA Annual Energy Review 2005. U.S. Energy Information Administration, U.S. Department of Energy.

[2] 2003 U.S. DOE Buildings Energy Data Book.

[3] U.S. Geological Service, 1995 data.

[4] Lenssen and Roodman, 1995, "Worldwatch Paper 124: A Building Revolution: How Ecology and Health Concerns are Transforming Construction," Worldwatch Institute.

[5] U.S. EPA Characterization of Construction and Demolition Debris in the United States, 1997 Update.

[6] U.S. EPA Characterization of Municipal Solid Waste in the United States, 1997 Update. Report No. EPA530-R-98- 007.

[7] McKinsey & Company, Reducing Greenhouse Gas Emissions: How Much at What Cost?, available at http://www.mckinsey.com/client service/ccsi/pdf/US_ghg_final_report.pdf.

[8] Pacific Northwest National Laboratory (operated for the U.S. Department of Energy by Battelle), Sustainable Building Rating Systems Summary (July 2006), completed for General Services Administration under Contract D E-AC05-76RL061 830, available at https://www.usgbc.org/Show File.aspx?DocumentID=1915.

[9] Letter dated Sept. 15, 2006 from GSA Administrator Lurita Doan to Sen. Christopher Bond, Chairman, Subcommittee on Transportation, Treasury, the Judiciary, HUD, and Related Agencies, Committee on Appropriations (accompanying report), available at https://www.usgbc.org/ShowFile.aspx?DocumentID=1916; see also Pacific Northwest National Laboratory (operated for the U.S. Department of Energy by Battelle), Sustainable Building Rating Systems Summary (July 2006), completed for General Services Administration under Contract D E-AC05-76RL061 830, available at https://www.usgbc.org/ ShowFile.aspx?DocumentID=1915.

[10] Letter dated Sept. 15, 2006 from GSA Administrator Lurita Doan to Sen. Christopher Bond, Chairman, Subcommittee on Transportation, Treasury, the Judiciary, HUD, and Related Agencies, Committee on Appropriations (accompanying report), available at https://www.usgbc.org/Show File.aspx?DocumentID=1916.

[11] U.S. General Services Administration, Sustainable Design Program, available at http://www.gsa.gov/Portal/gsa/ep/channelView.do?pageTypeld =8195&channelPage=%252Fep%252Fchannel%252 FgsaOverview.j sp&channel Id=-1 2894.

In: Recycling and Green Programs at the Capital… ISBN 978-1-60692-980-3
Editor: H. Y. Kim, pp. 203-211 

*Chapter 7*

# EXECUTIVE SUMMARY TESTIMONY OF JEAN CARROON, FAIA IMPROVING ENERGY EFFICIENCY, INCREASING THE USE OF RENEWABLE SOURCES OF ENERGY, AND REDUCING THE CARBON FOOTPRINT OF THE CAPITOL COMPLEX

In the United States, more than 40% of our carbon emissions are attributed to the construction and operation of buildings. While buildings represent a threat to the health of our planet, the reuse and greening of these structures also presents an enormous opportunity to reduce our nation's carbon emissions. Through improved energy efficiency and an increase in the use of renewable sources of energy at the Capitol Complex, the United States Senate has the opportunity to demonstrate to the American public the important role our older and historic buildings play in reducing carbon emissions.

## EMBODIED ENERGY AND ENERGY USE IN EXISTING BUILDINGS

Older and historic buildings are often not the energy hogs that many people assume. Data from the Department of Energy indicates that commercial buildings constructed before 1920 use less energy per square foot than buildings from any other decade up until 2000. A 1999 study by the General Services Administration found that utility costs in the GSA's inventory of historic buildings are about 27% less than in non-historic structures.

According to a formula produced for the Advisory Council on Historic Preservation, about 80 billion BTUs of energy are embodied in a typical 50,000-square-foot commercial building, the equivalent of about 640,000 gallons of gasoline. Tearing a building down, not only wastes this energy but more energy is required to construct a new building. The United Nations Energy Programme estimates that it takes 20 years of a building's 100 year operation to offset the expenditure of energy and materials in the construction.

The Carnegie Mellon Green Design Institute calculates the greenhouse gas emissions from renovation as 30 to 50 percent less than an equal investment in new construction at the same time 20 percent more jobs are created. The greenest building is one that already exists.

## Holistic Evaluation, Implementation and Maintenance Plans are Key

Successful greening of existing buildings begins with the holistic evaluation of facilities through energy audits and "green teams" followed by a consistent strategy of implementation and maintenance. The most cost-effective energy use reduction is often achieved with many relatively small gestures such as efficient light bulbs, regular replacement of radiator steam traps, programmable controls, attic insulation and the standard repair of windows.

A holistic approach recognizes the interaction of multiple elements and addresses direct energy consumption within buildings in relationship to the larger environment. For example, reducing the heat islands in a campus or city and shading a building with trees and awnings lowers air conditioning requirements and may also limit glare and improve interior day-lighting.

The categories frequently used in evaluating the greening of buildings - sustainable sites, water efficiency, energy and atmosphere, materials & resources, and indoor environmental quality – are interwoven and have a far reaching impact on our carbon footprint. Reducing water use in a building decreases the energy needed elsewhere to process and transport water. Conversely, reducing energy use in buildings reduces the significant amounts of water used in energy plants and building chillers. The synergies of environmental stewardship are endless. As we create healthier places to live and work in walk-able communities rich in heritage we improve our quality of life and lower health care costs as an offshoot of reducing our carbon footprint.

# Testimony of Jean Carroon, FAIA Principal, Goody Clancy and National Trust for Historic Preservation Sustainable Preservation Coalition Member

**Before**
**The Committee on Rules and Administration**
**United States Senate Hon. Dianne Feinstein, Chairman**

**Hearing on**
**Improving Energy Efficiency, Increasing the Use of Renewable Sources of Energy, and Reducing the Carbon Footprint of the Capitol Complex**
**Wednesday,**
**June 18, 2008**

Thank you for the opportunity to share the views and concerns of the National Trust for Historic Preservation regarding the potential for improving the energy efficiency and reducing the carbon footprint of the capitol complex. My name is Jean Carroon and I am the Principal for Historic Preservation with the design firm of Goody Clancy and a member of the National Trust for Historic Preservation's Sustainable Preservation Coalition.

## Background of the National Trust

Congress chartered the National Trust in 1949 as a private nonprofit organization to "facilitate public participation" in historic preservation, and to further the historic preservation policies of the United States. 16 U.S.C. §§ 461,468. With the strong support of our 287,000 members around the country, the National Trust works to protect significant historic sites and to advocate for historic preservation as a fundamental value in programs and policies at all levels of government. In addition to our eight regional field offices throughout the country, and our Washington, DC headquarters, we have 29 diverse Historic Sites open to the public around the country.

Through improved energy efficiency and an increase in the use of renewable sources of energy at the Capitol Complex, the United States Senate has the opportunity to demonstrate to the American public the important role our older and historic buildings play in reducing carbon emissions. I would like to provide the Committee with some specific recommendations for accomplishing this.

## Buildings and Climate Change

In the United States, more than 40% of our carbon emissions are attributed to the construction and operation of buildings [1]. While buildings represent a threat to the health of our planet, the reuse and greening of these structures also presents an enormous opportunity to reduce our nation's carbon emissions.

In recent years, there has been much enthusiasm among architects, green building experts and environmentalists about reducing the environmental footprint of buildings – but the green building movement has been principally focused on greening new construction. While greening new buildings is undeniably an essential element of any effort to combat global warming, even construction of the greenest new building uses significant energy and other natural resources, thereby contributing to global warming.

We simply cannot build our way out of our environmental crisis, we must conserve our way out by making better, more efficient use of our existing buildings. The approximately 300 billion square feet of existing built space in the United State may well be our most significant renewable resource.

## Embodied Energy and Energy Use in Older and Historic Buildings

Older and historic buildings are often not the energy hogs that many people assume. Data from the Department of Energy indicates that commercial buildings constructed before 1920 use less energy per square foot than buildings from any other decade up until 2000 [2]. A 1999 study by the General Services Administration found that utility costs in the GSA's inventory of historic buildings are about 27% less than in non-historic structures [3].

According to a formula produced for the Advisory Council on Historic Preservation, about 80 billion BTUs of energy are embodied in a typical 50,000-square-foot commercial building, the equivalent of about 640,000 gallons of gasoline. Tearing a building down, not only wastes this energy but more energy is required to construct a new building. The United Nations Energy Programme estimates that it takes 20 years of a building's 100 year operation to offset the expenditure of energy and materials in the construction [4].

The Carnegie Mellon Green Design Institute calculates the greenhouse gas emissions from renovation as 30 to 50 percent less than an equal investment in new construction at the same time 20 percent more jobs are created.5 The greenest building is one that already exists.

## Holistic Evaluation, Implementation and Maintenance Plans are Key

Successful greening of existing buildings begins with the holistic evaluation of facilities through energy audits6 and "green teams"7 followed by a consistent strategy of implementation and maintenance. The most cost-effective energy use reduction is often achieved with many relatively small gestures such as efficient light bulbs, regular replacement of radiator steam traps, programmable controls, attic insulation and the standard repair of windows.

A holistic approach recognizes the interaction of multiple elements and addresses direct energy consumption within buildings in relationship to the larger environment. For example, reducing the heat islands in a campus or city and shading a building with trees and awnings lowers air conditioning requirements and may also limit glare and improve interior day-lighting.

The categories frequently used in evaluating the greening of buildings - sustainable sites, water efficiency, energy and atmosphere, materials & resources, and indoor environmental quality – are interwoven and have a far reaching impact on our carbon footprint. Reducing water use in a building decreases the energy needed elsewhere to process and transport water. Conversely, reducing energy use in buildings reduces the significant amounts of water used in energy plants and building chillers. The synergies of environmental stewardship are endless. As we create healthier places to live and work in walk-able communities rich in heritage we improve our quality of life and lower health care costs as an offshoot of reducing our carbon footprint.

## Possible Strategies for Reducing the Carbon Footprint of the Capitol Complex

Holistic evaluation and multiple interwoven actions as a strategy for energy reduction was recognized by the National Trust for Historic Preservation in 1981 with the publication of New Energy from Old Buildings [8] and is a central part of the education and holistic guidelines currently offered on the National Trust website and presented in the metric systems created by the U. S. Green Building Council. Strategies common to historic buildings include, but are not limited to:

- *Public Transportation:* The proximity of the Capitol Complex to a large Intermodal Transportation Hub and the incentive programs created for Senate employees to use public transportation, shared vehicles and bike racks sign can significantly reduce the impact of the Complex allowing for increased green space where cars might once have parked, a reduction in heat islands, a decrease in polluted storm run-off and increasing the potential shading of the buildings.
- *Green Roofs:* The flat roofs and even sloped roofs of many historic buildings often easily accept planted or green roofs which reduce storm water run-off, increase building insulation and lower the summer air temperature.
- *Solar Panels:* Historic buildings with metal and slate roofs can often accept solar panels without damaging the existing fabric. Placement can be discreet and the installations can be reversible.
- *On Site Wind Generation:* Historic sites in Great Britain have taken advantage of new technologies in wind for an almost sculptural element carefully placed on sites with review of the supervising historic groups.
- *Awnings:* Once ever present on all buildings including the most historic, awnings, just like modern light shades, can be used to significantly reduce the solar gain. It is an application that is both reversible and renewable.
- *Interior storm windows*: Windows are a source of great tension between advocates of tight building envelopes and people that appreciate the durability, beauty and repairability of historic wood windows. Existing windows can be improved with good maintenance, interior storms windows and newly developed films that offer similar properties as low-e glass.
- *Lighting Strategies:* Evaluate existing lighting. Make sure it is appropriate to the space and task and only on when needed. Install occupancy sensors and daylighting sensors.
- *Office Equipment and other electronics*: Consider the efficiency of all electronics in the building and what the potentials for energy savings are – powering down and turning off computers, printers, copiers and vending machines.

- *Green Purchasing:* This includes Energy Star-qualified electronics and products used for cleaning, office supplies and in the kitchens and restrooms.
- *Water Conservation:* Modifying existing toilets and faucets to aerate water and limit the operating time of fixtures can reduce water use by 40 percent in existing facilities. Provide filtered water and NOT transported bottled water.
- *Improve Day-lighting:* Where retrofitting is possible, add skylights and movable glass partitions that bring light deep into a building and share it among spaces.
- *Increase Building Use Density*: Take advantage of unused and underutilized spaces by careful space planning and renovations. We calculate energy consumption by square foot without considering whether a building is fully and actively utilized.
- *Install Walkoff Mats and Clean Greening Plans:* Take advantage of new knowledge to decrease the amount of materials carried into a building and the utilization of green cleaning which by itself can significantly reduce the use of chemicals, paper and plastic trash bags.

The potential for greening an existing building and its operations is almost limitless and is an ongoing process of evaluation and change as new technologies, new tools and new information become available. Maintenance and the education and dedication of the facilities staff is absolutely essential, however the rewards for all are significant. The workplace is healthier and often more visually and physically comfortable. New documentation indicates significant increases in productivity and decreases in absenteeism. If implemented effectively, the multiple benefits of more environmentally sensitive O&M practices should also include reduced operating costs.

## About the National Trust for Historic Preservation's Sustainability Initiative

The National Trust for Historic Preservation's Sustainability Initiative, which was launched in 2007, promotes the idea that existing buildings are the ultimate renewable resource, and are crucial to any effort to address climate change. Our work promotes the reuse of existing buildings, reinvestment in older and historic communities, and retrofitting older and historic buildings to achieve energy efficiency. Finally, these principles of sustainable stewardship can be achieved with respect for historic fabric.

## Building Reuse

A sound older building that is abandoned, underused, or demolished is a wasted asset. Putting existing buildings to good use reduces demolition and construction waste and lessens the demand for energy and other resources for new building and materials. We are much too inclined to think of our buildings as disposable, rather than a renewable resource. A 2004 report from the Brookings Institution projects that by 2030 we will have demolished and replaced 82 billion square feet of our current building stock.

It will take as much energy to demolish and reconstruct 82 billion square feet of space (as predicted by the Brookings study) as it would to power the entire state of California – the 10th largest economy in the world with a population of about 36 million people – for 10 years. If we were to rehab even 10% of this 82 billion square feet, we would save enough energy to power the state of New York for well over a year [9].

Construction debris accounts for 25% of the waste in the municipal waste stream each year. Demolishing 82 billion square feet of space will create enough debris to fill 2500 NFL stadiums.

## Reinvestment in Older and Historic Neighborhoods

Each year in the United States, we pave over or otherwise convert to human uses an area equal to the state of Delaware [10]. While sprawl is devouring our landscape, many neighborhoods in the inner city and the inner ring of suburbs are vastly underused. Revitalization of existing neighborhoods promotes efficient land-use patterns and focuses public and private reinvestments in areas where infrastructure is already in place, already paid for. Furthermore, older neighborhoods are typically compact, centrally located, walkable and mass-transit accessible – characteristics that are promoted by advocates of smart growth and the "new urbanism".

Nevertheless, many older buildings are badly in need of energy-efficiency upgrades. There are plenty of techniques and products on the market that make these upgrades much less challenging than they once were.

## Respect for Historic Integrity

An increasing number of sensitive and successful rehabilitation projects demonstrate conclusively that historic buildings can go green without losing the distinctive character that makes them significant and appealing. Architects, developers and property owners do not have to choose between getting the energy-efficiency they want or keeping the character they love; they can have both.

## REFERENCES

[1] Pew Center on Global Climate Change, "*Towards A Climate-Friendly Built Environment*," 2005. Available at: http://www.pewclimate.org/global-warming-in-depth/allreports/buildings.

[2] U. S. Energy Information Agency. Consumption of Gross Energy Intensity for Sum of Major Fuels for Non Mall Buildings. 2003. Available at: http://www.eia.doe.gov/emeu/cbecs2003/detailedtables2003/2003set9/2003 pdf/c3.pdf

[3] Bradley Wolf, Donald Horn, and Constance Ramirez, "*Financing Historic Federal Buildings: An Analysis of Current Practice*." (Washington, D.C. General Services Administration,. 1999.)

[4] United Nations Environment Programme, "*Buildings and Climate Change; Status, Challenge and Opportunities*", 2007, ISBN:978-92-807- 2795-1.

[5] Carnegie Mellon Green Design Institute Life Cycle Assessment Tool, located at www.eiolca.net.

[6] U.S. Government Accountability Office, "*Energy Audits are Key to Strategy for Reducing Greenhouse Gas Emissions*", 2007, GAO-07-516.

[7] U. S. Dept. of Energy, "*Greening Federal Facilities, An Energy, Environmental, and Economic Resource Guide for Federal Facility Managers and Designers*", 2001, DOE/GO-102001-1165.

[8] National Trust for Historic Preservation, New Energy from Old Buildings, The Preservation Press, Washington, D.C. 20036.

[9] Nelson, *Arthur C. Towards a New Metropolis: The Opportunity to Rebuild America.* (Washington, D.C. The Brookings Institution, 2004.)

[10] Sierra Club. "*Sprawl: The Dark Side of the America Dream.*" 1998. Available at: http://www.sierraclub.org/sprawl/report98/report.asp

In: Recycling and Green Programs at the Capital… ISBN 978-1-60692-980-3
Editor: H. Y. Kim, pp. 213-228 

*Chapter 8*

# TESTIMONY OF STEPHEN T. AYERS, AIA ACTING ARCHITECT OF THE CAPITOL JUNE 18, 2008

For the past four decades, the Office of the Architect of the Capitol (AOC) has undertaken initiatives and we continue to implement programs to improve energy efficiency and reduce the environmental impact of the Capitol complex. Our Agency's commitment to reducing energy consumption is integrated into our Strategic Plan, and is carried out through our mission to serve Congress as we serve as stewards of some 16.5 million square feet of buildings and nearly 450 acres of land.

As we develop our long-term plans to address and prioritize the maintenance, renovation, and construction of facilities, we also consider the long-term impact of investments in projects and technologies needed to make our facilities more energy efficient, and are working with Congress to strike the necessary balance to successfully accomplish all goals.

In its efforts to meet the requirements of the Energy Policy Act of 2005 (EPAct) and the Energy Independence and Security Act of 2007 (EISA), the AOC exceeded the EPAct goal of two percent by reducing its energy consumption by 6.5 percent in FY 2006. In addition, for FY 2007, the AOC achieved a total cumulative energy intensity reduction of 6.7 percent over the FY 2003 baseline.

The AOC achieved these goals through a number of practical and effective projects and programs including installing dimmable lighting ballast systems, replacing conventional incandescent light bulbs with CFLs, installing modern heating/cooling systems, auditing the energy consumption of facilities to identify energy saving opportunities, using Energy Savings Performance Contracting, and encouraging and managing a vibrant Capitol complex-wide recycling program.

The AOC's Senate Superintendent's Office has also spearheaded a comprehensive energy program for the Senate Office Buildings. Some of their efforts include, installed more than 4,000 CFLs, replacing steam traps, installed various water conservation measures in restrooms and kitchens, installing bi-level lighting in hallways and renewable, solar energy source lighting in parking lots, and studying the feasibility of installing photovoltaic solar cells or vegetative roofs on Senate Buildings.

The AOC also is working with two Energy Saving Performance Contractors (ESCOs), and we plan to utilize them to achieve a portion of the required energy reductions under the EPAct and EISA. To ensure that our efforts save energy and save taxpayer dollars, we also are planning to conduct additional energy audits. In addition, we have completed studies to identify projects, techniques, and policies which can be implemented to save energy.

There are a number of projects, programs, and initiatives that we have planned to ensure a continued reduction in energy intensity across the Capitol complex. A short list includes improving utility metering, evaluating opportunities for onsite renewable energy such as use of photovoltaics and supplementing existing fuel with biodiesel, analyzing currently-planned facility repairs and upgrades for energy and water savings opportunities, and developing the Capitol Complex Master Plan/Sustainability Framework Plan to ensure an overarching sustainable approach to facilities and grounds administered by Congress.

The AOC is working to identify and implement long-term projects that will fulfill our mission to care for the historic buildings and assets entrusted to our care, and attain the required energy saving goals, while at the same time providing Congress with the best return on its investment.

# TESTIMONY OF STEPHEN T. AYERS, AIA
# ACTING ARCHITECT OF THE CAPITOL

**Before**
**The Committee on Rules and Administration**
**United States Senate**

**Regarding**
**Improving Energy Efficiency, Increasing the Use of Renewable Sources of Energy, and Reducing the Carbon Footprint of the Capitol Complex**
**June 18, 2008**

Madam Chairman, Senator Bennett, members of the Committee, thank you for inviting me here today to discuss the efforts the Office of the Architect of the Capitol (AOC) has undertaken over the past several years, and the initiatives we are currently implementing to improve energy efficiency and reduce the carbon footprint of the Capitol complex.

We appreciate the Congressional leadership's commitment to reduce energy consumption and conserve natural resources, reduce costs, and protect the environment. Our individual actions can add up to a tremendous collective effort and can produce significant results in saving taxpayer dollars and conserving our natural resources. Our Agency's commitment to reducing energy consumption is part of our Strategic Plan and carried out through our mission to serve Congress with a commitment to excellence.

With the addition of the Capitol Visitor Center and several new facilities to our jurisdiction over the past several years, including the National Audio Visual Conservation Center, the National Garden, and the U.S. Capitol Police's Fairchild Building, the AOC is now responsible for some 16.5 million square feet of buildings and nearly 450 acres of land. In recent years, the number and magnitude of our projects has also greatly increased.

It is our mission to ensure that the buildings and facilities in the Capitol complex continue to effectively serve Members of Congress and their staffs for generations to come. This includes ensuring that fire and life-safety deficiencies are corrected and that significant resources are devoted to protecting the people who work in and visit the Capitol complex.

As we develop our long-term plans to address and prioritize the maintenance, renovation, and construction of facilities, we also consider the long-term investment in projects and technologies needed to make our facilities more energy efficient, and are working with Congress to strike the necessary balance to successfully accomplish all goals.

Part of our efforts to strike the right balance is the development of a Capitol Complex Master Plan. The way in which we design, construct, manage, and maintain our facilities can have a major impact on environmental issues such as energy consumption, resource management, pollution, and environmental impact. Sustainable design and construction is a holistic approach to facility management that considers impacts on human health and well-being as well as the natural environment at every stage of the building life cycle.

The AOC has embraced the principles of sustainable design in the ongoing planning, building, operations, and maintenance of the facilities and grounds entrusted to our care. The Master Plan includes a Sustainability Framework Plan. The 20-year goal of this Framework Plan is to consider alternate sources of energy production, improve energy and water efficiency, and use alternative and renewable forms of energy. These goals will also, ultimately, minimize operating costs.

The Capitol Visitor Center (CVC) is an excellent example of our use of sustainability principles as it was designed to incorporate as many green features as possible within the constraints of its unique requirements. A few of the CVC's specific "green" features include:

- Built below an existing parking lot, the CVC is a "redevelopment" of an urban site which has not increased the amount of hard surfaces relative to run-off.
- A storm water management system was incorporated into the design to mitigate the impact of run-off and sediment into the city's storm sewer system.
- Compact Fluorescent Light (CFL) fixtures were used wherever possible and light fixture occupancy sensors are provided.
- Low-flow bathroom fixtures and automatic faucets and toilets were installed.
- Low-volatile organic compound emitting construction materials (paints, solvents, carpets) were used.

## COMMITTED TO SAVING ENERGY SINCE THE 1970S

The AOC has been engaged in energy-saving activities since the energy crisis of the 1970s. In 1978, the AOC presented a report to Congress entitled, "Program for the Energy Conservation and Management for the United States Capitol Complex Buildings," which proposed the concept for the Program for Energy Conservation (PEC). The purpose of PEC was to investigate and implement measures for energy conservation.

A pilot program was launched to test a number of initiatives before implementing it campus-wide. Some of the strategies executed included developing an automated energy management and control system to achieve specific efficiencies in the operation of mechanical and electrical systems. By the early 1980s, the system had proven itself and it was expanded to other Congressional office buildings and refined. Since 1992, our Energy Management Control System has produced significant energy savings annually.

Over the years, we expanded our efforts from a pilot program to a campus-wide effort. In the late 1990s, we completed a campus-wide lighting upgrade, replacing more than one-half million fluorescent lamps and ballasts resulting in a savings of more than $1.5 million annually. We have continued these lighting upgrades to the present day which includes our group re-lamping program and comprehensive lighting fixture ballast replacement in selected buildings.

## PUBLIC LAW 105-275, SEC. 310

When H.R. 4112, the Legislative Branch Appropriations Act for FY 1999, was signed into law, the AOC was required "to develop and implement a cost-effective energy conservation strategy for all facilities to achieve a net reduction of 20 percent in energy consumption . . . not later than 7 years after the enactment of this Act." The AOC responded by fulfilling the requirements of the legislation and developed a comprehensive energy conservation and management plan; performed energy surveys of some facilities; continued to install energy and water conservation measures, and considered Energy Savings Performance Contracts to finance energy conservation projects and to help achieve energy consumption targets.

# Energy Policy Act of 2005 (EPACT), Energy Independence and Security Act of 2007 (EISA), and Recent Energy Savings and Efficiencies

Most recently, we have demonstrated our commitment to energy conservation by complying with the requirements and goals of the Energy Policy Act of 2005. Under the Act, the AOC was required to reduce energy consumption in the Capitol complex in FY 2006 by two percent, as compared to the baseline set in FY 2003.

The long-term requirement of the Energy Policy Act is to increasingly reduce energy consumption per gross square foot per year in fiscal years 2006 through 2015. The AOC exceeded the goal of two percent by reducing its energy consumption by 6.5 percent in FY 2006. In addition, for FY 2007, the AOC achieved a total cumulative energy intensity reduction of 6.7 percent over the FY 2003 baseline.

We were able to exceed our goals the past two years through a variety of projects and pilot programs.

The AOC:

- Implemented a pilot program to install dimmable lighting ballast systems with daylight and occupancy sensors in overhead lighting to maintain consistent lighting levels in Senate offices.
- Is replacing conventional incandescent light bulbs with compact fluorescent lamps (CFLs) across the Capitol complex.
- Is installing occupancy sensor light switches for offices, and installing restroom fixture motion sensors and additional low-flow devices for water conservation.
- Upgraded elevators and escalators with energy-efficient solid state equipment.
- Initiated a feasibility study to replace the Dirksen Senate Office Building and the Rayburn House Office Building roofs with a vegetative roof for decreased storm water run-off and improved insulation.

Initiated a feasibility study to replace the Hart Senate Office Building and Rayburn House Office Building roofs with partial building-integrated photovoltaic roofing systems.

- Implemented a pilot program to install dimmable lighting ballast systems with daylight and occupancy sensors in overhead lighting to maintain consistent lighting levels in Senate offices.
- Is replacing conventional incandescent light bulbs with compact fluorescent lamps (CFLs) across the Capitol complex.
- Is installing occupancy sensor light switches for offices, and installing restroom fixture motion sensors and additional low-flow devices for water conservation.
- Upgraded elevators and escalators with energy-efficient solid state equipment.
- Initiated a feasibility study to replace the Dirksen Senate Office Building and the Rayburn
- House Office Building roofs with a vegetative roof for decreased storm water run-off and improved insulation.
- Initiated a feasibility study to replace the Hart Senate Office Building and Rayburn House Office Building roofs with partial building-integrated photovoltaic roofing systems.
- Is installing modern heating/cooling systems and adjusting and controlling HVAC schedules.
- Installed a storm water management rain garden at First and D Streets in 2004.
- Is installing an E-85 refuel station.
- Implemented a policy requiring the purchase or leasing of alternate fuel vehicles when replacing aging vehicles in the AOC fleet.
- Is auditing the energy consumption of facilities to identify energy saving opportunities and planning to add new steam and chilled water meters to all buildings to monitor actual energy use.
- Incorporated standards from the Leadership in Energy and Environmental Design (LEED) Green Building Rating System into our design standards.
- Is using Energy Savings Performance Contracting to increase building energy efficiencies and upgrade infrastructure.
- Recycled approximately 2,300 tons of paper from the House and Senate Office Buildings in FY 2007. This is the equivalent to saving approximately 38,573 trees, 6,807 cubic yards of landfill space, and 9,076,000 Kilowatts of energy.

The AOC also implemented a procurement policy that establishes our preference for the use of biobased products. We require the use of USDA-approved bio-based products when practical and cost effective.

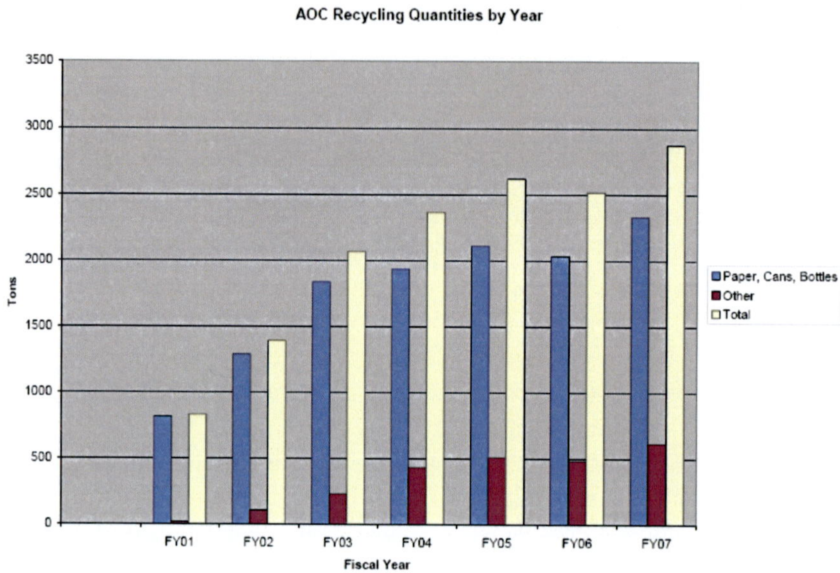


Reducing energy consumption is another important component of our overall energy-savings campaign. To encourage end-users to reduce energy use, the AOC has been conducting a public education campaign by providing materials on how to save energy to Member, Committee, and AOC offices. A new outreach program is currently being developed which will engage in new and various approaches and methods to inform those who work in and visit the Capitol complex of Congress's efforts to save energy.

Active participation by Congressional and other offices in the recycling program has been significant to its success the past several years. In both the House and Senate Office Buildings, offices are outfitted with recycling bins under the AOC's recycling program.

Over the past five years, the total tonnage of recycled waste has doubled from 1,400 tons to 2,900 tons. In addition, over the past two years, we have recycled 100 percent of all AOC computer and electronic waste which includes monitors, keyboards, computers, printers, laptops, and other types of computer hardware.

In the Senate alone, 993 tons of material was recycled in 2007, a 15 percent increase from the previous year. This past year, two more materials were added to the Senate recycling program: paper take-away trays from the cafeteria and CDs/DVDs.

In fact, over the past several years, the Senate has been very proactive in its energy saving efforts. The following is a short list of projects and initiatives that are ongoing or have been accomplished.

- Implemented projects in FY 2008 projected to reduce electricity consumption by one million kilowatt hours per year. This is equivalent to the annual greenhouse gas emissions from 142 passenger vehicles.
- Installed more than 4,000 compact fluorescent light bulbs.
- A study assessing the feasibility of installing a vegetative roof on the Dirksen Senate Office Building was completed.
- A study regarding the use photovoltaic solar cells on Senate Office Buildings was completed.
- Completed the Dimmable Ballast Pilot Program in 11 Senate/Committee office suites. Currently purchasing and designing the system for another 10 offices. The pilot program typically saves 11,400 kilowatt hours per week or 40 percent of lighting energy used in an office suite. Over the first year, the pilot saved 692,000 kilowatt hours of electricity.
- Selected a renewable, solar energy source for lighting in Lot 18. Scheduled to be completed this fall, these new lights will save 1,825 kilowatt hours per year.
- Replacing steam traps in the Senate Office Buildings which will save 5,000 MBtu per year.
- Installed various water conservation measures; dual flush valves (Dirksen and Russell), low flow flush sensor valves (Hart), low flow sink sensor valves.
- In the Senate Restaurants, the Senate Superintendent's Office has installed CFL lighting in the eating and service areas; installed low-flow water pre-rinsing stations in the food prep areas; installed dimmers and timers in all lit areas, and installed motion sensor lighting systems in low-traffic areas.

Installing energy efficient ceiling tiles in 15 Senate/Committee office suites in the Hart Office Building. The new tiles have a higher insulation value, (R= 4.3 vs. 0.33) and higher light reflection which allows a lower light output from the dimmable ballast.

- Installing bi-level lighting in Hart Building emergency stairways. The lights operate at 30 percent output when not occupied to maintain code-required lighting levels. When motion is sensed in the stairway, the light fixtures adjust to 100 percent light output.
- Since March 2008, cove lights in the hallways of the Dirksen Senate Office Building are dimmed every weekday night from 10 p.m. to 6 a.m., and each weekend. This effort saves 75 percent of the energy normally consumed by the cove lighting when fully illuminated.

Another major initiative underway is our effort to improve metering at the facility level for steam and chilled water, domestic water, and where necessary, electricity so that the impact of energy and water conservation projects can be measured rather than estimated. By thoroughly assessing utility usage, we can better target our long-term investments in projects that will yield the greatest payback over time.

The AOC has established a meter plan for the Senate Office Buildings, which includes the installation of chilled water, steam, domestic water, and electrical meters in each building. In addition, the plan includes sub-metering of utilities within the building for chilled water, steam, and electricity to further refine potential sources of energy usage. The plan is scheduled for completion in February 2009, and is subject to the availability of funding.

The AOC also is working with two Energy Saving Performance Contractors (ESCOs), and we plan to utilize them to achieve a portion of the required energy reductions under the EPAct and EISA. Energy Saving Performance Contracts (ESPCs) allow the AOC to initiate energy saving projects with little upfront funding. An ESCO studies the facilities and identifies improvements with short-term payback periods. Based on these studies, the AOC and the ESCO then select projects to perform under terms of an ESPC. A negotiated portion of any savings generated by the project pays the ESCO in accordance with the terms of the ESPC. Once the negotiated term of the contract is over, the government retains the energy savings of the project.

Because there can be risks associated with this arrangement, the Department of Energy (DOE) provides program guidance and assists with the ESPC evaluation. Additionally, the AOC consulted with the U.S. Air Force (USAF) and Naval Facilities Engineering Command (NAVFAC) to benefit from their experiences with ESPCs. The following are key considerations for using ESPCs for the Capitol complex.

To be successful, proper validation of savings and the ability to maintain valid baselines to measure savings are critical; we will evaluate alternatives to identify the most economical method for reducing energy consumption before awarding ESPC contracts. In addition, we will work to ensure that financing rates are competitive and quantify the baseline data and revisit these contracts annually.

To ensure that our efforts save energy and save taxpayer dollars, we also are planning to conduct additional energy audits. The Government Accountability Office, in its report entitled, "Energy Audits are Key to Strategy for Reducing Greenhouse Gas Emissions" validates that energy audits are a key "because these audits identify cost-effective systemwide energy-efficiency and renewable-energy projects." To date, energy audits have been or are being performed on five Capitol complex facilities. The goal is to perform energy audits on all buildings on a five-year rotating schedule.

Although funding was requested in FY 2007 to continue these audits, the funding level of the continuing resolution precluded any projects from receiving funding. In FY 2008, we received $400,000 for energy audits, and we will be conducting two new audits this summer. As funding allows, energy audits will be performed on each building in the Capitol complex as part of our five- year plan. For FY 2009, the AOC requested $1.4 million to conduct additional audits.

In addition to the energy audits, we have completed studies to identify projects, techniques, and policies which can be implemented to save energy. For example, we have been evaluating the viability of cogeneration capacity at the Capitol Power Plant, which could provide steam, supplementary electricity, and backup power to the Capitol complex and reduce regional emissions by more efficiently capturing the energy output.

It is important to note that the largest, single contributor to our energy reduction efforts is the Capitol Power Plant. Between FY 2003 and FY 2006, the Capitol Power Plant, as a result of new and improved energy efficiency measures implemented there, reduced its electricity consumption by six percent and consumption of gas, oil, and coal, measured as total million BTUs of energy, by 12.3 percent. To continue to achieve our goals, it is necessary to continue to invest in new technologies and equipment at the Capitol Power Plant. With that in mind, we have included important energy-saving projects and upgrades there in our FY 2009 budget request.

## Capitol Power Plant and Energy Efficiency

Madam Chairman, because the Capitol Power Plant (CPP) plays a critical role in our efforts, I would like to provide a brief history of the facility. The CPP operates 24 hours per day, 365 days per year to provide steam and chilled water service. Since the first initiation of steam service in 1910, the CPP has never been offline.

When it was first placed in operation, the CPP provided the Capitol complex with steam and electricity. However, in 1952, the electrical generation plant was decommissioned and modern steam and refrigeration plants were built to provide buildings with steam and chilled water for heating and cooling purposes. Today, the CPP generates steam and chilled water used for heating and cooling of 23 buildings located on Capitol Hill. The electricity used today throughout the Capitol complex is provided by PEPCO. The steam plant contains seven boilers that utilize a combination of three fuels (natural gas, low-sulfur coal, and fuel oil) to generate steam. Fuel selection is made based on a combination of economics, equipment availability, and Congressional requirements. The refrigeration plant contains nine electric driven mechanical chillers that utilize refrigerant to produce chilled water used for cooling purposes.

The Capitol Power Plant operates under the Title V permitting program established under the Environmental Protection Agency's (EPA's) 1990 Clean Air Act Amendments. The Title V program requires all new and existing major sources of air emissions to obtain a federally-approved, state-administered operating permit. All Title V operating permits include applicable requirements from federal and state emission standards. We take great pride in abiding by the permit because the permit is designed to protect the public.

The Title V operating permit currently held by the CPP is administered through the District of Columbia Department of Health, Air Quality Division. In addition, the CPP has a complex emissions monitoring system in place, and is required to certify the emissions monitoring systems quarterly, with a certification performed by an independent third party testing firm annually. The CPP must submit quarterly reports to the District of Columbia and Semi-Annual reports to the Director of EPA Region III.

The AOC has improved and will continue to improve efficiencies and reduce emissions at the CPP. Several initiatives have been completed over the past several years to expand environmental controls at the Capitol Power Plant.

A few of these projects include:

- Baghouses were added in the 1990's to reduce the amount of particulate matter emitted from boilers.
- Added new, high-efficiency filter-bags in the baghouses in 2005, which provide improved filtration and lower restrictions to air flow resulting in reduced energy consumption and lower emissions.

- Completed the expansion of the West Refrigeration Plant to upgrade refrigeration systems to increase overall efficiency, including the use of environmentally friendly 134-A Freon.
- In 2005, new coal under-throw stokers were installed to replace the original coal feeder systems. In addition, the CPP is replacing the stoker grate drive system in both coal boilers in 2007 and 2008. These modern systems should provide more efficient operation and coal combustion.
- The CPP is required to continuously monitor opacity, nitrogen oxides (NOx), and oxygen emissions. The Continuous Emissions Monitoring System (CEMS) and the Continuous Opacity Monitoring System (COMS) were installed in 2005. They provide constant monitoring of emissions from the boilers, which allow us to adjust our fuel mix in real time, and maintain compliance as set forth in Federal and local regulations.
- In addition, the Plant only uses low-sulfur, low-ash coal.

We are working to make the CPP more energy efficient and to reduce emissions. This is a longterm effort and one that will take considerable investment. However, this investment is reasonable compared to the impractical and cost-prohibitive potential of eliminating the CPP. Existing, centralized heating and cooling systems have been studied and proven to be most cost-effective for a large campus such as the Capitol complex. The ability to burn three fuels at the CPP assures reliability, provides flexibility, and provides some protection against rapidly rising fuel costs as we can switch to a lower cost fuel depending on system load and fuel use requirements. However, to cease using one fuel completely would require significant capital improvements to the CPP, necessitate disruptive infrastructure changes to the Capitol complex, and potentially increase average annual fuel costs by millions of dollars.

## New AOC Energy Saving Projects, Programs, and Initiatives

In addition to improving efficiencies at the CPP, there are a number of initiatives that we have planned to ensure the Capitol complex's continued compliance with the Energy Policy Act of 2005 and the Energy Independence and Security Act of 2007. To meet these requirements, we plan to undertake the following projects, programs, and initiatives.

- Improve metering so that the impact of energy and water conservation projects can be measured rather than estimated.
- Continue use of Energy Savings Performance Contracts (ESPCs) as a means to pursue projects that offer l ifecycle cost-effectiveness.
- Evaluate opportunities for onsite renewable energy such as use of photovoltaics and supplementing existing fuel with biodiesel.
- Evaluate opportunities for energy recovery both at the Capitol Power Plant and within individual buildings.
- Continue analysis of currently planned facility repairs and upgrades for energy and water savings opportunities.
- Continue development of the Capitol Complex Master Plan/Sustai nabi lity Framework Plan to ensure an overarching sustainable approach to facilities and grounds administered by Congress.

By practicing efficient energy management, we save taxpayer dollars and protect the environment and natural resources. As you can see, the AOC has taken considerable action over the years to save energy across the Capitol complex. There is more we all can do to further conserve energy; however we need to ensure that the projects we chose to invest in are fiscally responsible, energy efficient, preserve the historic integrity of these landmark buildings, and have minimal adverse effects on the buildings' occupants, the local community, or on Congressional operations.

## CONCLUSION

Madam Chairman, we greatly appreciate this Committee's support and the investment Congress has made in our facilities and infrastructure over the past several years as we continue to make the Capitol complex safer and more energy efficient. We are working to identify and implement long-term projects that will fulfill our mission to care for the historic buildings and assets entrusted to our care, and attain the required energy saving goals, while at the same time providing Congress with the best return on its investment.

In addition to using and installing new, modern, energy efficient technologies and equipment, other changes will need to occur in order to realize additional savings. This includes changes in behavior and practices by building occupants, and modifying building operations and methods. While we have been successful in reducing energy consumption in the Capitol complex the past two years, the work ahead will be much more challenging and will require significant investment.

Once again, I'd like to thank this Committee and Congress for their leadership on this issue. We should be leaders in the national effort to conserve energy. As stewards of the Capitol complex, we will continue to do our part to make this goal a reality.

Stephen T. Ayers, AIA
Acting Architect of the Capitol and Chief Operating Officer

On February 4, 2007, Stephen T. Ayers, AIA, AOC's Deputy Architect/Chief Operating Officer, in accordance with P.L. 108-7, began serving as Acting Architect of the Capitol until a new Architect is appointed by the President and confirmed by the Senate.

As Acting Architect, Mr. Ayers is responsible for the mechanical and structural maintenance of the Capitol, the care and improvement of more than 450 acres of Capitol grounds, and the operation and maintenance of 16.5 million square feet of buildings including: the Congressional Office Buildings, the Library of Congress Buildings, the U.S. Supreme Court Building, the Thurgood Marshall Federal Judiciary Building, and the Capitol Power Plant. He is responsible for the care of all works of art in the Capitol under the direction of the Joint Committee on the Library and is responsible for the maintenance and restoration of murals, outdoor sculpture, and other architectural elements throughout the Capitol complex. In addition, he serves as Acting Director of the U.S. Botanic Garden and the National Garden under the Joint Committee on the Library. The Architect of the Capitol also serves as a member of the Capitol Police Board and the Capitol Guide Board as well as an ex officio member of the United States Capitol Preservation Commission

Mr. Ayers completed his Bachelor of Science degree in Architecture at the University of Maryland and received his Master's of Science degree in Systems Management from the University of Southern California.

After attending Officers Training School at Lackland Air Base in San Antonio, Texas, Mr. Ayers was commissioned as a second lieutenant in the U.S. Air Force and assigned to Edwards Air Force Base in Edwards, California. While stationed at Edwards, he served as a Staff Architect with the 6510$^{th}$ Civil Engineering Squadron managing numerous design and construction projects. He was promoted to Design Team Chief and progressed to the rank of Captain. Mr.

Ayers was awarded the Meritorious Service Medal for his military service and after five years of active duty, resigned his commission to pursue a civilian career.

After working in the architectural and engineering community in the Washington, D.C., area, Mr. Ayers joined the Voice of America in Washington, D.C., as a General Engineer in 1991. In 1992 he transferred to Rhodes, Greece, to lead construction efforts at several Voice of America sites in Greece and Germany. Mr. Ayers returned to the United States in 1997 and joined the Architect of the Capitol as an Assistant Superintendent for the Senate Office Buildings. In 1999, he was promoted to Deputy Superintendent. He was then promoted to Superintendent of the Library Buildings and Grounds in 2002.

In October 2005, Mr. Ayers was appointed as the Acting Deputy Architect/Chief Operating Officer (COO). In March 2006, following a rigorous interview process before a selection panel comprised of the Chief Administrative Officer of the House of Representatives, the Comptroller General, Senate Sergeant at Arms, and senior AOC officials, Mr. Ayers was selected as the Deputy Architect/COO. In this role, he oversees approximately 2,200 employees and manages the day-to- day operations of the Agency.

Mr. Ayers is a licensed architect in California. He resides in Maryland with his wife and two children.

In: Recycling and Green Programs at the Capital... ISBN 978-1-60692-980-3
Editor: H. Y. Kim, pp. 229-232 

*Chapter 9*

# Testimony of Daniel P. Beard, Chief Administrative Officer US House of Representatives

# Before Select Committee on Energy Indepence and Global Warming February 26, 2008 Food for Thought: Sustainability from Counter to Compost

Thank you Chairman Markey and Members of the Committee for the opportunity to discuss the success we have achieved in greening the House food service operations.

As Chief Administrative Officer of the House I am responsible for implementing Speaker Pelosi and Majority Leader Hoyer's Green the Capitol Initiative. This wide ranging initiative covers all aspects of the way we do business in the House including the food service operations.

Our goal with the House food services operations is to make it a premier showcase of sustainable, green, and healthy food operations. The House food service touches virtually all of the visitors to the Capitol from constituents, citizen advocates to lobbyists, federal employees and the press corps. And of course there is the House staff and Members of Congress who eat here almost every working day.

We have worked closely with our new food service vendor Restaurant Associates to implement the green changes. With each of the 240,000 meals served each month we can set high standards and send a green message in a tasty way.

Our highest priority was the banning of all plastic and Styrofoam from the cafeterias. The knives, forks, spoons, sandwich clam shells are among the items made from corn. Plates and coffee cups are made from paper. Entrée containers are made from sugarcane.

And contrary to urban myth already circulating the spoons do not melt in the soup!

All of these food service items are fully compostable. This sandwich clamshell or this fork will become dirt in 90 days at a commercial compost facility. Our biodegradable items are made in places like Maine and Nebraska, Pennsylvania and Georgia. New small businesses are being created to meet demand as food services are moving from the experimental and educational phase to actually using increasing amounts of biodegradable food service ware.

The House is demonstrating with every meal served that there is a market for U.S. manufacturers to provide green sustainable recyclable products.

While we are striving for perfection there is currently no compostable lids for coffee and hot drinks. We have been examining lids made from potatoes and are looking to implement a solution soon.

We send the compostable food service items along with all of the food waste from the front of the cafeteria and from the kitchens to a pulper. The pulper is like a giant garbage disposal that breaks down and dewaters the compost material. This reduces the volume of the compost material by a ratio of 10-1 and reduces the weight by as much as 4-1. The result is reduced hauling costs and reduced tipping fees by 60%-75%.

The food service waste that was being sent to landfills is now being taken to the Department of Agriculture composting facility at Beltsville, Maryland or to a commercial composting farm in nearby Crofton, Maryland. There we are literally turning what was garbage and going into a landfill into a commercially viable product.

Ultimately what we would like to see is some of the compost come back here to beautify the Capitol grounds.

But perhaps the real beauty is to the bottom line. While the new operation has only been up and running about 60 days, preliminary results are very encouraging. The waste hauler for the landfill picked up approximately 20 tons less material for the last 3 weeks of December, 2007 compared to 2006. This reduces the hauling costs and with tipping fees 30% less at the commercial composting facilities savings are realized on tipping fees too. And at the USDA facility there are no tipping fees at all! As noted above the pulper is reducing the weight of the compostables further reducing disposal costs by as much as 75%.

Sending the food service waste for composting also reduces our carbon foot print, a key issue for this committee. By diverting the food service waste from the landfill we are preventing it's conversion to methane--one of the most powerful greenhouse gases. We are examining ways to calculate the methane reduction and use the savings as carbon offsets for other House operations. And we are not eating our food off items made from petroleum products.

Fully integrating a compost solution from the fork you pick up to the kitchen trimmings and sending it to be composted is a good business decision, saves taxpayer's money and is the right action for the environment.

We also looked at the food itself. The House is the largest account for Pura Vida coffee which is fair trade, bird friendly by being shade grown, and organic.

The beef, chicken, and pork are all hormone free. The seafood served is certified sustainable caught as defined by the Monterey Aquarium seafood guidelines. The shell eggs used are from chickens in a cage free environment.

When one of the workers was asked what his job was under the previous food vendor his response was "Opening cans." Under Restaurant Associates the amount of fresh produce and meat is approximately 85% up from an estimated 35% under the previous vendor. This switch to fresher food and the resulting trimmings is complemented at the back end with the pulper and composting solutions.

The House is promoting the buying of food locally defined purchasing food produced in a 150 mile radius from the Capitol when possible. The House is also emphasizing the purchase of organically produced food, and providing a market for new and existing farms and businesses to meet these needs. We are also reducing our carbon foot print by reducing the distance food has to be transported.

There are other greening stories to tell in the food service operations. The recycling stations are made from recycled glass and other material. The paint used to spruce up the cafeterias was low in volatile organic compounds. We are using electronic signage in the cafeterias to highlight daily menu specials. Bamboo flooring was used in the convenience store.

Energy and water conservation are also critical areas. All new equipment in the kitchens will meet the highest energy efficiency standards. New dish washers are being purchased to conserve water.

Vending machines is a little thought about area where significant energy savings can be found. The House is swapping out the approximately 80 old machines with the most energy efficient or Energy Star machines available. We are also changing the way the machines are operated to maximize energy savings. This includes delamping machines in well lit areas, changing compressor operations, and letting temperatures rise in soda machines in the middle of the night. These changes are estimated to save as much as $20,000 annually.

We have made a good start. But we know there is much more to do to be more sustainable, greener, and continue to reduce our carbon foot print. We will constantly review our purchasing and operations to be at the leading of green cafeteria operations.

Chairman Markey and Members of the Committee thank you for the opportunity to tell the story of our green food service operations. Restaurant Associates has been a hard working partner in putting together one of the greenest food service operations in the United States.

Bon Appétit!

# INDEX

## A


abatement, 188, 234, 235, 267
access, 13, 67, 72
accountability, 266
accounting, 27
accuracy, 232
achievement, 267
acid, 215, 225, 235
acoustic, 41
acoustical, 46
Adams, 131, 133, 217
adjustment, 48
administration, xii, 83, 97, 119, 191
administrative, 116, 117, 171, 174
aerosol, 43
age, 27, 28, 31, 110, 216, 266
agents, 143
aging, 56, 296
aid, 67, 113, 227, 229, 238, 239, 240, 241, 242, 243
air, 10, 17, 18, 43, 44, 46, 48, 49, 61, 62, 68, 70, 78, 81, 104, 163, 234, 235, 243, 244, 245, 275, 279, 280, 302, 303
air emissions, 302
air pollutant, 234, 245
air pollutants, 234, 245
air quality, 44, 70, 78, 235, 243, 245
AL, 178, 181, 188
Alaska, 238
Alaskan pipeline, 238
alternative, 8, 14, 33, 63, 64, 80, 88, 104, 189, 262, 291
alternatives, 64, 300
aluminum, 160, 244
amendments, 99
AOC, xv, xvi, xvii, 4, 6, 12, 13, 15, 17, 19, 24, 34, 35, 39, 40, 50, 54, 55, 56, 57, 64, 66, 68, 72, 92, 107, 134, 139, 173, 203, 204, 205, 206, 207, 208, 210, 211, 212, 213, 214, 217, 218, 220, 221, 223, 224, 227, 228, 229, 230, 231, 233, 247, 248, 249, 250, 251, 287, 288, 289, 290, 291, 292, 293, 294, 296, 297, 300, 301, 303, 304, 305, 308
application, 39, 62, 281
appropriations, 109, 112, 146, 148, 149, 154, 156, 164, 166, 173, 204, 211, 213, 253
appropriations bills, 146, 148, 164
Appropriations Committee, 140, 149, 164, 165, 166, 167, 168
aquatic habitat, 59
aquatic habitats, 59
ash, 8, 25, 33, 304
assessment, 19, 49
assets, 127, 198, 289, 306
assumptions, 92, 224, 228, 232, 233
asthma, 234
atmosphere, xi, xvi, 1, 3, 16, 21, 61, 76, 121, 130, 220, 235, 275, 279
atmospheric pressure, 254
atoms, 16
attacks, 235

auditing, 224, 252, 288, 296
authority, 99, 116, 117, 118, 127, 132, 156, 259, 268
automobiles, 67, 253
availability, 66, 94, 265, 300, 302
averaging, 232
awareness, 174

## B

ballast, 102, 288, 293, 294, 295, 299
barrier, 104
barriers, 226, 241
batteries, 160, 168, 171, 175, 198
battery, 48
beef, 312
behavior, 63, 306
benchmarks, 15, 35, 37, 38, 73
benefits, 8, 33, 38, 41, 61, 64, 65, 66, 93, 96, 105, 130, 132, 162, 172, 174, 212, 215, 222, 225, 234, 245, 282
benign, 47, 48
Best Practice, 52, 131
binding, xvi, 220
biodegradable, 68, 69, 95, 96, 97, 161, 181, 310
biodiesel, 289, 305
biodiversity, 58, 60, 61, 62
blackouts, 241
blog, 115, 136
boilers, 5, 22, 25, 28, 50, 51, 80, 108, 111, 214, 221, 225, 227, 229, 239, 246, 247, 250, 253, 254, 302, 303, 304
Botanical Garden, 158
bronchitis, 235
BTUs, 274, 278, 301
buffer, 240
bulbs, 9, 39, 40, 77, 89, 100, 101, 102, 122, 176, 253, 275, 279, 288, 294, 295, 298
burn, 113, 214, 221, 225, 227, 230, 240, 241, 243, 245, 246, 250, 304
burning, 8, 33, 90, 218, 222, 226, 239, 240, 246, 253
business model, 35
bypass, 48

## C

calibration, 37, 38
Canada, 238
candidates, 53
capacity, 58, 214, 221, 225, 226, 239, 240, 241, 242, 254, 301
capital cost, 109, 213, 240
capital expenditure, 215, 227
Capitol Hill, xii, xiii, xv, 11, 15, 49, 64, 72, 73, 83, 84, 93, 116, 119, 145, 166, 174, 176, 203, 204, 205, 207, 208, 211, 302
carbon, viii, xi, xv, xvi, 1, 2, 3, 4, 5, 6, 8, 9, 11, 15, 16, 17, 19, 20, 21, 22, 23, 24, 25, 26, 32, 34, 35, 36, 39, 49, 56, 61, 63, 73, 75, 76, 79, 82, 84, 86, 87, 88, 89, 90, 91, 92, 98, 108, 113, 114, 121, 123, 129, 135, 161, 201, 205, 206, 207, 208, 213, 215, 217, 218, 220, 224, 234, 235, 245, 247, 252, 253, 257, 262, 273, 275, 276, 277, 279, 280, 290, 311, 312, 313
carbon credits, 5, 25, 88, 90, 91, 113, 114
carbon dioxide, xv, 3, 16, 17, 19, 21, 26, 76, 80, 82, 92, 108, 121, 209, 215, 217, 218, 220, 221, 224, 234, 235, 245, 247, 253
carbon emissions, xi, xvi, 2, 4, 5, 6, 11, 23, 25, 26, 49, 98, 108, 245, 273, 277
Carbon footprint, 16
carbon monoxide, 25
cardboard, xiii, 137, 139, 149
carpets, 69, 70, 78, 90, 292
cell, xiv, 98, 138, 158, 161, 162, 175, 176
cell phones, xiv, 98, 138, 158, 161, 162, 176
centralized, 45, 46, 47, 65, 175, 304
certification, 258, 259, 262, 264, 266, 267, 303
CFI, 25
channels, 59
chemicals, xv, 122, 220, 235, 282
chicken, 312
chickens, 312
childcare, 13, 34
children, 87, 308
CHP, 17, 55
citizens, 172

civilian, 265, 307
classes, 66
Clean Air Act, 66, 302
cleaning, 10, 14, 44, 49, 51, 56, 68, 70, 71, 123, 261, 281, 282
climate change, xi, xvi, 1, 2, 19, 70, 78, 79, 94, 108, 127, 220, 260, 261, 282
Co, 118, 128
CO2, xvi, 3, 4, 5, 11, 15, 16, 17, 19, 21, 22, 23, 24, 26, 32, 35, 37, 38, 39, 41, 51, 63, 66, 71, 73, 80, 81, 82, 92, 257, 261, 262
coal, 4, 5, 8, 22, 23, 24, 25, 28, 32, 50, 90, 91, 92, 108, 111, 112, 206, 209, 213, 214, 215, 218, 220, 221, 222, 223, 224, 225, 226, 227, 230, 234, 235, 236, 237, 238, 239, 240, 241, 242, 243, 244, 245, 246, 247, 249, 250, 251, 252, 253, 254, 301, 302, 303, 304
coal-burning, 226, 246
coefficient of variation, 251, 255
coffee, 89, 95, 310, 312
Colorado, 259, 266
*Columbia*, 57, 62, 91, 179, 181, 303
combustion, xvi, 17, 108, 203, 206, 208, 214, 220, 221, 234, 235, 239, 240, 246, 250, 303
Committee on Appropriations, 119, 122, 123, 124, 167, 192, 193, 194, 195, 199, 200, 201, 219, 222, 253, 271
Committee on Environment and Public Works, 146
Committee on House Administration, xii, 84, 85, 86, 97, 98, 114, 116, 119, 128, 136, 141, 143, 147, 156, 157, 161, 172, 183, 189, 190, 191, 196
Committee on Oversight and Government Reform, 100
Committee on Rules and Administration, viii, 85, 100, 101, 103, 107, 114, 117, 119, 129, 144, 164, 166, 167, 168, 172, 201, 257, 276, 289
Committees on Appropriations, 155
communication, 74
communities, xvi, 258, 260, 262, 269, 275, 279, 282
community, 64, 67, 95, 172, 174, 258, 263, 305, 307
competition, 99
complexity, 60
compliance, 155, 235, 245, 304
components, 39, 42, 43, 51, 53, 70, 78, 208, 212, 259, 268
compost, 62, 96, 127, 158, 162, 310, 311
composting, xiv, 68, 89, 95, 96, 97, 126, 138, 161, 162, 175, 197, 311, 312
compounds, 78, 90
computer technology, 100
concentration, 16, 259, 268
concrete, xiv, 97, 101, 138, 168, 171, 199
conditioning, 10, 18, 44, 46, 47, 275, 279
Conference Committee, 194
configuration, 52, 89, 115
conflict, 156
congress, 185, 187, 188
*Congressional Record*, 124, 126, 152, 159, 177, 178, 179, 180, 181, 190, 191, 194, 196, 197, 199
consensus, 258, 263, 269
consent, 128, 145, 188, 190
conservation, xi, xii, xiii, 13, 19, 24, 76, 79, 83, 84, 86, 107, 118, 130, 132, 133, 173, 197, 221, 266, 267, 270, 288, 292, 293, 294, 295, 299, 305, 312
Consolidated Appropriations Act, 167, 201, 253
consolidation, 45
constant rate, 255
constraints, 226, 236, 246, 250, 291
construction, xiv, xvi, 27, 97, 101, 105, 108, 116, 138, 158, 176, 240, 243, 244, 261, 262, 263, 264, 266, 267, 273, 274, 277, 278, 283, 287, 291, 292, 307
construction and demolition, 261
construction materials, 97, 101, 261, 292
consultants, 154
consumers, 229, 243, 244, 269
consumption, xii, xvii, 2, 6, 7, 9, 11, 13, 14, 15, 19, 20, 28, 29, 30, 31, 32, 36, 37, 38, 39, 43, 45, 47, 48, 50, 56, 57, 58, 60, 69, 71, 73, 78, 82, 83, 87, 88, 89, 92, 98, 99,

100, 101, 103, 107, 108, 109, 115, 133, 161, 174, 208, 209, 225, 228, 238, 245, 250, 261, 275, 279, 282, 287, 288, 290, 291, 293, 294, 296, 297, 298, 300, 301, 303, 306
contaminants, 59
contamination, 50, 51, 148, 154
continuity, 17, 66, 117
contractors, 67, 151, 158, 196
contracts, xiv, 5, 25, 90, 109, 138, 147, 150, 158, 163, 169, 213, 300
control, 10, 13, 38, 43, 44, 46, 48, 49, 50, 51, 52, 53, 80, 81, 103, 152, 188, 225, 227, 229, 243, 247, 292
conversion, 39, 48, 53, 55, 81, 82, 226, 234, 241, 311
cooling, xvi, 4, 6, 10, 12, 17, 28, 29, 38, 42, 43, 45, 46, 51, 52, 53, 55, 56, 57, 85, 91, 103, 217, 220, 261, 266, 288, 296, 302, 304
copper, 105, 162
corn, 26, 97, 158, 161, 310
corporations, 269
corridors, 9, 39, 40
cost effectiveness, 165
cost saving, 46, 99, 110, 117, 205, 208, 213, 268
cost-effective, xv, 29, 32, 107, 108, 132, 204, 205, 206, 207, 208, 211, 213, 215, 216, 225, 226, 229, 234, 240, 241, 275, 279, 293, 301, 304, 305
costs, xv, 6, 8, 9, 14, 26, 32, 34, 39, 57, 66, 70, 77, 92, 96, 100, 105, 108, 109, 111, 116, 118, 132, 149, 150, 154, 156, 162, 167, 172, 204, 206, 207, 209, 212, 213, 214, 215, 221, 222, 224, 226, 227, 228, 229, 230, 231, 232, 233, 234, 235, 236, 238, 240, 243, 244, 245, 250, 254, 255, 274, 275, 278, 280, 282, 290, 291, 304, 311
counterbalance, 90
courts, 105
coverage, 61
CRS, xiii, xiv, 83, 84, 89, 122, 123, 126, 127, 128, 130, 131, 132, 133, 134, 136, 137, 138, 188, 197, 202
CRT, 18, 41
culture, 174
customers, 69
cycles, 169, 263
cyclists, 65

## D

database, 26, 249
decision making, 234
decisions, xii, 2, 47, 49, 204, 211, 225, 229, 247
definition, 254, 258, 263
Delaware, 283
delivery, 12, 53, 231
demand, 8, 32, 44, 48, 57, 91, 145, 195, 205, 206, 208, 212, 215, 222, 223, 226, 227, 232, 233, 236, 237, 238, 239, 240, 250, 251, 263, 283, 310
Democrats, 120, 136
Demonstration Project, 99
density, 267
Department of Agriculture, 311
Department of Energy (DOE), 82, 98, 109, 110, 130, 133, 210, 217, 222, 223, 224, 248, 251, 253, 270, 271, 274, 278, 300
Department of Housing and Urban Development, 152
Department of Transportation, 18, 63, 64, 66, 67
designers, 259, 268
desire, 117, 162, 175
Diamond, 75
direct cost, 65
directives, xi, 2, 215
disabled, 65
disposition, 118
disseminate, 72
distribution, 10, 12, 42, 43, 44, 48, 49, 54, 55, 239, 240
district heating, 42
District of Columbia, 57, 59, 62, 91, 179, 181, 303
domestic demand, 238
draft, 74, 99, 211, 227, 247
drainage, 104

durability, 281
duties, 114

## E

earth, 68
eating, 299, 311
economics, 302
Education, 14, 55, 71, 201
educational programs, 174
Edwards Air Force Base, 307
efficiency level, 47
election, 169
electric cars, 262
electric power, 4, 39, 76, 77, 80, 86
electrical power, 55
electrical system, 292
electricity, xvi, 4, 5, 8, 17, 22, 23, 24, 25, 28, 29, 30, 31, 32, 36, 37, 39, 41, 45, 51, 55, 76, 82, 88, 90, 103, 111, 112, 203, 205, 206, 207, 208, 209, 210, 212, 213, 214, 215, 220, 221, 222, 224, 226, 227, 235, 236, 237, 238, 240, 241, 242, 243, 244, 246, 251, 254, 298, 299, 300, 301, 302
electronic waste, 155, 297
emission, 6, 15, 26, 71, 80, 245, 302
emitters, 221
employees, xi, xvii, 1, 12, 19, 34, 64, 65, 66, 79, 88, 93, 94, 96, 125, 146, 161, 166, 210, 280, 308, 310
employers, 64, 65
end-users, 297
energy audit, xv, 20, 43, 108, 109, 203, 204, 206, 207, 208, 210, 212, 213, 218, 234, 274, 279, 288, 301
energy consumption, xii, xvii, 2, 6, 9, 11, 15, 19, 20, 28, 29, 32, 36, 37, 38, 39, 43, 45, 47, 48, 50, 57, 73, 82, 87, 88, 89, 98, 99, 100, 101, 103, 107, 108, 109, 115, 133, 161, 174, 261, 275, 279, 282, 287, 288, 290, 291, 293, 294, 296, 297, 300, 303, 306
energy efficiency, xvii, 6, 7, 8, 9, 10, 11, 12, 15, 16, 20, 26, 29, 33, 36, 37, 40, 43, 45, 46, 47, 48, 49, 50, 73, 77, 86, 88, 98, 99, 100, 107, 108, 109, 130, 132, 205, 207, 212, 223, 233, 259, 260, 262, 268, 273, 276, 277, 282, 287, 290, 301, 312
Energy Independence and Security Act, 107, 108, 132, 287, 294, 304
Energy Information Administration (EIA), 82, 92, 217, 223, 242, 248, 253, 270
energy management system, 81
Energy Policy Act, 6, 8, 18, 29, 31, 33, 104, 107, 109, 233, 250, 287, 294, 304
Energy Policy Act of 2005, 8, 31, 33, 104, 107, 109, 233, 250, 287, 294, 304
energy recovery, 305
engagement, xvi, 258, 260
enthusiasm, 277
environment, xi, xii, 1, 2, 12, 16, 17, 19, 34, 45, 54, 73, 95, 98, 112, 115, 156, 161, 246, 258, 260, 261, 264, 269, 275, 279, 290, 291, 305, 311, 312
environmental audit, 58
environmental control, 303
environmental crisis, 278
environmental effects, 19
environmental impact, xii, xvi, xvii, 2, 14, 70, 144, 161, 204, 205, 208, 212, 215, 258, 259, 260, 261, 262, 268, 287, 291
environmental issues, 291
Environmental Protection Agency, 74, 146, 210, 302
environmentalists, 277
EPA, 14, 58, 82, 146, 261, 271, 303
estimating, 225, 232
ETA, 228
ethanol, 13, 63, 253
Ethanol, 79
European Union, 234
evapotranspiration, 61
evening, 153
e-waste, xiv, 97, 101, 138, 160, 168, 171, 175, 197, 198
Executive Office of the President, 132
Executive Order, 151, 155, 191, 193, 195, 266
exercise, 105
expenditures, 92, 115, 205, 208, 213, 223, 228
expert, iv
exports, 238

Exposure, 123, 244

## F

fabric, xvi, 258, 260, 281, 282
family, 66, 126
farmers, 113, 114
farms, 312
fat, 95
February, viii, 96, 162, 205, 209, 214, 250, 300, 306, 309
federal government, 99, 142, 143, 145, 146, 259, 268
Federal Register, 152, 191, 193, 195
feedback, 15, 35, 73
fees, 96, 162, 200, 311
feet, xvii, 27, 110, 225, 231, 266, 267, 278, 283, 287, 290, 307
fertilizer, 62, 227, 244
fertilizers, 61
fiber, 152
fiber content, 152
films, 281
filters, 61, 81, 104
filtration, 44, 103, 303
finance, 11, 13, 34, 50, 154, 213, 266, 293
financing, 8, 33, 133, 300
fire, 50, 290
fitness, xiv, 10, 94, 138, 156, 167, 173, 201
FL, 77, 101, 177, 179, 180, 181, 182
flexibility, 80, 214, 221, 304
flooring, 312
flow, 13, 48, 58, 261, 292, 295, 299, 303
fluorescent lamps, 39, 77, 80, 293, 294, 295
fluorescent light, 39, 40, 89, 101, 122, 176, 298
food, xiv, xvii, 10, 13, 14, 34, 49, 58, 67, 68, 69, 89, 94, 95, 96, 97, 105, 131, 138, 145, 158, 161, 162, 175, 181, 253, 299, 309, 310, 311, 312, 313
food products, 68
Ford, xv, 27, 28, 74, 80, 94, 109, 126, 131, 133, 145, 151, 158, 196, 207, 211, 216, 225, 231, 249
Forest Service, 82
forests, 70, 78
fossil, xvi, 17, 22, 23, 203, 205, 206, 208, 209, 212, 220, 221, 245, 246
fossil fuel, xvi, 17, 22, 23, 203, 205, 206, 208, 209, 212, 220, 222, 245, 246
fuel, 4, 5, 14, 17, 21, 22, 23, 25, 28, 29, 36, 42, 50, 63, 91, 92, 98, 111, 112, 205, 206, 207, 208, 209, 212, 214, 215, 221, 223, 224, 226, 227, 228, 229, 230, 231, 232, 233, 234, 235, 236, 237, 238, 239, 240, 241, 244, 245, 246, 247, 248, 249, 250, 251, 254, 289, 296, 302, 304, 305
fuel type, 4, 21
funding, 8, 94, 109, 148, 204, 206, 207, 211, 217, 223, 248, 253, 267, 300, 301
funds, xv, 8, 33, 77, 80, 109, 112, 113, 148, 149, 150, 152, 153, 156, 166, 167, 173, 207, 211, 246
furniture, 14, 69, 85

## G

garbage, 96, 162, 200, 310, 311
gas, xvi, 4, 5, 8, 11, 22, 23, 25, 28, 32, 37, 44, 50, 51, 82, 86, 88, 89, 90, 91, 92, 98, 111, 112, 203, 206, 208, 212, 214, 215, 218, 220, 221, 222, 223, 224, 226, 227, 228, 230, 231, 233, 234, 235, 236, 237, 238, 239, 240, 241, 242, 243, 244, 245, 246, 249, 250, 251, 253, 254, 301, 302
gases, 130, 217, 254
gasoline, 123, 274, 278
General Services Administration (GSA), xiii, 108, 111, 138, 140, 141, 148, 157, 158, 159, 160, 164, 169, 170, 179, 181, 188, 225, 231, 249, 265, 271, 272, 274, 278, 284
generation, 5, 25, 55, 111, 141, 144, 222, 224, 226, 236, 238, 239, 241, 251, 302
Georgia, 74, 310
Germany, 131, 307
gestures, 275, 279
glass, xiv, 138, 160, 162, 170, 244, 281, 312
global demand, 238
Global Warming, viii, xi, 2, 3, 19, 21, 76, 96, 97, 119, 126, 127, 162, 198, 277, 309

goals, 2, 3, 8, 13, 14, 15, 16, 20, 33, 35, 36, 37, 66, 73, 87, 107, 112, 117, 142, 161, 166, 220, 231, 266, 287, 288, 289, 291, 294, 301, 306
gold, 162
government, 15, 37, 71, 72, 86, 99, 109, 111, 116, 140, 141, 142, 143, 144, 145, 146, 162, 224, 252, 259, 265, 268, 269, 277, 300
Government Accountability Office (GAO), 4, 18, 19, 21, 74, 75, 86, 114, 124, 132, 134, 135, 285, 301
GPO, 18, 122, 123, 124, 125, 135, 152, 189, 190, 192, 193, 194, 195, 196, 199, 200, 201
graph, 22
Great Britain, 281
Greece, 307
green buildings, 258, 262
green revolution, xvi, 258, 260
green tea, 274, 279
greenhouse, xv, 3, 5, 16, 17, 21, 26, 74, 76, 77, 78, 79, 86, 108, 163, 203, 204, 205, 206, 207, 208, 212, 214, 215, 217, 218, 220, 221, 246, 247, 259, 260, 262, 268, 274, 278, 298, 311
Greenhouse, vii, 82, 132, 133, 203, 217, 254, 271, 285, 301
greenhouse gas, xv, 3, 5, 16, 17, 21, 26, 74, 76, 77, 78, 79, 86, 108, 163, 203, 204, 205, 206, 207, 208, 212, 214, 215, 217, 218, 220, 221, 246, 247, 259, 260, 262, 268, 274, 278, 298, 311
greenhouse gases, xv, 3, 5, 17, 21, 26, 217, 220, 222, 311
*greening*, xi, xii, xiii, xvii, 35, 83, 84, 85, 87, 97, 98, 100, 106, 107, 112, 113, 116, 117, 118, 119, 120, 273, 274, 275, 277, 279, 282, 309, 312
groups, 35, 281
growth, 56, 239, 265, 284
GSA, xiv, 93, 94, 111, 138, 140, 147, 148, 158, 160, 161, 163, 169, 170, 188, 196, 199, 265, 267, 271
guidance, 11, 44, 79, 100, 118, 140, 147, 191, 300
guidelines, 65, 68, 69, 146, 210, 258, 264, 280, 312

## H

habitat, 60
handling, 10, 43, 44, 81, 225, 229, 235
harm, 62, 268
harmony, 268
Harvard, 13, 35, 75
hazardous materials, 267
health, xvii, 11, 44, 58, 60, 62, 71, 95, 215, 234, 245, 260, 273, 275, 277, 280, 291
health care, 275, 280
health care costs, 275, 280
health effects, 234, 245
healthcare, 264, 270
hearing, 101, 112, 114, 122, 123, 124, 125, 129, 134, 147, 165, 174, 190, 205, 260
heart, 235, 259, 268
heart attack, 235
heat, 12, 17, 22, 28, 42, 44, 50, 51, 54, 55, 61, 81, 90, 92, 104, 130, 243, 249, 275, 279, 280
heat loss, 54
heat transfer, 50
heating, xvi, 6, 10, 12, 28, 29, 42, 43, 44, 46, 55, 85, 91, 110, 130, 214, 217, 220, 221, 227, 233, 240, 250, 253, 261, 266, 288, 296, 302, 304
heavy metal, 69, 78
heavy metals, 69, 78
higher education, 265
hogs, 274, 278
holistic, 274, 275, 279, 280, 291
holistic approach, 275, 279, 291
horizon, 213
hormone, 312
hospitals, 111
hot water, 10, 30, 49, 54, 81, 130
House Administration Committee, 113, 140, 146, 154, 157, 191
House Appropriations Committee, 93, 214, 221, 253
household, 16

households, 67
housing, 46
HR, 94
HUD, 271
human, 283, 291
humidity, 48
hurricane, 236
hybrid, 14, 63, 93, 262
hydroelectric power, 222

## I

implementation, 12, 20, 34, 63, 87, 88, 89, 108, 117, 157, 164, 168, 184, 233, 250, 274, 279
imports, 238, 239
incandescent, 40, 77, 89, 101, 102, 288, 294, 295
incandescent light, 90, 101, 288, 294, 295
incentive, 154, 166, 173, 221, 280
incentives, 70, 111, 173, 265
inclusion, 142, 144
income, 111, 114, 244
independence, 94
indication, 209, 215
indigenous, 60
individual action, 290
industrial, 176, 223, 229, 233, 243, 244, 249, 251, 254
industry, 68, 86, 116, 236, 237, 239, 240, 241, 243, 244, 245
inefficiency, 54
infancy, 80
inflation, 98, 237
Information Age, 284
Information System, 185, 187, 188
Information Technology, 45
infrastructure, xvi, 46, 56, 59, 63, 65, 79, 104, 220, 222, 226, 233, 239, 240, 242, 246, 283, 296, 304, 306
initiation, 302
innovation, 69, 263
insight, 114
inspections, 98
institutions, 265
instruments, 5, 26
insulation, 12, 54, 55, 267, 275, 279, 280, 295, 299
integrity, 305
intensity, 39, 211, 212, 288, 289, 294
interaction, 275, 279
interstate, 240
interview, 224, 252, 308
intrastate, 240
intrinsic, 259, 266
Investigations, 114
investment, 16, 36, 37, 38, 47, 73, 80, 222, 239, 274, 278, 289, 291, 304, 306
iron, 244
irrigation, 13, 56, 57, 60, 104
IS, 185, 187
island, 61
isolation, 48

## J

January, 74, 113, 152, 250
Jefferson, 131, 216
jobs, 150, 274, 278
Judiciary, 131, 271, 307
jurisdiction, 11, 27, 50, 118, 119, 127, 191, 206, 290
jurisdictions, 151, 235, 265
justification, xiv, 138, 150, 151, 155, 173, 266

## K

Kyoto Protocol, 123

## L

Lafayette, 270
land, xvii, 60, 283, 287, 290
landfill, 96, 144, 161, 296, 311
landfills, xiii, xiv, 137, 138, 145, 311
landscapes, 60
land-use, 283
language, xiv, 138, 142, 145, 147, 155, 156, 164, 167, 168, 173

large-scale, 227, 239
laundry, 10, 49
law, xiv, 107, 138, 153, 293
laws, 118, 188
lead, xv, 12, 34, 159, 204, 205, 207, 208, 212, 213, 214, 215, 222, 224, 238, 244, 268, 307
leadership, xi, xii, xvi, 1, 2, 3, 11, 15, 19, 21, 50, 63, 69, 71, 72, 76, 78, 79, 86, 88, 90, 220, 223, 258, 259, 260, 263, 268, 306
leakage, 10, 43, 44, 54
leaks, 48, 209
LED, 18
LEED, 258, 259, 262, 263, 264, 265, 266, 267, 268, 269, 270, 296
legislation, xvi, 11, 50, 64, 99, 119, 139, 140, 143, 144, 145, 166, 172, 173, 220, 223, 233, 293
legislative, xiv, 98, 127, 138, 148, 151, 155, 171, 172, 173, 184, 188, 203, 206, 234, 253
legislative proposals, 98
life cycle, 78, 132, 133, 262, 291
Life Cycle Assessment, 285
lifecycle, 261
life-cycle, 7, 32, 69, 78
life-cycle cost, 7, 32, 69, 78
lighting systems, 208, 211, 299
limitation, 167
liquefied natural gas, 238
LNG, 238, 240, 245, 254
lobbyists, xvii, 310
local community, 305
local government, 111, 141, 265
location, 82, 175, 218, 262, 267
long-term, 6, 17, 26, 44, 66, 82, 118, 174, 287, 289, 291, 294, 299, 306
long-term impact, 287
losses, 12, 50, 51, 54, 55
love, 284
lower prices, 118, 148
low-income, 111, 244

## M

machinery, 62, 244
machines, 45, 49, 197, 281, 312
Madison, 131, 133, 216, 218
magnetic, iv
Maine, 310
mainstream, 263
maintenance, 11, 12, 13, 34, 41, 47, 50, 51, 52, 53, 54, 55, 58, 61, 62, 70, 81, 85, 94, 104, 106, 127, 130, 153, 176, 198, 217, 245, 258, 259, 263, 264, 265, 266, 268, 274, 279, 281, 282, 287, 291, 306
majority leader, 116
management, 9, 10, 20, 37, 41, 45, 46, 47, 48, 49, 56, 59, 60, 63, 75, 81, 107, 133, 152, 204, 207, 267, 291, 292, 293, 296, 305
manufacturing, 244
market, 80, 90, 95, 135, 143, 145, 148, 150, 154, 233, 234, 236, 238, 239, 243, 263, 265, 270, 284, 310, 312
market value, 154
markets, 165, 192, 195, 263
Maryland, 157, 161, 307, 308, 311
masonry, 160, 175
meals, 310
meanings, xv, 139
measurement, 44, 254, 267
measures, xi, xiii, 7, 13, 14, 16, 19, 29, 32, 37, 41, 68, 71, 73, 84, 108, 130, 132, 133, 140, 154, 191, 212, 213, 221, 233, 241, 251, 259, 264, 266, 267, 288, 292, 293, 299, 301
meat, 312
megawatt, 4, 24, 76
melt, 310
membership, 269
mercury, 235
metals, 162
methane, xv, 123, 217, 220, 254, 311
metric, 26, 53, 215, 234, 254, 280
military, 307
Millender-McDonald, 161
Millennium, 121
minority, 113, 114, 115, 116, 117
mirror, 173
missions, 17, 46, 76, 90, 224, 234, 247, 257, 261, 262, 304
modeling, 48
models, 10, 41, 44, 67, 80

modernization, 52
modules, 104
moisture, 62
momentum, 263
money, 51, 112, 113, 114, 115, 116, 147, 149, 163, 311
motion, 9, 40, 295, 299
motors, 10, 12, 43, 44, 52, 53, 54, 80
movement, xiii, 137, 277
municipal solid waste, 261
murals, 307

## N

nation, xi, 1, 19
*national*, 258, 260, 306
natural, 4, 5, 8, 11, 22, 23, 24, 25, 28, 32, 37, 50, 51, 58, 60, 88, 89, 90, 91, 92, 111, 112, 163, 206, 208, 212, 214, 215, 218, 220, 221, 222, 223, 224, 226, 227, 228, 230, 231, 233, 234, 235, 236, 237, 238, 239, 240, 241, 242, 243, 244, 245, 246, 249, 250, 251, 253, 254, 258, 264, 277, 290, 291, 302, 305
natural environment, 291
natural gas, 4, 5, 8, 11, 22, 23, 24, 25, 28, 32, 37, 50, 51, 88, 89, 90, 91, 92, 111, 112, 206, 208, 212, 214, 215, 218, 220, 221, 222, 223, 224, 226, 227, 228, 230, 231, 233, 234, 235, 236, 237, 238, 239, 240, 241, 242, 243, 244, 245, 246, 249, 250, 251, 253, 254, 302
natural resources, 58, 163, 258, 264, 277, 290, 305
Nebraska, 310
negotiating, 105
negotiation, 121
network, 45
networking, 14, 15, 35, 71, 72
New York, 91, 94, 121, 126, 188, 189, 192, 197, 283
New York Stock Exchange, 91
newsletters, 89
newspapers, xv, 139
NFL, 283
nitrogen, 25, 215, 234, 235, 303
nitrogen oxides, 25, 215, 234, 303
nitrous oxide, xv, 217, 220, 245
noise, 46
non-profit, 20
normal, 69, 78
normalization, 82
North America, 131
nuclear, 22, 222, 241
nuclear power, 222

## O

OB, 28, 133
objectivity, 265
obligations, 155
obsolete, 71, 184, 263
oceans, 17
OCs, 70, 122
Office of Technology Assessment, 141
Offices of Congressional Relations and Public Affairs, 248
Ohio, 267
oil, 4, 5, 22, 23, 25, 50, 56, 91, 92, 111, 112, 213, 214, 221, 223, 229, 230, 249, 250, 251, 301, 302
online, 56, 57
opacity, 303
operator, 91
opposition, 115, 116
optimal performance, 259, 264
optimization, 10, 48, 49, 52, 53
organic, 18, 62, 68, 70, 78, 90, 95, 122, 292, 312
organic compounds, 18, 70, 78, 90, 122, 312
organic conditions, 96
organic food, 68, 95
organization, 16, 68, 152, 172, 258, 260, 269, 276
organizations, 69, 75, 172, 258, 269
oversight, xii, xiii, 84, 85, 97, 119, 147, 149, 156, 157, 164, 191, 206, 227, 247
oxide, xv, 217, 220, 235, 245
oxides, 25
oxygen, 16, 304

ozone, 235

## P

Pacific, 271
packaging, 69, 146
pain, 98
paints, 14, 69, 70, 78, 292
palladium, 162
paper, xiii, xiv, 14, 68, 69, 71, 96, 97, 101, 137, 138, 139, 140, 141, 142, 143, 144, 145, 146, 147, 150, 151, 152, 153, 157, 158, 159, 160, 162, 163, 165, 168, 169, 170, 171, 172, 175, 177, 178, 179, 180, 181, 182, 183, 184, 186, 189, 190, 191, 199, 244, 270, 282, 296, 298, 310
particulate matter, 215, 234, 235, 303
partnership, 96, 161
passenger, 298
payback period, 111, 116, 132, 300
PDAs, 175
pedestrian, 105
penalty, 173
Pennsylvania, 310
performance, 11, 12, 37, 39, 40, 44, 45, 49, 51, 54, 59, 72, 107, 109, 258, 259, 262, 263, 264, 265, 266, 268, 270
periodic, 10, 41
permit, 61, 302, 303
personal, 67, 74, 98, 115, 158, 162, 175
personal communication, 74
pesticide, 13, 62
pesticides, 62
petroleum, 222, 254, 311
petroleum products, 311
Philadelphia, 89, 115, 122
phone, 163, 175, 197
photovoltaic, 108, 111, 288, 295, 296, 298
photovoltaics, 110, 111, 289, 305
pilot programs, 294
pipelines, 238, 239, 242, 246
planning, 19, 47, 50, 133, 281, 288, 291, 296, 301
plants, 60, 104, 105, 114, 222, 226, 227, 238, 239, 240, 241, 244, 246, 275, 279, 302
plastic, xiv, 69, 70, 78, 103, 138, 158, 160, 168, 170, 171, 198, 282, 310
plastics, 162, 175, 183, 244
play, xvi, xvii, 258, 260, 262, 273, 277
pleasure, 60
policymakers, 259, 268
pollutant, 25, 44
pollutants, 17, 59, 215, 225, 234
pollution, 59, 61, 91, 113, 163, 225, 227, 229, 235, 243, 244, 247, 291
poor, 38, 50
population, 60, 283
pork, 312
porous, 59
potatoes, 310
Potomac River, 59
power, 4, 10, 17, 18, 22, 24, 31, 39, 41, 42, 45, 46, 47, 48, 49, 52, 53, 55, 76, 77, 80, 86, 88, 90, 91, 92, 111, 112, 113, 214, 222, 229, 235, 241, 253, 254, 261, 283, 301
power plant, 22, 42, 91, 92, 111, 112, 113, 214, 222, 229, 235, 241
power plants, 222, 241
preference, 183, 195, 296
premium, 8, 12, 24, 32, 53, 54
premiums, 249, 251
President Clinton, 151, 153
pressure, 11, 50, 51, 52, 53, 243, 254
prevention, 154, 166, 195
price changes, 244
prices, 39, 91, 98, 208, 215, 222, 223, 225, 226, 227, 229, 231, 232, 233, 234, 236, 243, 244, 249, 251, 255
printing, 95, 150, 159, 177, 178, 179, 180, 181
private, xv, 8, 33, 103, 151, 204, 207, 211, 265, 276, 283
private sector, 265
private-sector, 33
proactive, 298
producers, 244
production, 11, 222, 226, 227, 228, 236, 237, 241, 244, 245, 291
production costs, 238
productivity, 165, 237, 282
profit, 20, 150

programming, xiii, 84, 117
promote, 64, 78, 98, 99, 108, 133, 143, 145
property, iv, 156, 200, 284
property owner, 284
protection, 59, 304
PSI, 11, 18, 50, 51
public, xvi, xvii, 8, 33, 35, 40, 65, 67, 72, 93, 103, 105, 174, 191, 245, 258, 260, 262, 265, 273, 276, 277, 280, 283, 297, 303
public court, 105
public education, 297
public relations, 245
public service, xvi, 258, 260
Public Works Committee, 120
pumping, 53, 56
pumps, 10, 43, 44, 51, 53

## Q

quality of life, 269, 275, 280
questionnaire, 157

## R

radius, 312
rain, 56, 59, 215, 225, 235, 296
rainfall, 61
rainwater, 60, 61, 104
range, 48, 50, 54, 93, 174, 210, 215, 224, 228
raw materials, xvi, 258, 261
real estate, 269
real time, 304
reality, 116, 306
recyclables, 154, 160, 162, 175
recycling, xiii, xiv, xv, 14, 62, 68, 70, 71, 96, 97, 101, 102, 127, 128, 129, 130, 131, 137, 138, 139, 140, 141, 142, 143, 144, 145, 146, 147, 148, 149, 150, 151, 152, 153, 154, 155, 156, 157, 158, 159, 160, 161, 162, 163, 164, 165, 166, 167, 168, 169, 170, 171, 172, 173, 174, 175, 176, 177, 182, 183, 184, 186, 188, 191, 192, 193, 195, 196, 197, 200, 201, 288, 297, 298, 312
recycling plant, 62
redevelopment, 292
reduction, xi, xiii, 6, 7, 15, 17, 22, 26, 32, 35, 49, 51, 61, 68, 71, 84, 85, 96, 97, 98, 100, 107, 108, 120, 162, 173, 175, 208, 218, 233, 250, 267, 275, 279, 280, 288, 293, 294, 301, 311
reflection, 299
refrigerant, 302
refrigeration, 111, 209, 302, 303
regenerate, 58
regional, 62, 63, 277, 301
regular, 51, 62, 275, 279
regulations, 93, 118, 140, 146, 167, 179, 181, 304
rehabilitation, 284
relationship, 85, 275, 279
relationships, 249
reliability, 46, 250, 304
renewable energy, 94, 114, 289, 305
renewable resource, 278, 282, 283
repair, 51, 53, 275, 279
Republican, 152
research, 200, 229
residential, 227, 243, 263
resolution, 117, 118, 127, 140, 141, 142, 144, 145, 178, 181, 186, 189, 301
Resource Conservation and Recovery Act, 143, 187
resource management, 60, 291
resources, 17, 58, 162, 212, 227, 247, 258, 264, 275, 277, 279, 283, 290, 305
responsibilities, 106, 107, 131
restaurant, 96, 161
restaurants, 95, 98, 105, 158, 161
retail, 264, 270
returns, 262
rewards, 282
rights-of-way, 243
risks, 300
roadmap, 3, 13, 16, 20, 35, 73, 87
rotations, 68
routines, 123
Rules and Administration Committee, xiii, 84, 103, 146, 174

Rules Committee, 129, 132, 133, 134, 136, 166
runoff, 13, 56, 59, 61, 104

## S

safety, 290
sample, 157
satisfaction, 100
savings, xvi, 6, 8, 9, 10, 11, 31, 32, 38, 40, 41, 43, 45, 46, 47, 49, 50, 51, 54, 57, 77, 99, 100, 101, 103, 115, 116, 118, 149, 156, 213, 258, 259, 266, 267, 268, 281, 289, 292, 293, 297, 300, 305, 306, 311, 312
sawdust, 160, 168, 171, 175, 198
scheduling, 45, 47, 109
school, 258, 263, 265, 269
sea level, xvi, 220
seafood, 95, 312
search, 94, 105, 189
security, 39, 40, 66, 100
sediment, 292
selecting, 104, 212
senate, 129, 201
sensitivity, 244, 251
sensors, 39, 102, 103, 212, 281, 292, 294, 295
separation, 141, 144, 146, 150, 153, 183, 189
series, 19, 35, 52, 77, 99, 157, 263, 270
service provider, 4, 269
services, iv, xvi, xvii, 9, 10, 15, 45, 46, 47, 64, 67, 69, 72, 78, 79, 93, 94, 105, 109, 118, 155, 233, 253, 258, 260, 310
sewage, 57, 59
shade, 61, 95, 312
sharing, 14, 66, 67, 88, 93, 94, 124, 125
Shell, 270
Short-term, 19, 65, 174
shoulder, 52
shrubs, 105
sign, 94, 125, 280
signs, 95
silver, 162
sites, 275, 276, 279, 281, 307
sleep, 41, 45
smog, 225
smoking, 123
socially responsible, 269
software, 52, 81
soil, 59, 60, 62, 104, 113
solar, 101, 103, 104, 109, 110, 133, 280, 281, 288, 298
solar cell, 288, 298
solar cells, 288, 298
solar energy, 103, 110, 288, 298
solar panels, 104, 133, 280
solar system, 111
solid state, 295
solid waste, 188, 200, 261
Solid Waste Disposal Act, 188
solutions, 99, 262, 312
solvents, 292
soot, 50
Speaker of the House, 87, 116, 120, 121, 135, 136, 150
species, 60
speech, 93, 95, 144, 152
speed, 12, 43, 53, 54
spot market, 243
stability, 265
stakeholder, 236, 238, 239, 240, 241, 243, 245, 246
stakeholders, 224, 226, 227, 236, 237, 238, 239, 240, 241, 242, 243, 244, 245, 251, 269
standard deviation, 255
standards, 57, 80, 86, 116, 118, 136, 143, 146, 224, 235, 252, 296, 302, 310, 312
statutory, 116, 119
steel, 244
stock, 47, 283
storage, 45, 48, 49, 108, 226, 235, 239, 240
storms, 281
stormwater, 56, 58, 59, 61
strategic, 118
strategies, 3, 4, 6, 10, 11, 20, 22, 23, 26, 32, 36, 41, 51, 52, 55, 59, 63, 74, 87, 127, 220, 261, 292
streams, 68, 226, 235
substances, 71, 215
suburbs, 283
sugar, 97, 158, 161

sugar cane, 97, 158, 161
sugarcane, 310
sulfur, 25, 111, 235, 245, 302, 304
sulfur dioxide, 235, 245
sulfur oxides, 25
sulfuric acid, 235
summer, 55, 114, 280, 301
supervision, 176
supplemental, 60
suppliers, 28, 238, 243
supply, 14, 40, 42, 43, 46, 51, 52, 53, 56, 57, 77, 91, 92, 104, 222, 226, 227, 229, 233, 236, 237, 238, 239, 240, 246, 247, 261
supply chain, 261
support staff, 85, 100
Supreme Court, 131, 217, 307
surplus, 156
surprise, 145
sustainability, 2, 11, 12, 13, 15, 19, 20, 34, 35, 50, 55, 69, 71, 72, 73, 78, 79, 86, 87, 88, 89, 126, 161, 258, 259, 263, 266, 267, 291
switching, 5, 8, 11, 22, 23, 25, 32, 36, 81, 92, 101, 172, 206, 207, 208, 214, 215, 221, 223, 224, 226, 227, 228, 230, 231, 234, 235, 236, 237, 238, 240, 241, 243, 245, 246, 247, 248, 249
synchronous, 52
syndrome, 90
systems, 9, 10, 12, 38, 43, 44, 45, 46, 57, 81, 100, 103, 104, 110, 115, 133, 165, 208, 210, 211, 213, 227, 240, 247, 258, 261, 263, 264, 265, 280, 288, 292, 294, 295, 296, 299, 303, 304

## T

targets, 49, 293
technical assistance, 75
technology, 18, 43, 59, 99, 104, 108, 111, 240, 262
television, 101
temperature, 17, 48, 52, 53, 81, 254, 280
tension, 281
term plans, 287, 291
terminals, 226, 240
test procedure, 165
testimony, 89, 91, 94, 96, 103, 107, 141, 149, 150, 151, 162, 165
Texas, 307
theory, 239
thermal efficiency, 255
third party, 303
Thomson, 178
threat, xvii, 98, 273, 277
threats, xvi, 220
TID, 126
time constraints, 250
time consuming, 175
total energy, 28, 29
toxic, 71, 146
toxic substances, 71
tracking, 9, 37, 38
trade, 89, 90, 95, 247, 269, 312
trade-off, 247
trading, 26
traffic, 66, 67, 299
training, 70
transfer, 50, 165
transformation, 263
transition, 46, 90, 126
transparent, 25
transport, 240, 275, 279
transportation, xvi, 13, 63, 65, 67, 72, 88, 93, 96, 126, 127, 134, 162, 198, 225, 229, 235, 245, 254, 258, 260, 262, 280
traps, 12, 54, 55, 104, 130, 275, 279, 288, 298
travel, 34, 63, 64
Treasury, 150, 167, 173, 271
trees, 61, 92, 105, 114, 121, 275, 279, 296
trend, 22, 29, 238
trimmings, 311, 312
trucks, 63
turnover, 166

## U

U.S. Treasury, 150
uncertainty, 211, 225, 229, 233
UNEP, 270
uniform, 80

unit cost, 233, 250, 254
United Nations, 270, 274, 278, 284
United Nations Environment Program, 284
United Nations Environmental Programme, 270
United States, xiv, xvi, 5, 25, 106, 110, 127, 133, 135, 138, 140, 155, 156, 158, 167, 173, 177, 178, 179, 180, 181, 219, 226, 236, 237, 238, 254, 271, 273, 276, 277, 283, 289, 292, 307, 313
universities, 13, 14, 15, 35, 71, 72, 269
updating, 11, 50
upload, 134, 201
urban areas, 60, 246
USDA, 82, 296, 311
utility costs, 274, 278

## V

validation, 300
values, 32, 251
variability, 233, 251
variable, 12, 43, 44, 53, 54, 80
variables, 53, 228, 233
variation, 251
vegetation, 56, 60, 61, 104, 105
vehicles, 14, 61, 63, 67, 79, 93, 98, 280, 296, 298
ventilation, 6, 10, 29, 44, 46
Vermont, 19
Vice President, 260, 269
visible, 246
vision, 144
voice, 99, 127, 142, 153, 188
volatility, 226

## W

wages, 96
walking, 262
*Washington Post*, 113, 115, 122, 135, 136
waste disposal, xv, 139
waste management, 267
waste products, xiv, 138
wastes, 104, 274, 278
wastewater, 56, 57
wastewater treatment, 56
water, xii, xvi, 2, 9, 11, 12, 13, 28, 29, 30, 37, 38, 42, 50, 51, 52, 53, 54, 55, 56, 57, 58, 59, 60, 61, 62, 79, 81, 103, 110, 111, 123, 130, 132, 133, 163, 205, 208, 213, 214, 217, 220, 221, 243, 257, 258, 261, 264, 266, 267, 275, 279, 280, 281, 288, 289, 291, 292, 293, 295, 296, 299, 300, 302, 305, 312
water quality, 13, 50, 58
watershed, 58
web, 65
webpages, 174
websites, 174
well-being, 260, 291
wellness, 95
wells, 237
wheat, 26
White House, 132
wholesale, 243
wind, 80, 90, 253, 281
windows, 44, 80, 103, 208, 211, 267, 275, 279, 281
winter, 38, 52, 81
wireless, 43
wireless technology, 43
wood, 14, 70, 78, 92, 281
wood products, 70
work environment, 37, 84
workers, 71, 312
workplace, xii, 2, 19, 83, 132, 210, 282
writing, 255

## Y

yield, 38, 77, 215, 234, 235, 259, 262, 268, 299